Reggae from Yaad

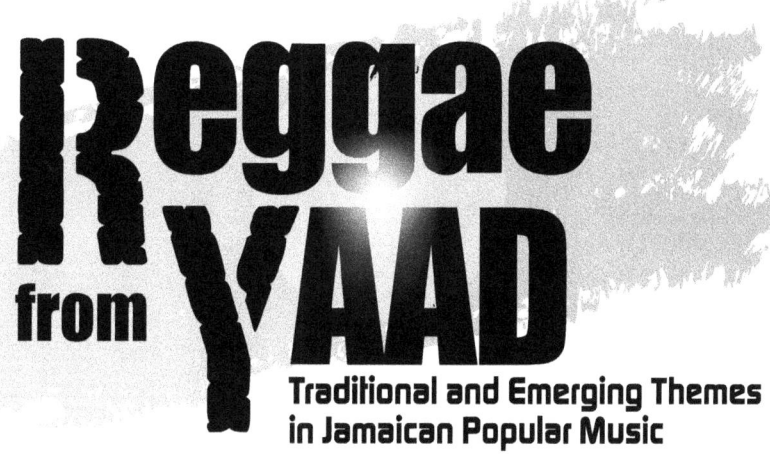

Reggae from YAAD

Traditional and Emerging Themes in Jamaican Popular Music

Donna P. Hope

IAN RANDLE PUBLISHERS
Kingston • Miami

First published in Jamaica, 2015 by
Ian Randle Publishers
11 Cunningham Avenue
Box 686
Kingston 6
www.ianrandlepublishers.com

Introduction, copyright selection
and editorial material
© Donna P. Hope 2015
ISBN: 978-976-637-891-2

A catalogue record for this book is available from
The National Library of Jamaica

All rights reserved. While copyright in the selection and editorial material is vested in Donna P. Hope, copyright in individual chapters belongs to their respective authors and no part of this publication may be reproduced, stored in a retrieval system or transmitted in any form or by any means electronic, photocopying, recording or otherwise, without the prior express permission of the author and publisher.

Cover and Book Design by Ian Randle Publishers
Cover Photo by Thomas Euler, Munich, Germany 19 July 2013

Printed and bound in the United States

Table of Contents

Acknowledgements —vii

Introduction
Donna P. Hope —ix

Section 1 – Legendary Reasonings

1. 'Bob Marley: The Man that I Know'
   Alan 'Skill' Cole; Transcribed and verified by Donna P. Hope —1

2. 'Production Something': David Katz in Conversation with Bunny 'Striker' Lee, King Jammy and Bobby Digital —28

Section 2 – Discourses Beyond Yaad

3. Expressions of Reggae in Havana:
   Processes of Foreign Influence and Cultural Appropriation
   José Luis Fanjul Rivera —51

4. 'You've got no time for me': Martin 'Sugar' Merchant, British Caribbean Musical Identity and the Media
   Shara Rambarran —64

Section 3 – Discursive Pathways in Jamaican Popular Music

5. Freedom Sound: Music of Jamaica's Independence
   Heather Augustyn —85

6. *Your Name A Mention*: Media Coverage of Clashes/Feuds in Jamaican Popular Music 1970–2010
   Donna P. Hope and Livingston A. White —100

7. From Dub Plate to Dancehall:
   Versioning as an Analogue Template for Digital Reggae
   Brent Hagerman —127

Section 4 – Dancehall Matters

8. Between 'Murder Music' and 'Gay Propaganda': Policing Respectability in the Debate on Homophobic Dancehall
   Patrick Helber —141

9. Good, Good Goodas Gyal:
   Deconstructing the Virtuous Woman in Dancehall
   Anna Kasafi Perkins — 164

10. The Lyrical Opus of Tommy Lee Sparta:
    Masculinity, Violence, Sexuality and Conflict
    Winston C. Campbell — 184

List of Contributors — 207

Index — 211

Acknowledgements

Reggae from Yaad represents the unified effort of a range of individuals, many of whom are not reflected as authors or contributors.

Special thanks go out to the entire team of faculty and staff members, students, assistants and others from the Institute of Caribbean Studies/Reggae Studies Unit, and other departments at the UWI Mona Campus in Jamaica, whose work on an exceedingly successful International Reggae Conference 2013 provided the launching pad for the presentations, panels, and papers in this collection. These persons include Drs Lloyd Waller, Christopher Charles and Livingston White; and Elizabeth Douglas, Georgette McGlashen, Robin Clarke, Jennifer White-Clark, Kenrick Alexander Sharpe, Ava-loi Forbes, Sherry Perrier, Tanya Francis-Thomas and Trojean Burrell.

The chapters benefited significantly from in-depth reviews from an impressive array of individuals with expertise in Jamaican culture, music, media and related arenas. Nuff, nuff gratitude to colleagues and friends who provided expertise as blind reviewers, translators and transcribers, often at short notice.

I am especially grateful for the unwavering support of Dr Kameika Murphy in providing academic and personal support to pull together diverse facets into a cohesive whole, and whose expertise proved exceedingly valuable. And the publication team at Ian Randle Publishers ensured that this work came into being with minor labour pains.

Special thanks to my son, Bertland Hope, whose skills at unearthing documents lost in cyberspace remain priceless, while extending a familial shoulder to lean on during moments of intense chaos.

Any omissions are accidental. Those who may fall in this category, do rest assured that your contribution is validated within these pages.

Introduction

Donna P. Hope

Jamaican popular music and culture continue to spread and expand far and wide, breaching borders and transforming new spaces. The more recent post-millennial shock and awe over the use of Jamaican talent, music, language and slang in diverse spaces, removed from Yaad – Super Bowl moments, VW ads and on popular North American programmes like the Voice and The Tonight Show – suggests a rather latent appreciation, amongst some onlookers, of the reach and appeal of the little 'island Jamaica' that is home to just over 2.7 million inhabitants. The appeal of Jamaican culture and the value of its music, musicians and cultural products to non-Jamaicans, many residing far beyond the very continent which houses the very particular Jamaicanness that is being bottled and sold under multiple labels, is well-established. Arguably, however, there is room for more discussion, debate, and ultimately documentation to highlight the diversity and multiplicity of the discourses around Jamaican popular music from within its indigenous spaces – Yaad, and from beyond Yaad, where cultures and ideas coalesce and often create new meanings that are similar, but inherently different.

In a world undergoing rapid and intense transformation, we are often transfixed by these Super Bowl moments, the moments of Voice-ing versions of Jamaicanness that are rapidly transmitted via new digital pathways…the Book with many Faces, and birds Tweeting rapid fire beats of text…with Insta-ntly-Grammed visuals and You on the Tube all swirling in a melee of overkill. This is new! Different! Never before seen! Create, create, create more content to feed the beasts and provide pathways to passive consumers who see all in a momentary blink. But within this fast-paced melee of cultural content, music at your fingertips, MyTunes, iTunes, everything Smart and portable and miniaturized, the opportunities for sharing and learning are overwhelming. It is within this opening that we continue to ruminate on musical meanings, to debate the traditional and new forms, and to put forward contemporary strains of thought and research that seek to unearth the cultural, social and related meanings that form the bedrock of Jamaican popular music from Yaad and beyond.

Reggae from Yaad retains the centrality of Jamaica, as Yaad, to the ever-expanding world of Jamaican popular music. The multi-focused chapters add to the growing number of dynamic and interdisciplinary works on Jamaican music and culture by offering contemporary scholarly interpretations on the history, cultural significance, media interactions, and gendered and social dynamics of Jamaican popular music from multiple geographical locations.

The papers in this volume represent a selection of the many and varied highly stimulating conference papers, panel discussions, and other oral presentations showcased at the International Reggae Conference hosted at the University of the West Indies, Mona Campus, Jamaica, in February 2013. The International Reggae Conference, then in its third staging, and hosted under the theme 'Traditional and Emerging Expressions in Popular Music', continued to provide a critical platform for debate and discussion, as well as an important networking and research opportunity for academics, researchers, cultural practitioners, artistes, entrepreneurs, music lovers and others from across the world. Under the conference theme, the thoughts, ideas, debates and research presented in this volume, represent a contemporary exploration of multiple issues around Jamaican popular music, in refreshingly novel fashion that adds significant value to the already existing body of work on the broader terrain of Jamaican culture. *Reggae from Yaad* engages new voices whose interpretations of Jamaican music and culture remain critical in the ongoing process of exploration and deconstruction of the meanings, symbols and value of the various genres highlighted in their work.

The first section, 'Legendary Moments', presents two seminal pieces from icons in Jamaican music and culture. Alan 'Skill' Cole's presentation on Bob Marley, at the annual Bob Marley Lecture 2013, is an exciting and timely treatise delivered in Cole's engaging style of dialogue. This chapter brings forward new information on Bob Marley, from the perspective of one of his closest friends and confidant for several years, until his death in 1981. Indeed, Cole 'tells it like it is,' highlighting crucial moments in the life of Marley, including the initiation of aspects of Marley's life and career, that set the stage for his post-mortem superstardom. Cole documents how Marley, the 'workaholic' and 'perfectionist', was haunted by the shadow of his prescient abilities...his gift from birth. The material in this chapter presages the publication of Cole's book-length work on his life and times with Bob Marley.

The second and final chapter in this section also engages with legendary voices to document the work of renowned pioneers in Jamaica's music industry. Here, David Katz engages with three of Jamaica's veteran music producers, Bunny 'Striker' Lee, Lloyd 'King Jammys' James and Robert 'Bobby Digital' Dixon, in a scintillating and harmonious journey within the terrain of Jamaican popular music. Spanning multiple genres, rocksteady, reggae, and dancehall, Katz and the producers provide a historical and almost linear trajectory of the development of major aspects of several genres of Jamaican music.

In section two, 'Discourses Beyond Yaad', Jose Luis Fanjul's essay brings attention to the development and impact of reggae spaces in Havana, Cuba, offering a timely introduction to issues surrounding Afro-Cuban identity and reggae. Fanjul provides an overview of how Rastafari, and particularly what he calls 'Rasta fan club sessions', emerged to become a significant part of Afro-Cuban culture, especially through the adaptability and proliferation of reggae music bands operating in 'salsa spaces', giving it a Cuban flavour. While recognizing there are limitations to the genre's reception and consumption in the island, Fanjul shows how Reggae is gaining currency in Afro-Cuban negotiations of religious, social and historical identity.

Shara Rambarran both explores the role of music in the relationship between Jamaica and Britain and investigates the relationship of multi-cultural groups of reggae music and the media, presenting arguments around the continued lack of understanding on the roots of reggae and Caribbean culture in Britain. The chapter focuses on the case study of Sugar Merchant who, Rambarran argues, was overlooked by the media as a musician. For Rambarran, the British media failed to highlight the creativity of genre-blending in the music of Merchant's group Audioweb, focusing instead on the incompatibility of a British Caribbean person, with a dub and reggae musical background, singing rock.

Section three, 'Discursive Pathways', opens with Heather Augustyn tracing reflections of national sentiments on independence in the music of the 1960s. Augustyn's essay offers the view that while independence marked a seminal period in nation-building for Jamaica, the celebrations, especially where music is concerned, reflected major divisions in the society – uptown vs. downtown, upper class vs. lower class, and the government vs. the people. It is during this time, however, that Augustyn sees ska emerging as the music of the people, providing them with a form around which they could coalesce and engage, influence and promote a national identity.

Donna Hope and Livingston White present a preliminary report emanating from their study on the role of media in the development and maintenance of popular music feuds/clashes in Jamaica. Drawing extensively from their content analysis of Jamaican newspaper articles between 1970 and 2010, this chapter provides clear indication of media bias in their use of inflammatory words and phrases and selective use of photographs and headlines, among others. The post-millennial Gaza/Gully clash between rival dancehall artistes, Vybz Kartel and Mavado, is a central plank of this debate and the extensive coverage of this engagement for over four years provides multiple media moments for examination. Hope and White's arguments resonate around the agenda-setting and meaning-making roles of the media as they zero in on the symbiotic relationship between dancehall feuds/clashes and the print media over several decades.

Brent Hagerman revisits the notion of versioning, reinterpreting same as a recurring negotiation between past and present elements that keeps music traditions relevant. Far from a mere recycling of the past, Hagerman finds that versioning, by continuously revisiting and processing previous songs, riddims, themes, musical motifs, and lyrics, plays a significant role in retaining the relevance and dynamism of reggae.

In the final section, 'Dancehall Matters', Patrick Helber tackles a contentious issue, using notions of decency to examine transnational social responsibility in dancehall, particularly as it relates to gay rights activism and contested lyrics in the music. Helber highlights how issues about homophobic dancehall lyrics are connected to general discussions on homosexuality and violence-inciting dancehall music in Jamaica. The chapter demonstrates how dancehall music and the debate on homosexuality and homophobia serve as projection surface to discuss general concepts of culture, nation, race and gender within Jamaica and the Jamaican diaspora. Helber argues for the parallels between the media discourses, which criticize homosexuality, and that which emphasizes dancehall music's responsibility for crime, particularly since conservative Jamaicans perceive both phenomena as a threat. He integrates both in a general crisis discourse arguably based on a variety of fears about the future of Jamaican nation, culture, gender order and morals.

Perkins uses the description of the virtuous woman in Proverbs 8 as a frame, and deconstructs the meaning of the virtuous woman in the Dancehall context by examining the lyrical array of several artistes who extol the virtues of this persona. In so doing, she questions this construction, as the total opposite to and/or rival of the skettel, and how her vaunted independence, as extolled, may in fact be contradictory or illusory. The chapter also explores how the righteous/cultural path this persona treads is to be reconciled with the public 'wining' and glamorous displays of self.

Winston Campbell's closing chapter explores broad themes in the lyrics of Tommy Lee Sparta, one of dancehall's contemporary and controversial deejays, whose moniker 'Uncle Demon' and dalliance with demonic symbols in his music and body art faced the ire of conservative Jamaica. Campbell argues, among other things, that the artiste's references to 'demon' (and its variants) and a perceived 'darkness' in his work could be reflective/descriptive of trends that are prevalent among the youth subgroup within the Jamaican cultural space, though there is an argument for a stronger prescriptive role being played by such utterances and visualizations.

The range and depth of intellectual inquiry presented in these essays constitute an appropriate and timely overview of issues that demand research and generate reasoning as we continue to germinate new mechanisms to spread cultural and academic exploration along new pathways.

Section 1
LEGENDARY REASONINGS

'Bob Marley: The Man that I Know'

Alan 'Skill' Cole
Transcribed and verified by Donna P. Hope

The following is a transcription of Alan 'Skill' Cole's presentation on Bob Marley under the aegis of the annual Bob Marley Lecture 2013 held on Thursday, February 6, 2013 as a part of the International Reggae Conference 2013.

It is the first time in a while that I have been asked to say anything about Bob Marley. It has always been people here and there on the corner and things like that. But I must tell you, I really always enjoy talking about Bob Marley because when I speak about Bob Marley it isn't what people tell me about Bob Marley, it is what Bob Marley told me about himself. So when I am talking about Marley, I don't have to go and write notes and things like that, it just flows because I am just telling it like it is and what he always told me.

Let me first tell you how we met. I was about 14 years of age and there was a major league football competition taking place and my team went to the finals. The finals was against Boys Town at Trench Town; minor league, sorry, I meant minor league. It was a full house crowd that evening in Boys Town after the game. Unfortunately, we lost. Boys Town had such a wonderful team and we lost the game; I think it was 2-1. And I met a young man that day by the name of Robert Nesta Marley. Very quiet unassuming young man, very shy looking individual and it was only for about 15 or 20 minutes that afternoon because, as I said, there was a crowd. After meeting that evening, we went our separate ways and we didn't talk much. I also remember that the first time this man looked at me he was so shy and unassuming and things like that and he looked at me like…and he had a little smile on his face and even after we met, he was like this. Anyhow, time went on and he started communicating (when I was going to school) with me – such as on a weekend when I was playing during the time of the football season – through a fellow by the name of Les Brown who is from Trench Town. So Les would bring greetings to me from Bob when I was in school every now and then. He said 'awe boy the bwoi score some goal dung deh how it guh, tell him say him fi come a Boys Town come play some football…'(Oh boy, the boy scored many goals [down there], tell him to come to Boys Town to play football….)

Anyhow, it was about, well it was about 19…the time elapsed, but before that I went to America and when I got back, there were some evenings when I got home from school and when I arrived; we got in from railway in those days and I would travel up Orange Street and in those days they had a shop where Joe Gibson is right now at the corner of Orange Street and Heywood Street.[1] There used to be a little shop right at the corner and occasionally we used to pass it and I remember one Friday I came from school with my hand in my bag and I went there [to the shop] and said, 'Where is Bob?' And they said, 'over in Randy's.'[2] Anyhow, I went up to the studio that night and that was my first time going to a studio, I should tell you, and I knocked on the studio door and people were there and nobody could go in when Bob was recording; only a few people were invited inside the sessions. And so I knocked and I knocked again and the guy said 'come in.' He put me inside and said, 'siddung, siddung don't leave don't leave'(sit down, sit down, don't leave, don't leave). Anyhow, they were recording a tune called 'Give Me a Ticket' – Peter Tosh made that song. I never forgot it; it was a Friday night and I stayed there a very, very long time and every time I was getting tired he said, 'no man I will carry you home I will carry you home don't worry I say.' Anyhow that night I left the studio very late and he took me home and he said 'I'm gonna come and look for you innuh. I know where you live now goin come and look for you.' (I'm going to come visit you, you know. I know where you live now, I'm going to come visit you.)

Time passed by and he went to America and after getting back from America, he went to Sweden and came back from Sweden. I met him, now this was 19…yes it was 1969. I was passing Downtown (Kingston) and I saw him and I went to him and said, 'what's up' and he said to me 'boy I want to get fit I want to get real fit. I want to play some football because boy I have to get myself in good shape.' So we decided to meet and we started to play football over in the Mountain View area. So he came there. Now this is a mystery that Bob even came to the field. And we were playing football over there and this young man named Gary Hall was involved in the music business – at that time he was actually the manager for Dynamic Sounds, Byron Lee's company.

And Gary Hall was watching us play football that evening and after we finished playing ball, Bob looked at me and said, 'yuh know dat man dere' (you know that man over there?) and I said, 'Yes, that man is in the [music] business you know. He runs a company by the name of Dynamic Sounds you know, (and) he knows about the business.'

'Suh you really know im?' (So do you know him well?) And I said, 'Yes mi know im.' (Yes I know him.)

Gary came across and he shook Bob's hand and we were there talking and he said, out of the clear blue sky he said to Bob, 'you know Bob why don't you work with 'Skill' and let 'Skill' be your manager get involved in the business you need somebody to help you in this business?' I looked at Gary and said, 'Gary Hall you crazy man I don't know nuhting about this business how you going to tell me to come work in this business?' (Gary Hall, you must be crazy. I don't know anything about the music business. How can you [invite] tell me to work in it?) Anyhow, Gary Hall said, 'don't worry man I can teach you the business' and I said, 'You can teach me the business? How you going teach me the business?' He said, 'well you know, I've been managing a club by the name of Liguanea, Mona and if you come and give me a season (help me for a season) I will teach you about the business.' I got a big slap right there in my hands. Bob said, 'yes, yes, yes, you affi do it, you affi do it.' (Yes, yes, yes. You have to do it. You have to do it). So I said, 'Gary wi will see how dat goin work I promised mah team and dats gonna cause a lot of problem.' (Gary we will see how that works out. I made a promise to my team and that will cause a lot of problems.) And Bob said, 'dat can work out, wi can work out dat.' (That can be sorted out. We can fix it). Then Gary said, 'how we going start the process now?' (How will we start the process?) I said, 'well if you come to training in the evenings.' He said, 'when you finish training in the evenings, I'm going to tell you, start giving you, start teaching you the secret about the business; like (such as) how the charts are made – everything.'

When (I) went up there the first time, Bob came to pick me up, I will never forget. He came and picked me up that evening and he was there early, (it) was so early. This man came up to my house and (it) was so early in the evening, it was about an hour before training started. So I went there. We went to Mona and the first evening we trained and Bob was there exercising and started jogging with us in the evening and in the last 20 or so minutes, he got to play in the game, because it was pre-season training and a lot of people were there. We finished the first evening and Gary took us to the bottom of the field and said, 'listen' and started to explain the process of the business, bit by bit, bit by bit. He said, 'you know you should form a company' and I said 'Gary you going too fast for me,' and Bob said, 'well I have a thing weh name, name Wailing Soul' (Well I have something called Wailing Soul). And he [Gary] said, 'no you want a new label.'

'Well,' Bob said, 'I have a ting name Wailing Soul and I really didn't want to change the name, Wailing Soul has been going on well big innuh, well big.' (I have something called Wailing Soul and I really didn't want to change the name. Wailing Soul has been going on quite well you know, quite well). He always released good music but he hadn't been getting any hit songs, so he wanted something new and so we decided to form a new label. So Bob came up with this idea about a gong.

There was a young man by the name of Tall…who worked at *Daily News*[3] as a graphics arts designer so I went to Tall and said, 'you know I want you to do a label for me, I want you to give me a design.' And Bob he started talking you know, and he said, 'I want something like a gong, you know gong?' And he was gesticulating and doing all sorts of things and Tall said, 'ok I think I got the idea.' So Tall drew a logo and brought it to Bob and Bob said, 'boy this logo look good, I think I can work wid dat but I need more dan dat.' (This logo looks good. I think I can work with it but I need more than that.) Tall asked him what more he needed and Bob said, 'I need a man like you to come and work with me.' Tall worked at *Daily News* and Tall said, 'boy I don't think I can leave *Daily News* and come right innuh now but I will try and do what I can do.' (I don't think I can leave *Daily News* and come right now, but I will try and do what I can do.) That's how the label Tuff Gong came into being. Tall said, 'Bob we got to form a company because with this Wailing Soul you nuh have nuh company or nutting set up.' (Bob we have to form a company because even with Wailing Soul you have no company or anything set up). Well we went and formed a company. So he and I went to Campion College to register (I went to Campion College for a year and a half for the record). So I went down and I met David Junior there. We went to Campion (together) and he had just started practising his father's business – and I took him down to David Junior. And we had a meeting and that's how Tuff Gong came into being.

After that, we started the journey and the journey was all about recording because Bob was a workaholic. This man was so involved in the music and in soccer it was unbelievable. Let me tell you, Marley would get up in the morning and we would go out and we would train and after training, well you know, my pattern was we had to eat properly so that was part of the whole coming together, the whole discipline and everything like that. And we started the whole routine. Now I was shocked because I didn't understand that man was a working – you'd call him a workaholic – and he would work in the studio and he would write a song and he would sit and work on the song all night (I mean unbelievable) until 2, 3, 4 o'clock in the morning. You know, Bob's head would be on his guitar, he would wake up and he would touch it again and come up with another song. Everything was recorded though. He always had his recorder and he would always record.

Afterwards, I would get there in the morning and he would say, 'I want you to hear this for me.' And he would pull me into a corner and say, 'listen to this,' and I would say, 'you do that all last night?' (You did all of that last night?) and he would say, 'yes.' And I would ask him, 'why won't you go to your bed at nights and sleep?' And he said, 'sleep, sleep? If you sleep too much you know what happen to you?' I said, 'no, tell me.' He said, 'any man sleep too much miss out.' (Any man that sleeps too much misses out.) I said, 'weh you mean miss out?' (What do you mean by miss out?) He said, 'yeah, if you sleep too much you are going to miss out because if I was sleeping all through the night I wouldn't come up with this.' I said, 'you're right but you need some rest' and he said, 'the rest will come. Don't worry about that, the rest will come.' But this man was really, you know, a workaholic. Believe me, he was just unbelievable, honestly speaking he was unbelievable I tell you. Sometimes they used to wonder when we just started Tuff Gong. You know the first song we had was *Trench Town Rock* and that was a big hit. And when I thought that the man [Bob] would just relax after we did the first song. He was week after week going to *Trench Town Rock*, and he was coming up with all of these songs. So I asked 'What happened to Peter and Bunny?' (What about Peter (Tosh) and Bunny (Wailer)?), He said 'I have the floor right now so let's just go now.' So I was the manager and Peter and Bunny were there now so I asked, 'what happened to Peter and Bunny?' (What about Peter and Bunny?) 'Why don't you let Peter....' He said, 'I have the floor right now and any man come, come.' (I have the floor right now. If anyone comes, so be it).

And he was working, working, working, working. And there's another thing I want to share with you. You know, doing the record is one thing, getting the product out there is another thing. It was just so important. Now, when Bob would be finished recording, there was a young man by the name of Family Man[4] and everybody knew Family Man. Now Family Man was the man Bob relied on the most of all the musicians. When I said 'rely on' I mean he was to me the musician who was closest to Bob. And he used to say to Family Man, 'Fams boy mi mix roun dem music yah innuh cause you know seh mi is a man, affi have dem pon the road innuh cause things looking a way cause wi an wi a get airplay now. From wi getting airplay you know seh dem cyaah stop wi now I.' (Fams, I mixed around the music because you know I am a man who has to have them out there [on the road] you know, because things are looking good because we're getting airplay now. Once we are getting airplay you know we are unstoppable.) Family Man was THE man. He [Bob] said, 'Fams you're the man in charge of mixing all music.' So, Family Man was given that, that power to do all the mixing, but when he went to the studio with Bob on a night with his mixing, we would be there (as well) – only Family Man, myself and Bob. And they were there mixing a song for three, four hours mixing. And I looked at Bob and said 'Bob is four hours we been here innuh.' (Bob, do you know we've been here for four hours?) They would say, 'I have to get it right. If I don't get it right I'm not leaving out here innuh,' (I have to get it right. I won't leave until I get it right you know) and I would say, 'I don't understand.' He says, 'it have to get right Family Man, Fams and me cyaah leave until wi get it right tonight' (Family Man it has to be right. We can't leave until we get it right tonight.) So, 2 o'clock (am) would come and Bob says, 'Family Man dat need likkle bass, innuh, too high innuh brethren and play it back innuh Fams yuh nuh hear a tell yuh seh…' (Family Man that needs a little bass. It's too high my friend. Replay it. Didn't I tell you that..). And Family Man would turn it down, the mix would be finished and he (Bob) would ask again, 'how the guitar sound? Play it back again.'

Sometimes I would feel sorry for the studio engineer…I remember Syd Bucknor.[5] Once it was Syd Bucknor and then it was Sylvan Morris.[6] It was different periods and these guys use to…I remember back then when we were paying them, we gave them a little extra because they worked hard, because if you look at it…in many instances they would stay over and Bob would wake them up and say, 'you cyaah sleep pon dis yah business innuh, this is a serious business.' (You can't sleep on this business (job), you know. This is a serious business [job].) Bob took his business seriously. He was a professional, he was…what would you call these people?…perfectionist? He was what you call a perfectionist. If there was one dot that needed to be taken care of, it had to be taken care of. I remember we had a song that we had to… he broke the stomper three times. We were mixing a song called *Rat Race* and he had to break the stomper three times. He said, 'Family Man come here, come here, come here.' And Family Man would go inside and nobody else, nobody else but Family Man, Bob or myself. And he would play the song and then say '(Do) you hear what I hear?' And Family Man would pose like this in his dark glasses, 'say weh yuh say.' (Say what you have to say). Bob would say, 'dis nuh soun good and it affi mix agen caaw mi ago throw the stomper, cause dis cyaah guh pon di road!' (This doesn't sound good. It has to be mixed again because I'm going to throw (away) the stomper. This can't go on the road [be released]). So, we're there and about two or three times I said, 'No, Bob. Three times you destroy the…' (No, Bob. This is the third time you've destroyed the...) and he said, 'destroy it cause mi a don't want nobody even seet, destroy it....' (Destroy it because I don't want anyone to even see it. Destroy it.) And so we took it down and we destroyed it. So, he was really a perfectionist in all aspects of his life and that was one of the important things of the man that I loved about him.

He was also disciplined and focused. I mean, when Bob went on tour or if he was going into the studio, he was so keyed up when he was going to do sessions it was unbelievable. He was so focused it's like he was going to a different world, he would just go crazy if you look at him. And people were afraid of him because when it was time for him to come to the studio...from he enters the studio area, it was a different personality and people were even afraid to smile because he didn't smile much and he was so focused. They used to say to me, 'so what is wrong? This man don't talk to people? I mean I don't understand it.' (So what's wrong? Does this man talk to other people? I mean, I don't understand it.) And I had to say, 'no a so him stay.' (No, that's just how he is.) He was so keyed up it was unbelievable. And you see him on tour it was the same thing, I mean he'd be there joyful, he'd be there doing his thing but when it came around to time for sound check or going to the venue he was the first man who was ready. He'd be there before anybody got on the bus, stage shows I mean for sound check and for shows he'd be there before everybody. Bob would be in the bus and he would sit down at the back and he would sit down looking and he's looking and...say if a guy was late, he'd frown...that was the time he'd frown and I mean he was just serious. When he had a mission and he knew he had a mission, he always used to say to me, 'Alan I'm on a mission and I have to do, I have to complete the mission.'

But I would like to share some other, some very important things with you, but I have to be careful because I can get carried away and I will talk for hours and hours. And I can tell you a lot of things that you didn't know before. But I'm going try and tell you a little. Most of you may understand that I am in the final stages of finishing a book and in it you will find most of the things that you did not hear tonight. What you hear (read) in the book you're going to be hearing (reading) for the first time, of all the books on Bob Marley. Probably I shared it with a few people, but did anybody in here know that Bob Marley was psychic? Psychic. Yes. As a youngster, as a little boy growing up in St Ann. Now, when I tell you this thing nobody told me this, Bob told me this himself.

Everything that I am telling you about the man is what we shared together. The days when we sold records together…let me tell you the story of how we used to sell records. We used to drive together every day – and Marley didn't speak to people – but when we were driving he was the one who did all the talking. He would talk to me until we got back to the shop and when we got back to the shop he would just turn off like a tape and he's gone again and nobody understood him. When we were on the road he would tell me stories (*such as*) 'when I was a likkle boy inna St Ann's innuh everybody use to come ah the village a morning time innuh come check mi innuh cause….' (When I was a young boy in St. Ann, everyone would come to the village in the mornings to see me you know, because….) I asked, 'How yuh mean?' (What do you mean?) And he said, 'yuh know tek dem hand an tell dem everyting.' (You know, I take their hands and tell them everything.) I asked, 'weh yuh mean…?' (What do you mean…?) and he said, 'yeah a say I can dweet' (Yes, I said I can do it.) And I said, 'den yuh stop doin it?'(Have you stopped doing it?) And he said, 'when I come to town the Rasta man dem say, "boy lego dem ting deh innuh."'(When I moved to Kingston, the Rasta men told me to stop doing things like that.) So I asked, 'weh yuh mean?' (What do you mean?) And he said, 'mi come a Back-A-Wall[7] and di Rasta dem say mi muss lego dem ting deh innuh cause dem ting deh a devil ting.' (I came to Back-A-Wall and the Rastafarians told me to stop doing those things because those things are of the devil.) And I said, 'eeh, well I don't see it dah way deh innuh.' (Really? Well I don't see it that way.) And he said, 'well I just let it go dah way deh…and when a guh back to mi village an tell dem say I don't innah it agen, dem bex.' (Well I just let it go that way…and when I go back to my village and tell them I don't do it again, they get upset.) I said, 'yuh a psychic.' (You are a psychic.)

And I had an experience with him and I can tell you he was really psychic because there are a lot of things he would tell me, and in telling me he would say…I would laugh and so he would come sometimes and hit me here. Each time I opposed what he said, he would hit me here and say, 'everything I tell yuh, yuh goin live an seet, you're going to live and seet.' (Everything I tell you, you're going to live to see. You're going to live and see it). Even in his last days when we were together, he was telling me something and I looked at him and he said, (he wasn't very strong) 'remember anything I tell yuh, yuh goin live an seet.' (Remember everything I tell you you're going to live and see it). And honestly speaking, everything that that man has told me I have lived and seen it manifesting. Let me share one thing with you. When we started selling records from Tuff Gong in the days, we went through a period where it was a struggle. You know, they had the Wailing Soul producing the best music in the business, as far as I am concerned, but it wasn't getting proper play you know, because the system wasn't open for a red, gold and green label. So, you know what transpired at that point? He said to me, 'yuh know every time I think about the music business I want to leave it.' (Do you know that every time I think about the music business I want to leave it?) And I said, 'why?' He said 'yuh have suh much problem, I doing all these songs and I getting fight yuh know.' (There are so many problems. I'm doing all these songs and I'm being pushed out, you know), and I said, 'what yuh saying?' (What are you saying?) He said, 'I can guh back a country guh plant my food, mi a farmer innuh.' (I can go back to the country [rural Jamaica] and plant my food. I'm a farmer you know.) And I said, 'yuh may be a farmer but yuh annuh farmer, yuh a musician, yuh a songwriter, extraordinary songwriter.' (You may be a farmer but you're not a farmer. You're a musician, you're a songwriter, an extraordinary songwriter). And he smiled and he said, 'yeah but boy, I don't understand this.' (Yes, but I really don't understand this). I said, 'why yuh nuh understand this?' (Why don't you understand?) I said, 'this is the struggle' and he said, 'yeah I know is a struggle but what kind a struggle diss would be ah mean, everything? And mah music cyaah sell.' (Yes I know it's a struggle. But what kind of struggle would this be, I mean, everything? And my music won't sell?) So I said to him, 'don't worry, don't worry about dat, dem gonna sell. Yuh music is gonna sell.' (Don't worry, don't worry about that, they will sell. Your music is going to sell). So when we started on this, I'm just going back to things, so when we started and Tuff Gong started making some money and getting together and so forth, I remember the first thing he said was, 'I am going to build a studio and I am going to build a pressing plant.' Now when we just sold *Trench Town*, we sold only 30,000 copies and 30,000 couldn't build a studio.

So I was there listening and he's driving me and he's there talking and said 'we are going to build a studio and we are going to build a pressing plant.' He didn't say 'I.' '*We* are going build a studio and *we* are going build a pressing plant' because he always used the word 'we.' 'We going to build a pressing plant and we going to have the best studio in Jamaica.' And I asked, 'better studio dan Byron Lee?'[8] (A better studio than Byron Lee's?) He said, 'better dan Byron Lee.' (better than Byron Lee). I asked, 'better dan Coxsone?'[9] (Better than Coxsone's?) 'Coxsone? Better dan Coxsone.' (Coxsone? Better than Coxsone). So I would say the name of the studio and he said, 'yes.' I remember I left in the '70s and when he came to Africa he said to me, 'suh hold out yuh hand.' (So, give me your hand). So I said, 'wahhpen what does dat seh?' (What has happened? What does that say?) '"Hol" out yuh hand man.' (Give me your hand). So I held out my hand but it was… BOOP! He hit me once and I said 'what is this all about?' He said, 'memba a tell yuh, memba ah tell yuh innuh it happen innuh but yuh naw pay it much since wi start the journey.' (Remember I told you, remember I told you. It has happened. But you haven't been giving it much attention since we begun the journey). So I said, 'is true?' (Is this true?) He replied, 'yeah yuh memba now.' (Yes. Do you remember now?) And I said, 'yeah I remember.' (Yes I remember.)

So, I'm trying to tell you how psychic the man was and other things too but we will read it in the book. But, but Marley was someone who in the ancient days, you know the prophesies of old like Nathan and Samuel when they call them 'seers' because a 'seer' was one who would read people's palms and tell them what would happen to them. But when we read the Bible, we will see these things and we will see them happening in our lives but we don't understand that nothing has changed, nothing is new. One teacher said when you are born psychic you come to this earth awakened and I think the man was one of those types of natural mystic who came awakened. He knew what he wanted, he knew where he was going, (and) he could tell you things that were going to happen. It's amazing, I mean because

I was so close to him and I think I was closer to him than anybody else because we spent so much time together and when I say time, I mean really valuable time. I would ponder sometimes when we were sitting down and Bob would tell me stories…an amazing thing about the man is that when he is telling you, he was so sincere and when he was talking sometimes you have to say, 'say that again', because sometimes he would take it out. The words were coming out of his mouth and he was like in a different world. See if you understand what I am saying to you. He was in a different world when he was talking and I saw that people who saw him in those days were afraid and would ask many different questions. I remember a minister once said to me in the 1970s, he said, 'this man don't talk to people?' (Doesn't this man talk to people?) I replied, 'Yes he speaks to people but he is just the type of person…he's very reserved.'

At that particular time in history, his mind was set in such a way that he would think about the days and the tribulations he went through you know. When I would spend some quality time with him at nights and I saw his personality, I would look at him and say, 'people is afraid of you innuh cause yuh don't talk.' (People are afraid of you, you know, because you rarely speak.) And he said, 'boy people see me and don't understand me but I'm just dat.' (Well people see me and don't understand me but that's just how I am). But inside him was not what was outside. See if you can see what I am trying to say. He was such a soft individual inside; if you understood him, he was soft inside and outside he was tough. 'Don't look at my face,' he says in a song you know; he recorded a song and in that particular song, Bob Andy came into the studio that night. I remember we were doing the cut, and Family Man and I were there alone. And he was doing this thing called *Talking Blues* and I remember when I let Bob Andy inside and he came inside and he looked up, he took off the earphone, because we never let people inside the studio cut and this is Bob Andy, he put back the microphone. Bob Andy heard when he was doing the cut and he said, 'I have been down on the rock it's like I'm wearing a permanent screw.' (I've been down on the rock, it's like I'm wearing a permanent frown.) And that answered the question; why he had a permanent frown. See, Bob Marley had sung his life story in so many different ways, his life, his experience I should say, in so many different ways that people don't understand, they didn't understand because they were looking in all different directions.

I remember the first time we went to England and he was doing a press conference and these reporters came. Both of us sat down doing the press conference, the English reporters (asked), 'How do you write all these, these types of songs? How do you write these songs?' And he started laughing. He was laughing, he was laughing in such a way that the reporters must have thought that he was jeering them. And he said, 'I get my inspiration from my people. I write the songs according to what I see around me.' And they just did not understand what he was saying. And he looked at me laughing, then he said simply, 'What (I) write…I get my inspiration from the people, what I write is my life, it comes from what goes (on) around me.' And it was true.

If I am permitted, I just want to share with you, because I have certain people here with me, who worked with me on a project and I hope they don't mind me saying certain things. When he wrote certain songs when you listened to it, you understood it because of the experience; because I was there through most of these experiences and I am telling you it was amazing. You know he did a song with Lee 'Scratch' Perry, a song by the name of 'Lost My Best Friend.' You know what I realize, what is the name of that song again? Lost my best friend that I ever had, 'My Cup Runneth Over', thank you very much, 'My Cup'. He did the *Soul Revolution* album with Lee 'Scratch' Perry and Bob was telling me about the experience; how he wrote that song and why he wrote it went back to the early days when he came to Kingston. He came into Western Kingston. His father took him to town and his father took him to West Kingston and his father left him with one of his ladies somewhere in the Oxford Street area, for his father didn't take him to his home because of…you know, what it was in those days. So he had a friend by the name of Eddie Fraser. Eddie Fraser you know in those days when you call half-caste. In places like West Kingston, Back-A-Wall, in those areas you were look down upon because you know, half-caste you know, and so on. Eddie Fraser was light-skinned like Bob and Bob clinged (clung) to Eddie. I don't know if anybody knows history, whose memory can take them back to that time in history. They were very, very close, as

I said. Eddie Fraser's father and mother were in charge of a school called Ebenezer High School where the cemetery was – it still is. And they became very, very good friends. That was the first friend Bob said he had when he first moved from the country. And Eddie Fraser was hanged in the early days for something that Bob said, (and I do believe), he was wrongfully accused. And he got hanged and they were very, very close friends. And he would say, 'Alan, Eddie Fraser was my very, very close friend.' And I never forgot it. And he wrote a song that was about that experience. If you listen the song carefully, 'I lost my best friend that I ever had,' that was Eddie Fraser.[10]

So Marley was someone different. As I said he was, he was what I would call a natural mystic. Let me just break it down, I don't want to go anywhere further. He was a natural mystic and he remained that way until the day he died. (A) very important thing about this man is that he always said to me, 'Alan, I'm on a mission and I have to just keep on a line.' It came to me why he said that. I remember we were in the rehearsal one day, we were both together and Sly's studio had released a song by the name of 'Family Affair'. Hopeton got some people and his big hit song and we were told that '79, or something like that, and he took some of Sly stories and he sung some of Sly's stories. He played a song for me, a love song and he said, 'this song will sell don't it?' (This song will sell [do well] won't it?) And, and I said, 'yeah cause people hardly accustomed to love song anymore.' (Yes, because people are hardly exposed to love songs anymore.) But he said, 'well I not writing song like that I am on a different road, I'm on a different road.' (Well I'm not writing songs like that, I'm on a different road, I'm on a different road). So he know all what he was all about; he kept his music on a certain road, on a certain line and pattern and that's what made him a potent Third World personality; because of his lyrical content. It wasn't really the music of Marley, although we know the music was favoured, but we know the lyrical content made him such a dynamic force in the Third World.

You know Marley was looked upon as a Third World prophet, as some people would call him, and as a hero, who was a spokesperson for the oppressed people in this, in the world. And he knew. He realized because he said to me, 'I have to sing to the people and talk to my people, the people with me. So I have to keep on that line, I cannot stray.' So, he knew what he was all about, you know. It's just as I said, you were born psychic, you come here, you arrive awake. I don't know if you understand what I am trying to say, if people get it, but when you are born with those types of gift, you come into this world awakened. Some of us, those who have been blessed that way, they are special. And I say to you he was really a special person, the way he did his thing, it was as if it was something designed by some other force, because he would tell me, because he would say to you, 'yuh know I want this to be done yuh know, but I don't want to rush it.' (You know I want this to be done but I don't want to hurry it). I said 'why yuh don't want to rush it?' (Why don't you want to hurry it?) 'Yuh don't rush tings.' (You don't hurry things.) I learned that from him, he said, 'yuh don't rush tings Alan, yuh mek it flow and if it flows, it alright.'(You don't hurry things Alan, you let it flow and if it flows, it's all right.)

And this man was amazing. He had so much patience and he developed a type of discipline that I don't know if we will ever see. I don't know, but I think it will be difficult for us to ever see a musician in this period who had that type of discipline, that type of commitment to what he was all about. That made him so special and today it still mystifies the world. That's how is it that a man's music keeps selling like it is after so many years after he has departed. It hasn't happened to any other artist in the world. His music is like good food. Let me share something with you. It may sound sad but it isn't sad. In the latter (last) days when we were together and we were talking, both of us, he was laying down on the bed on his back and we were talking; and he was telling me about what transpired on tours when I was away. He was bringing me up to date and he said to me, 'well, yuh know, I am here fighting for my life yuh know and everybody else is healthy.' (Well, I am here fighting for my life and everyone else is healthy). And I said to him, 'because you had slipped up.' He had missed out and it was what caused the problem and he said yes. He said, 'yes I know.' And I said to him, 'history will be kind to you.' And he gave me a big smile and I said, 'history will be kind to you Bob, believe me.' And he smiled and I asked, 'you believe what I said?' And he said, 'yeah.' And I know wherever he is today, if he is watching us, he must be smiling to himself, 'Boy, this man knew what he was saying,' because I did know that history would be kind to him and will continue to be kind to him because he was special.

One other thing I want to share with you is that in his last days that I spent with him, his spirit was jovial. And when I say jovial, we started to talk about death to define how I saw death and it was hard. It was hard in a sense to be telling someone who was about…We were so close together that it took me a little while, I took a deep breath and I sat there for quite awhile, and I was listening to him and he said 'I want you to give me your concept of death/.' And I said, 'You know people never die.' I said, 'we never die. You can't kill energy you know.' He asked, 'what yuh seh?' (What did you say?) I said, 'Yuh never die yuh mek a transition.' (You never die, you make a transition.) He was shaking his head and he was like this, his eyes were full and I said, 'man never die, we never die.' (man never dies. We never die). I said, 'life once created never ends we just make a transition.' I said to him, 'When this flesh can't take it nuh more im affi put it down but yuh never die.' (When this flesh can't take it anymore, you have to put it down but you never die.) And he was so happy when I shared that with him that it was just one of the times when he was very happy in his latter days when he was struggling. It sort of lifted his spirit because I could see it in his whole outlook. Because I remember he got up; he got up out of the bed you know, and he said, 'boy I want some food innuh, ah feel like ah want some food innuh.'(I want some food, you know. I feel like I want some food.) I asked, 'yuh sure yuh want something to eat?' (Are you sure you want something to eat?) He said, 'yeah, ah feel like ah want some food.' (Yes, I feel like I want some food). I said, 'what kind of food yuh want?' (What kind of food do you want?) He replied 'anything, feel good.' (Anything. I feel good).

That alone had a touch of, had that type of impact on him that it's as if he was cured of his illness. You know he was contemplating, and I think he was perplexed, because there were so many things going around and a lot of things, some of which I won't say here, and he was aware of this because believe me, he shared everything with me. You know he was saying all these things to me that I couldn't answer myself and he always hitting me and saying, 'talk nuh man, talk nuh man.' (Talk man, why don't you talk man.) I didn't want to get involved in that and he would say, 'why yuh naw talk?' (Why won't you talk (to me)?) And I would say 'mi nu want to get involved in dat' (I won't get involved in that.) And (he) knew I wouldn't talk about that. He was telling me what was going to happen after he passed away, believe me he was telling me what was going to happen after he passed away. And he wouldn't make a will and I think one of the reasons he didn't sign a will – I have always been asked why Bob didn't sign a will – I said people always brought a lot of documents for him to sign and he wouldn't sign it. And I said right because what he wanted they didn't bring it to him. Then they asked me why I said that they didn't bring what he wanted. He wanted something and that document was not presented to him. He would just shake (his head) and he wouldn't sign any documents. So when you hear people asking why Bob Marley didn't sign a will and you will hear people saying all different types of things….But I was there and I know why Bob Marley did not sign a will. We will talk about it in the book.[11]

But he was such an amazing character you know. Bob would sit down and talk to me about his kids and he'd tell me who patterned their mother and who's going to pattern their mother. And he was on the dot, believe me people, I shared it with him – the man was on the dot. It was amazing, believe me. I can't know how many people believe me because I am here to tell you the experiences that I shared with the man. What I am telling you is because I was so close and he would tell me all the stories. There is nobody that is alive in this world today that I think he shared what he shared with me. You know it went so personal that I can't, some of the things I can't even share it in the book; honestly, because that's how we were and as I said, there is nothing that he did that he wouldn't tell me, believe me there is nothing that Bob did that he wouldn't tell me. And I didn't ask him questions, he would tell me and then he would say, 'What you think about that?' (What do you think about that?) He was the talker and I was the listener.

Such as in the night when I started taking him out. I started taking him to the middle-class society. In the early days it was for Marley, it was Trench Town. We hadn't been to Bull Bay as yet; it was really like from Trench Town to the studio, Greenwich Park Road, Trench Town, Third Street, Second Street, whatever, football field, and so on. Like that, you know, it was just like that. But when I start taking him out now to Mona, some of my school friends that had gone to the university[12] and had finished, we would take him out in the nights and Bob…I remember sitting down and when Bob came into the crowd…only a few people who are here will remember those days. And I am talking about people, former athletes, and you name all different sectors of what you call it, of our lives. And Bob would sit down and he would listen. He wouldn't speak, he would rarely speak. And the following morning, Bob would tell me every single word that Tom, Dick and Harry had said. The following day, he was unbelievable. And I started saying to myself, 'What kind ah man this is? Yuh know he sit down there and yuh talk all night im listen?' (What kind of man is this? You know he just sat there and listened to you talking all night?) And with his spliff [joint]. He would make a spliff [joint] and the guys would talk and talk and he would listen and he listened to you talk and talk. And Bob would listen. The following day anything that struck, struck a chord that picked up – anything, like anything that he picked up, like what would you call it, like a current? The next day or two days following that will be on… either he would be on the guitar and he would call you and say, 'ah wah yuh hear dis.' (I want you to hear this.) Unbelievable, believe me, unbelievable.

Let me share an experience. We were going to do a *Natty Dread* album. We started preparing the *Natty Dread* album because the Wailers had parted and we had done two albums and he had a five album, they had a seven album deal with Island Records. And the first meeting he came to Twelve Tribe[13] at a place called Staan-Up-Hill. And it was private meeting, in those days you had to have a book. You had to be a registered member to be up at Staan-Up-Hill. Jerry[14] was there, Peter Phillips[15] was there, Sister Bunny,[16] a lot of people who are here tonight were there and Bob. Rupert was there and many of the brothers, some, Ivan was there. And I mean, if I missed anyone, I am sorry. So, we went to the meeting and Staan-Up-Hill was a place where you went to. Staan-Up-Hill the way people was on a hill…the hill had a little slant like that and it went down into a little valley. So Rick could see everybody. Oh, he was there too. Bob was sitting down with some guys, the Briscoe Brothers. And all of them were inside and it was crowded. And I was standing to the other side. And I remember the leader of Twelve Tribes was Brother Gad,[17] and Brother Gad had this thing about him, when he was talking to see who understood, 'Whoever have ears, let him hear.' That was one of his favourite lines. And the meeting, after the meeting we would run down from Staan-Up-Hill, myself, Jerry and Omar and quite a few (other people). Who remembers? We would run down from Staan-Up-Hill, down to Papine. Kenneth and Earl Belcher[18] and Rupert Hoilett…Shakespeare and all the Olympian Brothers. We would go up to Papine and sometimes we would say, 'Let's go to Half-Way-Tree.' And that night when we drove down Bob was driving the car. Mikey Free was there too, and we had some people in the car. And we drove and when we got to Papine, the man said it was Half-Way-Tree and we rough it [manned up], all of us and we took off…And we drove and drove…But we didn't get to Half-Way-Tree. We came out on Old Hope Road and I left him. That night I was wet and I went home and stayed home.

The next morning I went up, I went to Bob, who was there, and I saw him with the guitar…I never forgot. And he put down the guitar and he was smiling. So I said, 'what happen?' (What's up?) Listen to what he said, 'ah want yuh hear something innuh, seh ah waah yuh hear something.' (I want you to listen to something, I want you to listen to something.) And he plug in the Motorola tape. And anywhere we travelled to, the Motorola tape was there. And he put in the Motorola tape and he said, 'listen to this.' I guess you have figured out what the song is about. 'Picking up Rasta man Vibration.' I got just that one line from him and he sat there and this man is fact, and he plugged the tape and he walked away. And this is what's going to freak me out. He walked away and he plugged it in now and he started and I heard him on the guitar 'picking up' and he was spitting it out. So I said, 'oh my gosh' and then I said to him 'yuh is a dangerous man,' (You are a dangerous man) and I said, 'I affi be fraid how I even talk because yuh might write tings to weh I probably don't want yuh write.' (I have to be careful of how I talk because you might write things that I probably don't want you to write.) So just to show you his creativity, how this man was just…This one time, just that one line and he wrote a song. Bob would just listen to you and we sat down inside the house and we would sit down there many nights. And Earl Belcher, Hugh Booth,[19] Hugh is not here, Professor Booth, Mr Edwards all these brothers would come there at night and when we finished talking in the night, Bob would take up the guitar and come out with a song out of, out of the norm just listening to what people had to say.

So I'm just telling you, when we started breaking him in and so on, he got that, that type of inspiration from people. 'Trench Town.' We were driving one day. A car had an accident in the street and he had to drive on the sidewalk. This was 1970 and the song we were writing a song together 'children playing in the street broken bottle and rubbish heap'[20]...because we couldn't pass the car. All I get was 'in the ghetto bed was sweet' and he had this song there and it was troublesome and I never forget the year; it was 1970. That song was difficult for him. 'Ah song nuh fi gi a man suh much trouble it a give me headache but a going put it down but yuh going hear back from mi.' (A song shouldn't cause a man so much trouble. It's giving me a headache. I'm going to put it down for a bit but you'll hear from me again.) I think I was in Africa when this song was released. That's how he was. These types of things were generated from the man. He would do things like that. If Bob heard you say something using one of the old colloquial terms or whatever, he'd take something from it and he would give you something from it. You would be surprised; he was phenomenal and I don't know if you can find songwriters of that calibre again. They were special you know, because he was such a man he was so creative, because of as I said insight, I would say Bob wrote songs about the people around him, you know about the people there. When I listen to some songs, I have to go to him and say, 'hol' on deh now what is this all about?' (Just a minute now, what is this all about?) and he said, 'yuh know weh mi a talk bout man.' (You know what I'm talking about.) And I am telling you because when I really listened to it I had to go back and say, 'but brethren what is this all about? Is this....' (But brother, what is this all about? Is this....) And him said, 'yeah man same way.' (Yes. Just like that). Because I knew where he was coming from. But I guess you want to know some more about Bob Marley.

Let me tell you now, his love for football was amazing. And this is what I wanted to tell you all about, why he loved the game so much. I am just trying to tell you my personal view (of) why he loved the game so much. You know, he said to me, 'Football is like music. Rhythm, coordination.' I said, 'yes yuh know it's true.' (Yes, you know, that's true). So I remember when we started, I started exercising and he was there with me and every few weeks he said to me, 'this the rhythm, this rhythm yuh know.' (This is the rhythm, this is the rhythm you know). I said, 'yes this is rhythm.' He said 'yeah rhythm and coordination.' He said, 'Yeah that's what music is all about yuh know; rhythm and coordination.' (Yes, that is what music is all about; rhythm and coordination). He would say to me, 'You know I want to master this ball I want master it.' I asked, 'Why do you want to master it?' He said, 'ball come to me like the world when I see a football it come to me like the world.' (Ball is like the world to me. When I see a football, it is like the world to me). I said, 'yeah.' I said, 'ah tink yuh right innuh.' (I think you're right, you know). He said, 'yeah.' He said, 'The ball to me is like the world when yuh have that ball and yuh control when yuh have it, it is like the globe, rhythm and coordination.' (The ball is like the world to me. When you have the ball, you have control. When you have it, it is like the globe, rhythm and coordination). I asked, 'yeah, but what yuh do with the globe?' (Yes, but what do you do with the globe?) He said, 'well yuh tek this ball and yuh talk to it like how I see yuh talk to it, yuh talk to it.' (Well you take this ball and you talk to it like I see you do. You talk to it). And he said, 'this is the way I want to talk to the world, this is the way I want to talk to the world.' And I'm listening and I said I don't understand what this man is saying, he wants to talk to the world, but I understood it afterwards. When he is sending his message, he wanted to get to the world. He kept training and I said, 'Bob yuh love football more than me.' (Bob, you love football more than I do.) He said, 'is two ting in the world I love innuh, football and music. Nuttin cyaah change dat, memba dat any part ah the world yuh go memba dat innuh because this is my life!' (There are two things in the world that I love you know, football and music. Nothing can change that. Remember that, anywhere in the world you go, remember that because it is my life!) I said, 'music is yuh life.' (Music is your life). He said, 'music is my life but football and the music they go together. Yes, yes he had a passion. I remember sometimes I would be there we're there, we're sitting in the hammock and we would roll the bearings and so on. And Bob comes out and showed his abdominals and said, 'how I look, how I look?' I said, 'coming on, coming on.' And he would say, 'ah wah dem get tough like your own innuh. Yah understand. Caaw wen mi tek off mi shirt suh dat wen a guy see mi im mus see something inside look like a gong, im mus see something inside look like a gong.' (I want them to get as hard as yours. You understand? Because when I take off my shirt and a guy sees me, he must see something inside that looks like a gong. He must see something inside [my shirt] that looks like a gong). I said, 'Alright, yuh know we have to go to the gym yuh know, its best we go to the gym.' (You know we have to go to the gym. It's best we go to the gym.)

I knew a man named Gerald Roche[21] and Gerald Roche, he was the first Mr Universe from this side of the world and Gerald Roche was my conditioner at that time. And so I took him. We would run in the mornings. We did a lot of running. Bob could run and he would get together with me and we would run for hours. So the first time I took him to the gym I said, 'well now if yuh want yuh abdominals to get like my own yuh have to come to the gym.' (Well, if you want your abdominals to look like mine do, you have to come to the gym). So first thing, I took him to the gym and I said, 'Abdominals, you need some abdominals.' He did some bench press. 'Suh what about the squat?' (So what about squats?) He said, 'No I don't ready fi the squat yet.' (No I'm not ready for the squats yet). Anyway, after the first evening he was able to…you know I worked very hard in those days, and he was there watching but he wouldn't go through the exercising. We usually went to Papine to bathe near the pipe near Water Commission on the right hand side there going up. The pipe usually ran there and we would go alone in the nights and bathe close to the… What's the name of that school on the left? Water Commission, yes I think it's still there. People went there, I think people went there by the numbers. We would go there late in the nights, late in the nights we would go there and bathe and we were there bathing in the night and he said to me, 'yuh know boy, I will run with from here to Montego Bay pushing the iron ting I feel I fraid a it yuh know.' (You know, I will run with it from here to Montego Bay, (but) pushing the iron thing. I am afraid of it you know.) I said, 'weh yuh mean, yuh affi work the iron if yuh want this yuh know.' (What do you mean? You have to work the iron if you want this.) He said, 'boy mi will work everything else but yuh see that ting name the iron, ah cyaah, a fraid a a dah one deh innuh.' (I am willing to work everything else but you see that thing called the iron, I can't. I'm afraid of that one.) I said 'boy a dem feeling deh yuh have is the first day innuh.' (You feel that way because it's the first day). He said 'boy is mi first day? Is not mi first day, is mi last day dis.'(Is it my first day? It's not my first day, it's my last day). So I said 'But yuh seh yuh love dat abdominals but yuh seh yuh want dat abdominals to show up unless we going work on the board.' (But you said you love the abdominals. But you said you want the abdominals to show up. Unless we're going to work with the board.) And Rupert made him a medicine board just like mine. Alright, we were going to work on the medicine board but he never went to the gym with me. He'd watch and I said, 'come man' and he'd do a little push-up, and he would take off his shirt and say, 'how this look?'(How does this look?) 'Yeah it look good, it look good, but you must do the...' (Yes it looks good, it looks good but you have to do the....) And he would say, 'no, no, no' and he would never do any of them. He would do the push-ups and some abdominals, but I could never get him to do some squats or anything else, not another exercise because he would say, 'No I can't do this one.' And you know it's the only thing that we tried to do together that he didn't really get involved. But he was up to everything else.

This man was something else. Let me tell you something about the man. He was quick with the ball and he saw for the first time and he said, 'tink seh yuh a gaah road tomorrow morning and mi nuh learn fi do dat yuh mad.' (Don't think you're going on the road tomorrow and I don't learn how to do that. You must be mad.) He said, 'anyting yuh do mi affi learn dat.' (I have to learn everything you do.) And he would go out there, and for hours he would be there working and then 'Skill!' 'Wah?' (What?) 'It right? Look weh mi a do. It right?' (Is this right? Look at what I'm doing, is it right?). And I said, 'keep going, keep going' and he come back, very quickly. He would say, 'old man a wah yuh tell mi if it right innuh.' (Old man, I want you to tell me if it's correct.) I said, 'yeah man yah ketch it yuh know.' (Yes, you're getting it now). 'Mi nuh like dat innuh old man. Mi want when a man see mi, a man seh mi is a pro.' (I don't like that old man. I want to be seen as a professional.) I said, 'yeah man, yah yuh look like a pro. Don't worry bout dat,.' (Yes, you're looking like a pro. Don't worry about that.) And he worked and worked and worked…

That's the type of individual he was. This man, I mean, I was so amazed sometimes when he would sit down and tell me the things he did when he was a little boy growing up. As I said he would tell me stories and some of the things fascinated me. When he was going to school, his teacher would tell him, 'Nester yuh not a bad boy innuh, but it looks like yuh is a dreamer.' (Nesta, you're not a bad boy, but it looks like you're a dreamer.) I asked him the name of the teacher, she died couple years ago, she was his teacher in St Ann's and he said, 'This woman seh I am a dreamer.' (This woman said I'm a dreamer.) And I said, 'But you are a dreamer.' He said, 'Yeah but I'm seeing things that she didn't see.' And I realized what he was saying because when he was in the classroom when he was younger and he would gaze, he went out, he went away, he went somewhere else and when he got back everything was over, yes everything was over and it amazed the teacher because she said, she would say, 'Yuh u go a wah different world and when yuh come back my class over.' (You went to a different world and by the time you got back, my class was over.) But she didn't understand that he was psychic and I don't think she knew that he was psychic because when he was doing his, what you would call his readings in the morning, he usually did it early in the morning and so on.…

You know we could talk all night about Marley. We could go on and on, let me tell you please. My experience. When you read my little (book) you will see so many little things unfolding I pray and hope that we get it pretty soon but I need to answer any questions because people need to be asked questions. I hope I did a good job. It is just a little insight of Bob Marley I wish I could share more with you all. But as I said, you will read it. I think after you read the book you won't need to hear anything more about Bob Marley. It will be told there, all the stories and the things that I really know about him and the things that I can't afford to say here tonight, I tried to put it in writing so the world can enjoy it and know the man that I knew. And trust me, that is going to be very interesting.

Notes

1. Orange Street and Heywood Street are located in downtown Kingston, Jamaica.
2. 'Randys' refers to Randy's Records/Studio; Vincent 'Randy' Chin's record store and recording studio, first at the corner of East and Tower Streets and then relocated to North Parade in downtown Kingston. With the Chin's relocation to the USA, Randy's Records /Studio changed to VP Records in 1979.
3. The *Daily News* was a Jamaican daily newspaper in circulation from 1973–1983. It was one of the first major competitors to the longstanding Jamaican *Gleaner*.
4. This reference is to Aston 'Family Man' Barrett, sometimes called 'Fams' for short. He is a Jamaican bass player and one of the Barrett Brothers who played with Bob Marley and The Wailers. Family Man is said to have been actively involved in co-producing several of Marley's albums and also responsible for many of the bass lines on Marley's greatest hits.
5. Norman 'Syd'/'Sid' Bucknor was an engineer/producer who worked with some of the biggest names in Jamaica's music history. He worked at legendary Jamaican studios such as Channel One, Studio One and Dynamic Sounds. One of his greatest achievements as an engineer was his work on ***Natty Dread***, Bob Marley and the Wailers' 1974 breakthrough album. He died in London on May 9, 2010 after living and working in England for more than 30 years.
6. Sylvan Morris is an engineer who worked with many greats in Jamaica's music history working at legendary Jamaican studios such as Dynamic Sounds recording studio and later joining Syd Bucknor at Studio One. He also worked at Treasure Isle and Harry J's among others. Morris was an engineer on Bob Marley and the Wailers' 1974 breakthrough album, ***Natty Dread***, and was also engineer on the 1976 album, ***Rastaman Vibration***.
7. Back-A-Wall or Back-O-Wall, was a Rastafarian settlement in West Kingston. It was notorious in the 1950s as the worst slum in the Caribbean area, where 'three communal standpipes and two public bathrooms served a population of well over 5,000 people.' (See 'Out of the bowels of desperate poverty, a true Jamaican political success story is scripted .' *News. Jamaica Observer*. March 21, 2004). Between 1963 and 1965, Back-A-Wall was demolished and re-developed to form the community of Tivoli Gardens.
8. Byron Lee, a Jamaican musician, record producer and entrepreneur, was renowned for his work as leader of the band, Byron Lee and the

Dragonaires. Lee purchased West Indies Recording Limited (WIRL) from Edward Seaga and renamed it Dynamic Sounds. Dynamic Sounds was one of the best equipped studios in the Caribbean during the late 1960s and 1970s, attracting both local and international talent.

9. Clement Seymour 'Sir Coxsone' Dodd was a Jamaican record producer who influenced the development of Jamaican musical forms like Ska and Rocksteady in the 1950s–1970s. In 1963 he opened Studio One on Brentford Road in Kingston. Studio One holds a seminal place in the history and development of Jamaican ska, rocksteady and reggae as Dodd attracted some great Jamaican talent to the Studio One listing.

10. Eddie Fraser, apprentice radio technician of 69 Pink Lane, Kingston was found guilty by a jury of his peers of the August 1968 murder by gun of a 29-year-old coconut vendor, Artell (Othneil?) Brown. The 22-year-old Fraser was sentenced to death by Justice Uriah Parnell. He was hanged on January 19, 1971. George Fraser, his younger brother, was sentenced to 12 years hard labour. (See *Gleaner* of December 10, 1968 and June 4, 1969 and the *Sunday Observer*, November 24, 2013.)

11. Alan 'Skill' Cole is working on his forthcoming book titled, *The Bob Marley That I Know*.

12. University of the West Indies located in Mona, St Andrew (Kingston 7).

13. The Twelve Tribes of Israel is a mansion (house/branch) of the Rastafarian religion.

14. Robin 'Bongo Jerry' Small, from a middle-class family, was an active participant in the political and cultural transformation in 1970s Kingston and related activities at the UWI, Mona Campus, and a member of the Twelve Tribes of Israel. He currently hosts a popular radio talk show, 'Straight Up', on NewsTalk93 FM at the University of the West Indies, Mona Campus.

15. Peter Phillips, from a middle-class family, was also an active member of the political and cultural transformation of 1970s Kingston and a member of the Twelve Tribes of Israel. Now Dr Peter Phillips, he is the Member of Parliament in the People's National Party (PNP) for East Central St. Andrew, and as at 2014, is the ruling PNP Government's Minister of Finance and Development.

16. 'Sister Bunny' affectionately refers to Angela Heron, also a member of the political and cultural transformation of that era.

17. Prophet Gad or Brother Gad (Dr Vernon Carrington) founded the Twelve Tribes of Israel, a mansion of Rastafari, in Trench Town in 1968 (some reports say 1969). In the 1970s, the Twelve Tribes of Israel, was the most visible Rastafari 'mansion,' drawing its membership mainly from

middle-class Jamaican families. Among them were Dr Peter Phillips (see note 15) and Bongo Jerry (Jerry Small) (see note 14), brother of former government minister, and Attorney-at-law, Hugh Small, QC.

The Twelve Tribes of Israel was also the dominant force in the local music industry, having within its ranks the likes of Reggae superstars Bob Marley and Dennis Brown, Israel Vibration, Freddie McGregor, Fredlocks, Little Roy, Hugh Mudell, and deejays Brigadier Jerry, Sister Nancy and Sister Carol, among others. (See Basil Walters, 'Patriarch of the Twelve Tribes of Israel Passes On', in the *Jamaica Observer*, Wednesday, March 30, 2005.)

18. Earl Belcher was the founder of the legendary sound system, Jah Love.
19. Hugh Booth was also a member of the Twelve Tribes of Israel. He is credited with initiating Twelve Tribe of Israel's funding for Israel Vibration's first album.
20. This song, 'Children Playing in the Streets', was reportedly written by Bob Marley in 1975. In 1979, during the United Nations' celebration of the International Year of the Child, it launched the career of the group of four of Bob Marley's children – Ziggy Marley and the Melody Makers – comprising Ziggy, Stephen, Cedella and Sharon Marley. Proceeds from the single were pledged to the UN to assist with the efforts for the International Year of the Child. The song appeared on the Melody Makers' 1985 debut album *Play the Game*.
21. Gerald Roche was a Jamaican bodybuilder. He placed fourth in the Amateur Short Class 3 of the 1973 National Amateur Bodybuilding Association's Mr Universe competition.

'Production Something': David Katz in Conversation with Bunny 'Striker' Lee, King Jammy and Bobby Digital

DAVID KATZ: The rich tapestry that is reggae music has a lot of different elements that make it as it is: you have lyricists, vocalists, and musicians, but sometimes an element that can be neglected when we think about the greatness of reggae music and its richness is the contribution of the producers. And I think we can consider the producers of reggae music here in Jamaica as something akin to a film director – the directors of those classic works of cinema that have made such an impact all over the world. Jamaica's music producers are the gentlemen behind the scenes who harness the creativity of the players in the same way that the film director harnesses the creativity of the actors and draws the best out of them. They are really the crucial element that helps shape the music in Jamaica, perhaps more so than any other element. Additionally, they need to be concerned with the finance, with getting everything in place so that the recordings can be made, and so that the resultant music can then be released into the world. And as we consider the crucial contribution of Jamaica's music producers, we are very privileged to have with us three gentlemen who have been responsible for changing the shape of reggae music several times over, so I would like you to please give a warm welcome to King Jammy, Bunny 'Striker' Lee, and Bobby Digital.

So as we consider the role of the producer, the role you each have played in shaping this incredible music that has made such an impact around the world, I would like to begin this special roundtable session by having some opening remarks from the veteran in the business, Bunny 'Striker' Lee. I would like you to illuminate for those in the audience who may not already be aware, how and when did you become to be involved in music?

BUNNY LEE: Good evening to one and all. It's a pleasure to be here to talk about reggae music. I've been around the business for a long time, over 50 years, but I started doing my thing in 1967 at Duke Reid's Studio, and from right then till now, I'm in the business, for myself over 40-odd years. We bring in the name reggae, and we're in from rocksteady.

DK: Tell the people a little bit about what you were doing before you were a record producer. And how did you come to make your first production?

BL: Well, I was a record programmer. I used to go to Teenage Dance Party,[1] take records from Duke Reid, Beverley's (Leslie Kong), Coxsone,[2] and get it played on the radio.

DK: And how did you then make the change? How and when did it happen that you actually made your first break into production?

BL: Well, Duke Reid gave me the first studio time free, and I had £20, get four musicians: [guitarist] Lyn Taitt, [bassist] Brian Atkinson, [drummer] Joe Isaacs and [pianist] Gladstone Anderson.

DK: What were some of the actual first recordings that you made?

BL: It actually name 'Do It To Me Baby,' with Derrick Morgan doing the introduction with Lloyd and the Grovers. It's still good to hear the sound of music, the beat is good, so it really rock steady. The second one is 'Music Feel' with Roy Shirley.

DK: What would you say characterized rocksteady? How did rock steady differentiate itself from ska?

BL: Well, rocksteady is slower than ska, but ska never leave the Jamaican music; even when it slows down to rock steady, you have a ska guitar playing, and a piano. Ska is the backbone of the Jamaican guitarist, so ska never leave the music. When Duke [Reid] and them [other producers] start, them start doing the rhythm and blues thing, and we had a man named Clue Jay,[3] who was trying to get the guitar to play something, and him say, 'Let the guitar go ska, ska,' and so the name 'ska' was born. You know, [after] the rocksteady, we had a beat in-between the rocksteady to reggae, it start at Studio 17,[4] with [Delroy Wilson's] 'Better Must Come,' and all them tunes, [John Holt's] 'Stick By Me,' and they call it 'John Crow Skank' –that's the crossover. School kids just call that beat 'John Crow Skank.'

DK: Now King Jammy, I'm sure that there are some people here who are aware of the work you did in the digital era, but some of them might not be aware of how long your contribution has been to the music. Could you tell me a little bit about that type of shift, from ska to rocksteady, and on to these other genres?

KING JAMMY: Good evening ladies and gentlemen. I started my career in 1972. I produce a song in Canada[5] which didn't do well, but that was the first song. So I came back to Jamaica in 1976 and because I had a love for that song, I decide to record it again, with different musicians, so I got Steelie and Clevie[6] together, and that time it did better. But before I did that song, I used to stay over with Bunny Lee, that's where I get my teaching from about the business. Bunny was the teacher. He taught me most of the things I know in production.

DK: Bobby Digital, tell us a little bit about your experience with sound system in the beginning.

BOBBY DIGITAL: Good evening ladies and gentlemen. It's nice to be here to share our experience with the world. My experience with sound system, we grow up in the Waterhouse area, and when you grow up in an area like that, you find you grow up among so many sound systems in one community, you don't even know which of the parties to attend. You have Earl's Disco, you've got King Tubby's, you have King Attorney, you have King Jammy,[7] and everybody vying for a spot. So, it lead from that to my friend and I, said, back in the early '80s, say, 'We have to start something weh name Heatwave, cause our thing have to burn, scorching hot.' We come up with the name from an American group by the name of The Heatwaves, and it grew over the years to be like a little community sound system; it take not long before the name was all over the community, and everybody start to attend our parties, and getting crazy. So it was a good experience.

DK: We'll be looking a bit more at further developments along those ways a bit later, but at the moment, one of the main points of this session is to be looking at the evolution of reggae, and the producers' key role in helping to aid that evolution. So I would like to turn the spotlight back on Bunny Lee, momentarily, to ask about the shift into reggae, the very first reggae song, and I know at the last International Reggae Conference, Michael Barnett presented a very intriguing paper, looking at that very topic. So, Bunny Lee, in your point of view and from your memory, how did rocksteady shift or evolve into reggae, and what was the first reggae?

BL: Well, it was Duke Reid who slow down the beat. You used to have a bad man in Jamaica, them call him Busby – Colin Busby from Trench Town. Him used to come in the dance and dancing with all six girls, you know. And then we used to say, 'Buzz and the girls, them ah rocksteady,' and then the name was born, rocksteady. Same like how the ska name was born with Clue J.

DK: So how did the reggae come about? How did it come that reggae superseded rock steady, how and when and why.

BL: Well, Lee Perry and myself, when, when we was experimenting with the 'John Crow Skank,' in '68, we start doing reggae with a thing name 'Bangarang.'[8] Glen Adams,[9] we have this session, and no keyboard man never turn up, and Duke Reid say, 'Bunny, Glen can help himself.' Glen, him never tell me [that he could play organ]. So I say, 'Thank you, Mr Reid, the session is on,' and me go upstairs, and the rest is history. Glen play the first reggae tune. Is the organ going 'reggae reggae' in the music, you know. If you take the organ shuffle out of the music, it go right back to rock steady. You hear that organ shuffle, that is why they call it reggae. Well, let me tell you something about this tune here, when we was doing it…you know a guy from England, a jazz musician named Kenny Graham, he had a tune named 'Bongo Chant', it is what we were going do, but Glen Adams and the other musicians couldn't hold the chords for the music, and [saxophonist] Lester [Sterling] say, 'Bunny, make we do something new.' I say, 'Turn it into a two-chord tune, and they can come into it again,' and Lester say, 'How Bangarang sound?' Me say, 'Yes, Lester,' and call in Stranger Cole and Lloyd Charmers to sing, 'Woman no want bangarang', and the rest of that tune is history.

DK: So basically, you're saying this is an adaptation of a record that was made in England called 'Bongo Chant'.

BL: Yes, that's right, 'Bangarang' coming from 'Bongo Chant'. If you listen to 'Bongo Chant', it's the same. The only difference is the beat, 'cause my guys them was too young, them couldn't hold the chords.

DK: Now, King Jammy and Bobby Digital, can you cast your minds back to 1968 and think about when this new sound came on the scene, do you have any memories yourself of what the impact was like, and what it was like for you when you first heard it? Or were you even hearing it at that time?

KJ: Well, you mean 'Bangarang?'

DK: Yes, or reggae in general. That new sound that came in, in '68.

KJ: Well, being the type of person who move with Striker Lee, I was well up to date because I came in as Striker Lee's second; I used to drive Striker Lee's car and a lot of other little things, before I start doing production. So I used to changes coming along, so the reggae music was like, just a little faster thing from the rocksteady, but it was impressive, because they develop a little dance for the reggae straight away. So it was a trend coming down. Ska came with a dance, rock steady came with a dance, and the reggae came with a dance. So most of the music that were developing came with dances, different dances, that's how I remember it.

DK: And, Bobby Digital, what kind of memories did you have of that era, if any?

BD: Well, that era, I'm not that old, you know, I'm just 51. I'm not that old, but growing up and hearing this type of music was pretty impressive, and to know this type of music was coming from 'Yard', yard here. So we start to grow up on that vibe of music, what really keep you on track, cause this type of music really motivate me, this type of energy what give off, to make the people dance. You feel love, party, and you don't have to mash a man, and him thump you. Yeah, good vibes. From my upcoming until this time, when you still hear this music, you just feel real good about that.

BL: We had a music before it, they call it calypso or mento, and quadrille in Jamaica, that is real Jamaica roots music you know, because most of our songs even build up with some of those melodies, up to now. If you look at the Jolly Boys,[10] you understand.

DK: So as we trace the further developments, once we're in the reggae era, we just heard that reggae came in as this fast-paced beat with this organ shuffle, but after about a year, the music changed again. What happened and why?

BL: Well, it still going on in a different fashion, cause when King [Jammy] come in with 'Sleng Teng',[11] and the electronic music come in, King become Superman, you understand? Him was untouchable, this beat come overnight, like when U-Roy come and say, 'Wake the town and tell the people, a new sound come;'[12] 'Sleng Teng' just changed the whole thing, and everybody just gone to computer music.

DK: We'll be looking a little more closely at 'Sleng Teng' in just a few moments, but before that, there's a couple of other developments along the way that I'd like to bring up. There's one that happened in the mid-1970s that was very influential in Jamaica for about a year and a half, and I'm referring to this sound based on an open and closed high-hat, what they called the 'flying cymbal', or some know it as 'flyers'. So what can you enlighten the audience about the development of that style?

BL: That beat, it was a chicken wing I was eating. I used to like to eat Kentucky Fried Chicken, I like the wing, and the man say, 'Which part ah the chicken you like, Bunny?' 'I like the flyers.' So when they play that beat now, I just call it the 'flyers' and it take on, and we get the guitarist to play to match it, blend them together.

DK: So what was the first song to make use of the 'flyers' and who were the musicians that played it?

BL: Well, it was Family Man that was in the Bob Marley Band at the time, was playing ska guitar,[13] [Earl] 'China' [Smith] was playing lead guitar, Robbie (Shakespeare) was playing bass, Carlton Davis, we call him Santa, was playing drums.

DK: And the song was…?

BL: 'None Shall Escape The Judgement'. It was really a guy named Earl Zero,[14] and Earl 'Chinna' Smith, the guitarist, him wasn't playing in no band at the time, and him was rehearsing and I stop and hear him, but him only have the first verse, and I said, 'Gentleman, I have a session at Duke Reid's studio tomorrow, reach!' But, when we do it, the song was too short.

KJ: The same Earl Zero that sing 'Please Officer'.

DK: So, 'None Shall Escape The Judgement' was originally recorded by Earl Zero, but you didn't release Earl Zero's version?

BL: Earl Zero couldn't manage the song, so Johnny Clarke was there and Johnny learn the song.

DK: Johnny Clarke was already more established, or not really?

BL: He wasn't established neither. We used to call Johnny Clarke 'Studio Idler', because he used to come round the studio, and that's how him learn song. That night, I run off a cut to give King Tubby to cut dub, and Johnny go voice at the studio, and him make one cut, and that was the song.

DK: And then that sound, the 'Flying Cymbal', every producer wanted that sound on their record for a period of time.

BL: Because the sound system was playing it, everybody was listening. It take on.

DK: So, sound system was a crucial force in that as well?

KJ: Sound system, even now the sound system is crucial.

BD: Yes, sound system is crucial.

BL: Because sound system was like our radio station in the early days, and Merritone[15] sound, Merritone play a very big part in this thing too.

DK: There are all kinds of other innovations that we could cover, but since we don't have all day, were not going to go through them all. But you were mentioning a while ago 'Sleng Teng', which obviously revolutionized everything. But before we get to 'Sleng Teng', King Jammy, when you began to do your productions, when you were still known largely as Prince Jammy, you were doing roots music. Tell us a little about the roots reggae that you recorded. Who you were working with, and what made your sound stand out?

KJ: Well, because I used to listen to so many producers before I started doing my productions, I start to have an idea in my head that I wanted to come with something different. So, when I started my production, brand new, they had an Arabian sound, which Bunny Lee endorse that sound – he was the one that expected me to carry on that sound. So when the Black Uhuru [debut album *Love Crisis*] came, we went to England with the production, and Count Shelley[16] heard them and he said, 'Boy, this production wicked! It's a new thing, I love it!' So he released the album. It didn't really do big in England at that period, but everybody love the music. But because it was such a new thing, it didn't catch on right away. Later on, you know another company [Greensleeves] took the album and re-released it [as *Black Sounds of Freedom*] and it did much better.

DK: It sounds like it was somewhat ahead of its time, and you had a whole new community of vocalists that you were working with there in Waterhouse, where you were based.

KJ: Well, in Waterhouse, as Bobby Digital knows, there was a lot of sound systems, a lot of parties every weekend; you didn't even know which one to go to. So same way, you had a lot of artists, a lot of young talent, so when I started, I started with new talents, because I said to myself, 'I listen to Delroy Wilson, Johnny Clarke, I want to come with some new artistes to form a new crew.' So, we had The Travellers, Purpleman, Wayne Smith, Junior Reid. Those were the artistes I started out with.

BL: Half Pint.

DK: Lacksley Castell was another, with 'What a Great Day'.

KJ: Yeah, Lacksley Castell. There is a point that I really wanted to make: on all of my productions, I was the engineer; I mixed them, I record them. I used to work with Bunny Lee and a lot of other producers, and even for that specific song ['What a Great Day'], you listen to that phaser in the music, that was a new thing that I brought in the mix to change the everyday thing that they used to do.

DK: So you're basically saying that a part of what made your sound the way it was, and made it different, was all of that experience that you'd had as an engineer before you had gone into production yourself?

KJ: Both as an engineer and a sound operator, and being around experienced producers like Bunny. That's what gave me my experience.

DK: One of the things you became concretely involved with during the same era, before the music shifted to digital, is dub as an art form, and you were one of the chief architects of dub. So tell us a little bit about, how did dub come into being, how did it evolve, and what was your role within that process?

KJ: Well, that again was Striker Lee, because I used to mix so many songs with Bunny Lee; whenever we mixed a vocal song, Bunny Lee always insisted for us to mix versions straight away, without the vocal – you know, drop in the vocal, and drop it out. That's the dub culture, you know, and that was very famous, popular in Europe, so that is why we mixed the rub-a-dub styles, with reverb and delay. That is really the heart of dub mixing: drop out the voice, drop on bass, sometimes the rhythm section, and echo it a way, and then you have horns, hold it for a long time and keep on going. It's an influential music.

DK: Bunny 'Striker' Lee and Bobby Digital, what are some of your thoughts about when dub first emerged, and the impact that it made, and any role you may have had to play in it? When dub first came on the scene, what do you remember about that?

BL: Well, in the early days of recording, it was four-track, and Tubby and myself, was up Duke Reid's studio one day and a guy named Ruddy Redwood from Spanish Town was cutting some dubs.

DK: The man who had a sound system called Supreme Ruler of Sound.

BL: Yes. So he was cutting, and Smithy [Byron Smith], the engineer, forgot to put in the voice, and Ruddy say, 'No, man, make it play,' and when he play it, him say, 'All right, cut one with the voice.' So I went over to Spanish Town, where Ruddy was playing, and when I come back the Monday, I say, 'Hey, Tubbs, you see the joke business what happen up ah Duke Reid studio? You have to start doing that.' Then, we never say 'Version Two', them say 'Part Two', and when them say 'Part Two', the whole dancehall sing. So Tubbs start doing it now, and him start play some Slim Smith tune and him start drop out the voice, like 'Ain't Too Proud To Beg', him take out the voice and play the rhythm, pure drum and bass. And then people start to say, Tubby have an amplifier that can take out the voice!

DK: Bobby Digital, in your early days on sound system, was dub something that you featured? Or was it not really a part of what you represented on your sound?

BD: Yeah man, dub was always there. Because me coming up in that time is like, I always want to play the dub style of music first... because I usually sit and watch U-Roy deejaying on the version, sit and watch U Brown deejaying on the version, Ranking Trevor deejaying on the version, so that was one of the first things. I usually just go by Tubby's, dub off some Studio One, or Duke Reid, Striker Lee, and I usually just play the versions. And when I play the versions, I just listen to the different type of instrumentals that go with them arrangements….

BL: I'm going to tell you how Bobby Digital turned into an engineer. Bobby did come up to Jammy's to cut dub, and Jammy say, 'Bobby, you and me haffi work.'

KJ: It was a Pat Kelly album….

BL: A Pat Kelly album, and Jammy say, 'You have to learn to engineer too,' and from that, the rest is history.

DK: So this is how you first began working with Jammy?

BD: Yeah, he took me away from Sunday dinner, and said, 'Come ah the studio.' So from that day up til now….

BL: You have to start somewhere….

DK: Bunny Lee, in the clip we watched from Howard Johnson's 1982 television documentary, *Deep Roots Music*, you say that dancehall music is still the same rocksteady, and still has that same ska guitar; you say, 'If it doesn't have that ska guitar, then it's not reggae'. So would you say now that you still feel the same way?

BL: Ska is the original Jamaican music; rocksteady have ska, the ska itself, and reggae, the computer thing…. 'Sleng Teng' have ska in it too, you know, ska guitar. So ska is still the backbone.

DK: King Jimmy, in *Deep Roots Music*, you are seen mixing a dub of Junior Reid's 'Jailhouse' at King Tubby's studio. What do you remember about mixing dubs like that?

KJ: Well, those memories can't be forgotten, because those were the prime times of my upcoming in the music, and that was one of my first productions with Junior Reid, doing a dub version, so those memories cannot be erased.

DK: We mentioned before that it was still the roots reggae era when you began working with Wayne Smith. Now of course Wayne Smith is the man who went on to record 'Sleng Teng', and as they all say, 'the rest is history'. But tell us a bit about the early recordings you made with Wayne Smith in the roots era, and then tell us about 'Sleng Teng'. And Bobby Digital, feel free to join in.

KJ: This particular track, 'Ain't No Me', that was Roots Radics with Steelie on keyboards, and that was voiced at King Tubby's. That was one of the first recordings for Wayne Smith, that song and two other songs, and 'Jailhouse' with Junior Reid was done at the same session. Those rhythms were laid down at Channel One studio, then we took them to King Tubby's studio and voiced them there. That's how we usually work.

DK: So how long after that did 'Sleng Teng' happen? Was it a year, or two years, something like that?

KJ: We built 'Sleng Teng' coming on the end of 1984, then it was released in '85.

DK: So, how did the song really come about? How did this recording happen in that form? Bobby, don't forget, you can join in.

KJ: The initial stage of this rhythm was like a buck-up. It wasn't in a reggae format any at all, it was like a wild drum-and-bass thing going on, so we decided to slow down the tempo of it. So when we slowed down the tempo, we really heard the real licks; then we overdub the rhythm section and the bass, that's how 'Sleng Teng' was born. But the true 'Sleng Teng' now, the vocals, 'Under Mi Sleng Teng', Wayne Smith was singing about herb, you know? It's an herb, but he call it 'Sleng Teng'. So him sing about that herb, him under him sleng teng, like him under the weed, you know? That's how it came about.

DK: Bobby Digital, were you present when 'Sleng Teng' was being put together?

BD: Yes, in that area, I was present at last. Because before that, we usually go to Channel One studio to make rhythms, with Johnny Osbourne, and all those artists. So, it was like, with these instruments [that is, the Casio keyboard], we were just going through, but when we were going through, it slip…and we leave out…and when we leave out, a serious thing now! But King [Jammy] find Wayne Smith, and King say him ah go voice Wayne Smith, then we just say, 'Wow!' [And we voiced] Tenor Saw, Sugar Minott [on the same rhythm]….

KJ: As a matter of fact, when we found back the rhythm, because we didn't want to lose it again, we needed to voice Wayne Smith on the rhythm, and we put it back on tape, because we didn't want to lose it in the basket any more, so we put it on tape, and kept the tape.

DK: And of course, it ended up changing Jamaican music literally overnight, and the repercussions were felt very far across the globe.

BD: Yeah, a great impact of 'Sleng Teng'. I can't forget. From that time until this time, 'Sleng Teng' major, globally.

DK: And part of what comes out of this is a dynamic partnership that was taking place between the two of you, at King Jammy's studio.

BD: Yes, it is a partnership, no matter how we stay. I go out and do my thing, and we are family; we speak to each other the same way, we work together the same way, with the same love and respect.

KJ: Bobby Digital was one of my most brilliant engineers, most dedicated engineer and everything.

DK: Let's take a listen to another track which is a collaboration between the two of you, a track with Cocoa Tea, 'Tune In'.

BD: I'll tell you something about this music, this particular song, I cannot forget it. You see, I made a special for King Jammy's, a sound special you know, 'King Jammy's In The Lawn', and the rest is history again.

KJ: Yeah, Bobby Digital was a deejay! Because I voice him on a combination. I never released it, but I should release it now.

DK: Bobby Digital, tell us a little bit about when you decided to make your own way and begin to do your own productions.

BD: A long story, but we're going to cut it short, because of time. To me, I was looking…and say, 'Let me do some things on my own,' and from then, me just say me haffi go take this thing more serious, and Jammy, him couldn't manage the whole of the work, me can tell you, because me work with him and audition, every week or every couple of weeks, on a Thursday…so from then, I started with a one-one thing, then I start voicing. Then, I say, man like Shabba Ranks was my neighbour, up the street, so I say, 'Yo, come. I carry you to the studio. Me ready now.' Then, I usually thief studio time, because I go studio early, and I just say, 'You know what? Yes, a so it go, you haffi do a thing.' And me say, 'Alright, Shabba Ranks, we just a do we thing one-one.' One this month, one next month. We wouldn't say, do everything one day. And you know, this kinda give me a motivation. So when I blow out my first set a songs, I was like, 'Yeah!' I was really impressed with myself, cause you know you feel that drive. So is from that time to this time.

DK: What memories do you have about those days with Shabba, which yielded huge hits like 'Wicked In Bed?'

BD: Well that song, I'll never forget it. To tell you the truth, it voiced in the bedroom. That was voiced in the bedroom at King Jammy's house. King Jammy had the tape machine on these blocks, two concrete blocks on a piece of board…and Shabba just said, 'Boy, me come to voice you know'. Me say, 'Yeah?' So…the bedroom… the mike…him deejay, and him say, 'Me good.' So that was something he really achieved….

DK: In a few moments, I will be opening things up for question and answer with the audience, but first, there are a few other points, and some other music that I want to explore. And there has been a lot of talk recently about 'Revival' in the music, a revitalization of reggae in its present form, and I'm mindful that just a few short years after 'Wicked In Bed' was recorded, Bobby Digital, you had initiated a kind of reggae revival, and I'm thinking of the work that you did with Garnett Silk. What can you tell me about working with him then?

BD: Oh, well, that's another pioneer. I met Garnett when I was at Jammy's studio. Garnett came there to do specials for a sound system in Mandeville, so I really liked his singing. So when he came around to do specials, funny, he was deejaying. So I said, 'No, ah what kind of thing that? Ah sing you fi sing, man.' So I usually get some studio time on a Wednesday, and when Garnett Silk came, I was so disappointed. You know what happen? Steelie and Clevie, Sly and Robbie there, Garnett come every day until one morning me say, 'A foolishness that. Ah voice me ah go voice him today.' Him say, 'Lord Watch Over Our Shoulders,' that one, and the same day, we voice 'It's Growing'. So I think it start get big from that.

DK: Apart from the work you did with him, and his qualities as a singer and a lyricist, what can you us about Garnett Silk as a person?

BD: Garnett Silk was humble…and when he sing, something come over him. So you know this man was real. His projection, his delivery, he was sincere.

DK: The last few tracks we've been playing have been purely digital. And you were saying that 'Sleng Teng' came in the later part of '84, and these tracks that come out into the early '90s, everything is just computer rhythm, digitized. But then, another change starts to happen, a return, or some kind of renewal. And I'm thinking specifically again, of Bobby Digital. Your productions, coming into the mid-'90s, start to get more depth and three-dimensional, where you have a blend of digital instruments and live instruments, and it seemed to be something that other producers also began to explore and adapt. What can you tell us about that?

BD: To tell you the truth, I wasn't…I had a lot of experience in live recording with Striker at Channel One, so it was, in my head…I said, some man say they want to programme things, but I want to use a musician…so I start…Jammy and Striker Lee, I was like their student, so…we always try to blend together the thing.

DK: Let's take a listen to an example, Sizzla's 'Black Woman and Child'.

BD: Yeah, that particular song, memories about that song, the rhythm, I laid that song for Shabba Ranks, 'Ease The War, Increase The Peace'. It used to play every Sunday.

DK: I know you've all got plenty of questions that you'd like to put to these musical heroes, and mindful that time is short, in thinking about these continuities, and this evolution, what other comments can we get from our panellists about what has taken place from that time until this time?

KJ: Well, I'd just like to be honest about the current dancehall music that is being made by the youths in Jamaica and all over the world. There are some good efforts that is going on now in the music, but it doesn't progress as I would like it to be, in terms of musically speaking. In the days when we used to make dancehall music, it was musically inclined more. More people used to appreciate, not all of the lyrics, but the music, musically and instrumentally. And I'd just like to send a message to the younger producers out there: it's our music, it's our life. You don't just go in the studio and just do something because you want to make a money. You have to do it from your heart, for love, you have to love this thing to really penetrate it for real. Because if we didn't love the music, I wouldn't still be making a new studio right now, and we're still recording. So I'm just begging the new youths out there just to do something to keep the thing going so that it can remain Jamaican. We don't want to hear that other places just take away everything, and we don't get nothing from it. Just keep it going.

BL: What I will just say is, the music evolved from them times till this time. It's still, don't care what it change to, it's still dancehall music, you know. Because our music used to play in the dancehall, just the same. And the youths them must value the music and put more into it, but I wish them all the best. There are a few good singers coming in, and if they continue…but as the King just say, if we don't be careful them people abroad going to take it, because you see what is happening on the Continent now, most of the artistes are from Germany, France, and everywhere. So if the youths don't behave themselves, them will find themselves outside.

BD: If you don't know where you coming from then you can't know where you're going. And if you don't know the root you not going to know the branch nor the stem. The youths of today, them don't follow no elders. Those who teach, they don't want to associate themselves with us as students. Them no want to associate themselves with us who should pass on the knowledge and say, 'Well, this don't look too right', or 'This can go on'. Or to say, you want to do this, 'How do I get this done? How do I go forward? How to approach this?' Is like them feel that them is it, make a song on a rhythm that is playing and get a little break, and them ah the big man, them a top man. But you no top until you do a couple years in this thing like Striker and Jammy, Downbeat. Even me, me still growing. Me still take telling from these people, because me can't go near them, them done know how the business run. So you need to keep in contact with the elders of the music to get ideas from them and tell them your ideas to get feedback. Cause if you no know you roots, you cannot know the branches or the stem. Them youths here need to go back to them roots and research what was then, and how things set now, and what them need to do.

DK: Thank you. So we'll open up now for question and answer.

Question #1: I think the last point that you made about the machines, I don't know if you used the machines or the machines used you, but you did wonderful music, you all made wonderful music. But the biggest slavery to music is the machine, and Auto-Tune. What do you think about the way people use Auto-Tune to change their voice?

BD: Well, now you hear people sounding like a chipmunk. And in Jamaica, if you sound like a chipmunk on the song, is because you supposed to sound like a chipmunk. In our day, all the music was on key; we just used Auto-Tune to smooth out some edges. These guys, they use it right through the thing, the song no on no key, most of these songs no have no rhythm. Is like the rhythm dash on so, all you hear is 'Nyaa-nyaa-nyaa-nyaa'. Them is not artistes. Artistes are like Taurus Riley, Romain Virgo. When them ah sing, they differentiate themselves from the pack. But it's how you use the tool.

DK: King Jammy would you like to respond?

KJ: Well as Bobby Digital said, it's how you use the tool. And I think the only way that I would use Auto-Tune is if somebody voice a song for me and he's from another country, and he's not there to correct a mistake and he's unavailable, then probably I'd use it to just put it back in tune. But for the duration of the whole song, it would get monotonous to me. It's not really a cultural thing, it's just a style.

Question #2: I know you do not approve of the lyrics the youths sing, or put out to the public, but how do you think the youths, so to speak, can access the elders to get this knowledge how to produce, or think, or write, in the way that we want them to?

KJ: Well, that's a very simple thing. For youths to get in touch with me, my number is in the Yellow Pages, phone directory, it's on the Internet, it's everywhere. And to access me, even if it's not possible, there are other ways they can learn these things, by going to the Edna Manley School, or if they can't afford it personally, probably a government-sponsored method, you know. But access to this information is available.

DK: Bunny 'Striker' Lee, any comments before we close this session?

BL: Well, it's good to hear and listen to the younger folks, and what the King say, we can take it as the gospel.

DK: Bobby Digital, any comments about how Jamaican producers can make themselves accessible?

BD: My door is open for anybody. And I'll treat you like my sons, take them under my wings to learn production, and I don't raise no children. A man will just come ask you, 'How you do this?' and as an elder, you just have to tell the youths how to do it. So my door is wide open to anyone who really shows their interest. Any day, any time, feel free. Nuff time people say them no want to wake me, but ah true them no know that if them want something, I will jump up out of my bed and give them. So just tell them to call Bobby, or call Jammy.

Notes

1. Established by Sonny Bradshaw in 1959, Teenage Dance Party was a radio and television programme showcasing local dance talent. It was broadcast on Jamaica Broadcasting Corporation (JBC) radio each weekday afternoon, and on JBC television every Friday night.
2. Arthur 'Duke' Reid founded the Treasure Isle record label and recording studio, as well as the Trojan sound system. Leslie Kong founded the Beverley's label. Clement 'Sir Coxsone' Dodd founded the Studio One group of labels and recording studio, and the Six Coxsone Downbeat sound system.
3. Clue Jay and the Blues Blasters was led by bassist Cluette Johnson.
4. Randy's, a recording studio opened by Vincent Chin in the late 1960s, was located at 17 North Parade.
5. 'Single Girl' by Nana McLean.
6. Keyboardist Wycliffe 'Steelie' Johnson and drummer Cleveland 'Clevie' Browne joined together to form an unbeatable duo, building hit rhythms for countless producers during the 1980s.
7. King Tubby's Home Town Hi-Fi was founded by electronics specialist and sound engineer Osbourne Ruddock. King Attorney, originally known as Soul Attorney, was founded by Rupert Brown; it would later be known as Socialist Roots, after being acquired by Tony Welch. King

Jammy's sound system was founded by Tubby's protégé, Lloyd James. Earl's Disco was located towards the bottom end of Waterhouse.
8. 'Bangarang' by Stranger Cole and Lester Sterling, produced by Bunny Lee.
9. Glen 'Capo' Adams was a session organist that later played with Bob Marley and the Wailers and Lee Perry's Upsetters. 'Bangarang' was recorded at his first recording session.
10. Formed in Port Antonio in 1955, the Jolly Boys mento band was one of the most popular hotel acts of the 1960s and '70s. The group still performs with several veterans whose membership dates back to the 1960s.
11. Wayne Smith's 'Under Mi Sleng Teng' was Jamaica's first computerised hit.
12. U-Roy revolutionised deejay music with his fluid toasting at Treasure Isle in 1970, yielding hits such as 'Wake The Town.'
13. That is, playing rhythm guitar.
14. Earl Anthony Johnson, alias Earl Zero, was an aspiring singer from Greenwich Farm that was a close friend of guitarist Earl 'Chinna' Smith.
15. Founded by the Blake Brothers in 1950, Merritone is one of Jamaica's longest-running sound systems.
16. Sound system proprietor Count Shelley ran the Third World label in England. He later moved to New York and opened Superpower Records, one of the largest reggae record shops and labels in the USA.

Section 2
DISCOURSES BEYOND YAAD

Expressions of Reggae in Havana: Processes of Foreign Influence and Cultural Appropriation

José Luis Fanjul Rivera

> New people, new ideological trends,
> another emotional tuning,
> awaken new intonations or transform,
> and re-intone the ordinary ones (Asafiev 262).

In the 1970s, a new genre appeared on the Cuban music scene: reggae. It entered the island through various avenues which facilitated its spread through informal *underground* channels.[1] This perhaps accounts for the fact that when reggae made its appearance it did not receive the support and dissemination it might have deserved, due to its Caribbean references and the content or message of brotherhood expressed in its lyrics; this despite the interest or appeal it held for local and especially international audiences.

The entry of the Jamaican music genre into our island is linked to the diplomatic relations established with Jamaica, Barbados, Trinidad and Tobago, and Guyana in 1972 (Furé 2005), and with other islands which later established relations with Cuba. Such diplomatic relations led to the temporary immigration of English-speaking students, mainly Jamaicans, who were awarded Cuban government scholarships. Other contributory factors included the movement of Cuban construction workers to Jamaica, and vice versa, in 1976, as well as the cultural exchange between both countries announced that same year. This cultural exchange allowed reggae music to make its way into Cuba, as the introduction of cassettes, LP records, Walkman's as well as posters, T-shirts and typical accessories brought by sailors and travellers, familiarized Cubans with Rastafari culture and its related social construct.

Radio stations in Florida and different areas in the Caribbean gave an even greater boost to the spread of this music. During that period, reggae was heard only at parties in private homes in inner city neighbourhoods, mainly in Havana and Santiago de Cuba. Its peripheral status, which locates it within marginalized social sectors and non-commercial spaces, has remained unchanged up to the present. The situation continues but in other ways, and reggae now has a bit more freedom. Moreover, the prevailing feeling or attitude of Cuban society towards reggae music is, to a large extent, influenced and distorted by the prejudices that have been generated around Rastafarian culture, the culture that is committed to this genre and has identified with its roots, without changing the principles of the performance of the music in the early 1970s.

Social and musical changes in the late twentieth-century phase of the Cuban Revolution, which promotes social rights and racial equality, enabled the development of bands that play this genre of music, but without promoting the music directly. These bands have developed a style based on the individuality of the performers, who increasingly emphasize contributions from their Cuban heritage. As an example, we have Tierra Verde [Green Earth], which was one of the pioneering bands of this movement. Thereafter came other interpreters of the genre, a minority of them with academic training, who absorbed, innovated and transposed the codes of a foreign musical model with which they had some affinity because of its proximity and the similarity of the social problems.

Other bands worthy of mention are Insurrecto [Insurgents], Remanente [Remnant], Hijos de Israel [Children of Israel], Punto Rojo [Red Dot], Paso Firme [Firm Step], Mañana Reggae Band [Tomorrow Reggae Band], Raíces Negras [Black Roots], Elio Band, Príncipe Carlos [Prince Charles], Military Dread, Coco Man, Donato y los Sicarios [Donato and the Assassins], Crazy Man, Incognita, and El Médico [The Doctor].

SPACES, RELOCATIONS AND SOCIO-MUSICAL STRUCTURES

The current context of reggae in the city of Havana is somewhat peculiar as it is a situation in which the fans, both musicians and audience, assume responsibility for the promotion and dissemination of the genre, and the culture with which it is identified. La Casa del Tango [House of Tango], located on Neptune Street, near the corner of Galiano, hosts the reggae band Remanente and its followers on alternate Friday nights. This space, where Rasta fan club sessions are held, is not the most appropriate for performance by the band which presents another image. However, the Rastafarians' need for social validation transforms it into an appropriate space.

This space is designed for the anecdotal and nostalgic style of the tango, not for the features of the discourse of the Jamaican music genre, which, since its inception, has raised issues of social relevance and expressed criticism in the spirit of reflection rather than censure, in addition to the spiritual support it offers its consumers.[2]

The group dynamic operating around the Casa del Tango in the middle of Central Havana is highly unusual because of the influx of people into the location and the nearby establishments for buying alcoholic beverages (alcohol is consumed, though not sold, at that venue). As a result, participants in the club sessions can be seen all along Neptune Street. Havana comes alive every Friday for reggae night, and beginning early in the afternoon, Rastas heading to the venue can be seen on the streets. It is like the prelude to a ritual, a time that allows them to show themselves socially and stroll through that urban space in their outfits, seeking attention and new fans.

The frequent entry of foreigners into the space is due to interest in the genre, which is very appealing because of the abundance of Caribbean sound and visual imagery demanded by everyone who vacations on a Caribbean island. This promotes cultural exchange between the participants. Despite this, the strategies and cultural attractions that draw tourists to the island do not include reggae as part of the events presented in hotels, rendezvous and night shows.

Introducing such an internationally recognized music genre into an island with characteristics similar to those of the place where it originated, is quite difficult because of the language barrier. Over the years, many bands have ventured into reggae, and many musicians have been part of the Rasta movement in Cuba.

There are some reggae bands that have not been recognized by the music centres, institutions or agencies responsible for validating them within the current music scene. That is why they have become part of an underground movement that exists and survives in big cities worldwide, where those involved have a sense of belonging and are able to identify with marginal sectors of society that are not exactly the most recognized and accepted. They are the ones who hold their reggae club sessions in houses, patios and yards, looking for a place to be and to maintain contact, depending on their kinships or conflicts. This alternative socio-musical discourse on radio and television and in other communication media, is the expression of a whole chain of parallel events, beliefs, religions and lifestyles that coexist within societies and, in this case, within Cuban society.

As shown by the fieldwork, in Havana, only one reggae band is auditioned and hired by the National Centre for Popular Music: Remanente. This band, which performs at the Casa del Tango, is the bearer and creator of new musical repertoires that blossom from the cultural encounter between Cuban and Jamaican music, and this in turn facilitates a process of generic hybridization.

The members of Remanente nostalgically recall events held in the '90s in La Corea (Hernández 2010) on San Miguel del Padrón Street in a natural outdoor setting, where an entire socio-musical world was created by reggae and reggae musicians. In the twenty-first century, with changing concepts of space, stage design, the technology boom and the overwhelming emphasis on spectacle, musicians and managers of bands like this one, think about being in suitable venues that allow them to give visibility to their reality.

The contradiction involved in the act of presenting a reggae performance in a place that reflects a tango atmosphere directly influences the artistes and consumers, but in this case other resources are mobilized to stage a musical event with established multidimensional performances.

Having a space, a strategic space, is also a challenge because of Cuban aversion to Rastafarianism. The social prejudices that persist in Cuban society, despite the gains of the Revolution are obstacles facing Rastas every day.

SHIFTING IDENTITIES AND INTER-GENRE MUSICAL PERFORMANCE

> New identities come into being not only devoid of their metaphysical essence, but also stripped of their epic aura. Gone are essential identities; and so too are identities that drive history

or are responsible for history's great causes. Indeed, identity profiles are unstable; no longer do they create subjects with pre-defined positions but they often point to shifts and dislocations (Ticio Escobar).

Redefining Rastafarianism in Cuba has led the people who have adopted this culture to search for the means to fill and satisfy much of their spiritual needs as human beings so that life in the difficult environment where these individuals operate may consequently be lived according to the religious and spiritual values they embody. Thus, the posture of a Rastafarian in Cuban society would be that of a Cuban who has adopted certain religious, cultural and aesthetic ideals which contribute to the construction of an individual identity. This distinguishes him from what would be a typical member of the society and makes him into a living embodiment of a symbolic image that is alien to our nationality.

In light of this, the following questions are pertinent: if a person's attitude is based on certain ideals that are not part of certain established typologies of a given society like Cuba, what kind of identity construct would prevail in these cases if there is a dynamic that fluctuates from one side to another and vice versa? To what extent does one identity prevail if an individual has more than one identity? What does a Rastafarian represent in and for Cuban society? Is Cuban identity deconstructed by Rastafarian culture, to the point where Cuban identity disappears, or does Rastafarian culture construct a fluid Cuban identity within narrow social groups?

Undoubtedly, the dialectical principle illustrated by our current cultural problems, which are a feature of a globalized world, makes it difficult to give an exact definition of identity, given the shifts made at different levels of perception and assimilation of identities. A social analysis will reveal certain behaviours of Rastafarians in Cuban society, their acceptance, and the frictions created between individuals of diverse ideologies, religions, and cultures in different locations where people meet and interact. A musicological study could focus on the review, critique and analysis of the complete findings of an examination of the musical performance of different melodic, rhythmic, and intonational structures, which, in their turn, reveal changes in the creative impulses, hybridization and interpretation of a particular genre, in this case reggae, as a musical product of Rastafari culture in Cuba.

However, when played in an environment that is different from the original environment, by individuals who interpret and consume it, this genre changes its original feeling, that is, the feeling that generated it. Although it retains its principles, there are changes in concept, ingredients and dynamic, reflecting the musical sensibility of the place where it is performed and of the individual or individuals who perform it.

Because reggae is a genre whose lyrics convey a sense of protest, reflection, celebration of blackness and social conflict, it can be easily adapted to the present situation of Cuba, which shares the previously mentioned problems. This also makes it adaptable to the distinct musical personality of its producer.

In Cuba, racial discrimination, derogatory comments and the shock effect of Rastafarians are reactions and behaviours that persist today. Reggae producers or consumers are, to some extent, victims of the cultural limitations and ignorance of people and institutions that do not recognize or understand a way of life based on other and even more diverse aesthetic and cultural references. These references are an undeniable blend of Jamaican and African identities with the added input of Cuban elements.

Recognition of their Rastafarian identity by the members of Remanente does not imply a defined and static identity, with fixed musical roots located conventionally in the musical style of Bob Marley, nor does it mean that they follow established patterns. To some extent, their identity will therefore fluctuate between the Jamaican construct and their Cuban roots.

In this case study, the initial musical repertoire begins with what the agents of Remanente think, as against what happens during the musical event itself and the themes of the songs. This will then determine the performance to be presented at a show. Self-awareness plays a key role in their ideas about what they want to present as a cultural expression, and that is where the identity problem is reflected. This will subsequently determine the path taken by the band.

Being aware of what it means to be Rastafarian, projecting a certain image of Africa, slavery, blackness *I-an-I*,[3] Babylon[4] or Haile

Selassie,[5] and embracing a way and philosophy of life with its own thinking and attitudes, but at the same time being a Cuban with set codes of musical expression, leads to a rethinking and questioning of who am I and in what context do I create music?

The idea put forward by musicologist, María de los Ángeles Córdova, of what it means to be a Cuban musician supports this argument:

> It actually involves having the elements that constitute our historical musical experience, as well as possessing the creative and performance techniques that enable the relatively swift and precise assimilation of all those influences (both internal and external) that connect with one's own musical culture. The original artistic manner in which cultural experiences and assimilated influences are integrated will also be the result of the artiste's cultural identity, training and creative talent (Córdova 2007).

Closely related to this, is the fact that the production and execution of reggae music is as variable and performative[6] as the very identity of an individual who acts according to the typical behaviour patterns of a complex Cuban culture, but adopts the culture and philosophy of Rastafarian life.

In the process of thinking about what is to be said, written and expressed in a performatic[7] and musical manner, the ideas of the creators undergo modification, depending on the onstage interaction between musicians in the band and the participating dancers. Using what happens in rehearsals, the musicians create a repertoire that defines them as a band, and enables them to share a collective identity, but each band member, in turn, respects the other's musical ideas, allowing for the display of individual instrumental or vocal styles.

In one sense, the identity of each individual must play a key role in the sound of Remanente. Each band member has a history of which he gives an example organically in each performance, as he adds to the composition glimpses of his experience in other musical genres such as son, rumba and rock. Mention should also be made of other band members who, while not objecting to this performativity,[8] try to maintain sound stability and a feeling of pure reggae, though it is being reinterpreted in another time and space.

Thus, we see how, on a personal and group level, identity is constructed in the way these individuals define and identify themselves within a band, as they interact and develop an intangible sense of belonging, as bearers of a sound brand, conceived, created, adopted and expressed by the managers and players in the group.

One of the factors affecting the identity predicament is not having a suitable place to stage the reggae shows, taking into account not only space requirements, that is, a space with 'smart' lights, adequate lighting effects and décor, but also the scarcity of resources. The issue becomes a challenge because they try to find a space with the appeal and magnetic energy to fill the music scene with what in another context is referred to as spectacularity.[9] Using this term, we will try to explain what happens in this space, which changes its function when it is taken over by another type of stage-music performance.

Spectacularity, as a feature, exists where there is a musical repertoire with a large or small scale impact, which in the case we are studying can be seen in the inter-genre nature of the interpretation, and the musical and dance movements. The stage-music performance thus becomes a process of enjoyment, exchange, improvisation, giving rise to mixtures and hybridizations that interconnect and create close links between related identities in the same communication space. Therefore, approaching this subject from an inter-genre perspective would be a rather bold idea.

Remanente's musical output could not be defined and classified as inter-genre,[10] but this perspective could be applied to their behaviour in order to understand the complexity of the musical flows and influences, whether foreign or domestic. This is not the case of the samba-reggae that Gerard Behague (2000) produces with the Rastafarian community of Bahia in Brazil. There, the genre is located in a specific cultural context in a dynamic relationship with the social and political situation in Brazil, where samba reggae is a reflection of what happened there in the late 1990s.

The definition provided by musicologist Danilo Orozco is valid. He explains that inter-genres are:

> Genres with varying degrees of hybridity, especially those whose profile is usually characterized by extraordinary trans-genre mobility and a structure made up of juxtaposed elements, a high degree of counterpoint or dynamic clash at specific points, a phenomenon that is prominent at certain more or less critical historical moments (Orozco 2006).[11]

He notes, moreover, that:

> With respect to such inter-genre, the point is not how hybrid it is, but how much more dynamic and fluid are its elements and its constituent time-space factors, that is, the overwhelming predominance of either a dynamic clash between superimposed elements and spaces, juxtaposed to each other or of a discursive immediacy (which is rare in other types of hybrids or mixtures), and also how much that dynamic clash could tell us about the determining factors in the socio-musical environment (Orozco 2006).

Cuban reggae is not currently defined as a musical inter-genre, but to understand in depth what happens in its case, it is necessary to focus not only on the performance but also on the dynamics of the process, which is where one can appreciate the features described above. The fact is that because the music genre is linked to the culture of the society where it is produced, transformation and destabilization of what, in principle, was assumed as an original identity is inevitable. In this way, other identity features that will expand the socio-musical discourse are introduced.

The sound produced by the Remanente Band includes implicit strategies for an appealing and dynamic performance. This holds the audience's attention and for the listeners it represents familiar and typical features, depending on the context of each individual. It is also related to musical events experienced by the individual and the dialogue between different sound and social spaces.

It should be noted that in the maturation process or in his trajectory as an artist, the musician follows a line from which he will draw his preferences. This will cause him to interpret or compose new music and, at the same time, establish a trademark. These trademarks or tokens are retentions of other musical experiences that differ from the current ones, as well as narratives or references within the narrative itself. This can occur at the micro level, where the musician inserts a series of intonations or chord tensions in his improvisation (although in this genre ninths, elevenths and thirteenths are not common and are only used depending on the text).

At this time, when the musical discourse changes, each improviser will play his part in the act, when, for example, the pianist mixes the syncopated beats of a cha-cha-chá or a *tumbao* with reggae beats without losing the rhythmic quality. Then the guitarist accentuates the sound of rock, and the singers alternate with the percussion, creating a sudden crossing of discourses that move the identity markers towards one type of music or another. As a result, generic hybridization takes on a meaning that is suited to the current musical scenario

Included in the strategies employed by the band is the dynamism added to the repertoire by the band manager, based on a combination of well-known Jamaican themes and themes from Cuban authors. Improvisation and extension of aspects of the themes, with long sung and vocalized phrases are the result of repeated improvised and experimental techniques. The combination of melodic-rhythmic intonational features typical of Cuban music genres with Jamaican reggae points to changes in perception on the part of the listeners. The shifts in musical function and the venue changes affect the visual, spatial and instrumental situation on the stage; this in addition to the presence of some members of the audience moving freely on the stage, leading to a surprising change in the original musical effect. All this gives a performative quality to the space and to the show, and defies the expectations of a standard musical presentation.

What makes Remanente a unique musical group in the country is the contemporary concept of a stage managed by the band's agents who defend the values that they promote and who take the messages they convey as their very own and transmit them to the public. They play a leading role and use a very personal style of creating reggae. Spectacularity and the articulation of a Rastafarian musical discourse in the Casa del Tango sessions are guaranteed by the impact of the repertoire performed by the band, as well as by the form and the relevance of the content in terms of significant musical qualities and social values. That repertoire satisfies the spiritual needs of a devoted local or foreign audience that participates and interacts with the band contributing to the conscious and organic creation of imagery related to Rastafarianism and reggae in this party space.

Despite the obstacles presented by Cuban reality, lived experience shows that these people, with their philosophy of life, religion, culture, love and brotherhood consider themselves Cuban first and foremost because their Cuban identity is something that makes them authentic in the eyes of the public, the world and in their own eyes. Rastafarianism goes hand in hand with a Cuban identity, is part of the construction of this identity and is rooted in a process in which music is the main factor and the reason to meet, dialogue, and give expression to the most important content within this space and time. It is the very essence of who they are.

Given the limitations of finding suitable spaces for socialization in the Cuban Rastafarian movement, the effect of a reggae fan club gathering every Friday in a place that is associated with another scenario, is that Rastas experience the marginalization fostered by the country's cultural policies. They face not only these problems but also the problems associated with the racial factor, which continues to dog the island and are current topics discussed in various state, political and social forums as baggage to be eliminated. The aesthetic and philosophical conflicts, to some extent, create barriers between the population and the Rastafarians whose way of life is uncommon among Cubans.

Based on first impressions of a sector that, in its dynamism and social recognition, is defined as a small group in the population of the entire country, it can be said that Remanente and its audience, with their cultural significance, have been able to insert themselves into Havana's social life. The demand for reggae fan club sessions organized by them is increasing, due not to the high quality of the lighting and technological resources, but to the power of the identity values that are reflected and translated into the music and its performance on stage, and to the way is which its members identify with each other: greetings, hugs, hairstyles, caps and clothing. They have gone from being 'the other' to becoming 'us' because one thing is certain and it is that a Cuban identity is present in each of them, because in Cuba, in order to be Rastafarian and create reggae, one must first feel that one is Cuban.

Notes

1. The term *underground* refers to what becomes clandestine by existing at other levels of social recognition in this case.
2. According to Ana María Hernández, manager of Remanente, 'reggae speaks to current affairs and deals with everyday reality. Reggae lyrics do not convey nostalgia.' Interview, Casa del Tango, Friday May 7, 2010.

3. *I-an-I* is an expression of unity between two or more people, and also of unity with Jah (God). A sense of solidarity, brotherhood and identity is expressed in *I-an-I*. Each person is divine and the 'truth' brings equality for all.
4. Babylon is a term drawn from the Holy Bible and is identified with everything negative that affects the world. It symbolizes the force that dehumanizes the individual, resulting in a loss of values.
5. Haile Selassie I (1892–1975) was the last emperor of Ethiopia (Abyssinia, 1930–1974).
6. According to Alejandro Madrid 'it refers to the performative quality of an act, that is, its ability to do what it says at the time that it is said, taking into account the context and the repetition of the act to create discursive conventions,' (Sibe Forum, 2007).
7. Madrid defines it as that which 'speaks to how the actors in a theatrical piece (music in this case) operate, or the setting or relationship between performers and audience' (Sibe Forum, 2007).
8. I refer to the concept of performativity provided by Judith Butler in *El género en disputa* which she defines as follows: 'Performativity is not a singular act but a repetition and a ritual that achieves its effect through its naturalization in the context of a body, understood, in part, as a culturally sustained temporal duration.'
9. Spectacularity refers to a quality of something spectacular, which causes pleasure and wonder and is able to attract attention and move the spirit.
10. This category was used by Danilo Orozco in his studies of Cuban *timba* in the 1990s, where similar events occur.
11. Danilo Orozco: '... Detrás del qué sé yo y el no sé qué..."Borroso musicar transgenérico: espacio-tiempo, discursividad y cuerpo."'

References

Asáfiev, B.V. 1971. La Forma Musical Como Proceso. *Editorial Música*, Leningrado.

Behague, Gerard. 2000. La samba reggae: invención de un nuevo ritmo símbolo de la negritud Bahiana. Retrieved February 2010 from http://www.hist.puc.cl/historia/iaspmla.html.

Benavente Morales, Carolina. '¿Dónde está el toque jamaiquino? Reggae, rastafarismo y la cultura rasta en México', México. (s.n.) Retrieved February 2010 www.uc.cl/historia/iaspm/baires/articulos/carolinabenavente.pdf.

Butler, Judith. 2001. *El Género en Disputa*. México: Paidós.
Córdova, María de los Ángeles. 2007. Música y transculturación. Culturas musicales no hegemónicas: esencia y factores de transformación. Cuba, siglos XVI al XIX. Diss. La Habana Instituto Superior de Arte.
Furé Davis, Samuel. 2005. Lyrical Subversion in Cuban Reggae. In *Image and Narrative*, Online Magazine of the visual narrative. Retrieved February 2010 from http://www.imageandnarrative.be/inarchive/worldmusicb_advertising/samuelfuredavis.htm.
Hansing, Katring. 2001. Los Rastafaris: Guerreros del Amor. *Caminos*, No. 22.
Hernández, Ana María. 2010. Interview by author. Friday May 7.
Larenas Álvarez and Angie Alejandra. 2002. La Inserción Social del Rastafari en Cuba: ¿Tendencias Contraculturales? Undergraduate Sociology Thesis. Universidad de La Habana.
———. 2004. El Rastafarismo en Cuba: una Aproximación a Sus Dimensiones Sociales. *Catauro* (La Habana) Vol. 5, No. 9 (Enero-Junio).
Larrique, Diego P. 2008. Reggae e identidades en Caracas: una Introducción a los Mulatos Márgenes de la Modernidad. *Revista Venezolana de Análisis de Coyuntura*, Caracas Vol. 14, No. 2 (July–December): 341–61.
Madrid, Alejandro. 2009. Performativo y Performático. *Fragmento del Foro de Sibe*, Vol. 13.
Orozco, Danilo. 2006. Detrás del qué sé yo y el no sé qué... Borroso musicar transgenérico: espacio tiempo, discursividad y cuerpo.' *Inaugural Lecture of the IASPM Conference*, Havana, Cuba.
Serbin, Andrés. 1986. Los Rastafari: Entre Mesianismo y Revolución. *Nueva Sociedad*, Caracas, No. 82 (March–April): 178–86.

'You've got no time for me': Martin 'Sugar' Merchant, British Caribbean Musical Identity and the Media

Shara Rambarran

During the 1990s, Britain experienced 'Britpop' – a British cultural movement celebrating art, film, sport and popular music. While this movement was excessively praised by the media for the production of successful British talent, it appeared that British creative artists born of another ethnic origin were somehow ignored. To demonstrate this point, this article will focus on the British Caribbean singer, Martin 'Sugar' Merchant and his group, Audioweb, and how they struggled to gain recognition in the British media. To understand the possible reasons why they did not receive full support from the media, the discussion will be begin by briefly addressing the history and reception of early Caribbean culture and music in Britain. This will be followed by an overview of British Caribbean popular music from the 1950s to the 1980s, and its representation by the media. It will lead to a discussion on the main focus of this article, Martin 'Sugar' Merchant and his group, Audioweb. Here, this section will address Merchant's sociocultural and musical background – his group, and their placement in British culture – with reference to Britpop. The chapter will offer suggestions as to why Merchant and his group failed to receive media recognition despite having a loyal fan base and support from the music industry. This concept will be supported by examining the group's reaction to the lack of media attention. It will be followed by analysing a song and music video, 'Faker' (1997), which silently hints at their (dis)placement in British culture and society. The article will conclude with a summary of the research, and how the lack of media's support unfortunately led to the demise of Audioweb.

AN OVERVIEW OF THE HISTORY OF CARIBBEAN MUSIC IN BRITAIN

To understand the development of British Caribbean popular music in Britain, this section begins by offering an overview of the significance of the music in culture and society, this is then followed by a history of Caribbean music in Britain.

Caribbean music has maintained a continuous presence in British culture and society since the early twentieth century, whether it is experienced in imagined communities, underground and urban scenes. Aspects of Caribbean music, in particular, Jamaican reggae, dub and ska, have contributed to other musical genres such as jungle, drum and bass, grime, dubstep, and have fused with rock and punk. Musicians of these styles may have achieved some commercial success, but with the exception of exported artists (most notably Bob Marley and The Wailers) however, genres such as reggae tend to receive little recognition in the media and in British society. Indeed, some songs may be perceived as 'novelty' hits where they have a sense of longevity – whether it is marketed for the mainstream audience or for selected communities. Therefore, it is unlikely then that the musicians of these genres may not receive the full acknowledgment they deserve especially if there is no coverage from the media. This concept will be explored momentarily, but first, it is important to gain a sense of the history of Caribbean music and its reception in Britain.

The history of Caribbean music in Britain has been well documented by musicologist, John Cowley (1985, 1990). He argues that the music developed in two periods: 1900–45 and 1945–60. The first period in Britain (the 'Empire') consisted of calypso and jazz. Performed by professional musicians from Trinidad and Guyana with the likes of Iron Duke (real name Henry Julian) and Ken 'Snakehips' Johnson, the musicians were based in the London circuit, performing in venues such as the *Café de Paris* club. The marketing of their recorded works, however, were exported to the Caribbean and not sold in Britain, as the 'general acceptance for black West Indian big bands in Britain was difficult to achieve' (Cowley 1990, 4); which also meant that musicians found it difficult to make a decent income as professional performers. The first stage of the Caribbean music scene in London quickly demised due to the Second World War, and the tragic death of Ken 'Snakehips' Johnson and some of his band who were killed during the Blitz (Levine 2006, 400–401).

The second period of Caribbean music in Britain (1945–60) consisted of jazz (played by musicians such as the Jamaican saxophonist, Joe Harriott), and traditional Jamaican folk songs (sung by the likes of poet, Louise Bennett) (Cowley 1990, 7). Calypso music was revived in England by 'Al' Jennings and his All Star Caribbean Orchestra, Lord Beginner and Lord Kitchener. These musicians were discovered by Denis Preston, a record producer, personality deejay, jazz critic and journalist, who helped to raise the profile of Caribbean music in Britain (Cowley 1990, 5). In the early 1950s, Preston became an independent producer with his own label, Record Supervision Limited and the famous Landsdowne Studios. The music produced was consumed by the first wave of disillusioned migrants, mainly from Jamaica and Trinidad, who bonded together through music, where they could reminisce and celebrate their own identity and culture (for more information on this significant history please read the publications of the Centre for Contemporary Cultural Studies 1982; Gilroy 2002; Owusu 2000). The reason for this unity is because they struggled to integrate in British society owing to the unwelcoming tone from the local people (demonstrated in Lord Kitchener's song 'The Underground Train'). However, during the 1950s, it was Jamaican music that started to gain attention in Britain with the likes of Louise Bennett's song, 'Linstead Market' (1951) and Eric Hayden's 'Give Her the No 1' (1953).

In the 1960s, Bluebeat music, received some national recognition with imported Jamaican records such as Jimmy Cliff's 'Wonderful World' (1964) and Millie Small's 'My Boy Lollipop' (1964). Also, British based multi-racial groups formed such as the Equals, who, interestingly, were more popular in Europe than in Britain. However, as argued by Mike Alleyne, the popularity of music hits in Britain 'failed to generate ongoing success for Jamaican music in the pop market' (2012, 194), which could be due to the marketing and media. The marketing of music in Britain, particularly reggae, was generally poor. Dick Hebdige argues that it was rejected by the British Broadcasting Corporation (BBC) and radio stations as it was 'too raw and crude,

[and] the lyrics [were] too obscene and too difficult to follow for white tastes' (1987, 92). Other incredible reasons include: that the tempo was slow and the bass line was heavy. The credible reason is that the lyrical content presented in reggae, dealt with sociocultural and political issues (such as rejection and oppression in society), which resulted in the lack of interest from the media and broadcasting corporations as they thought it would not be appealing to the masses (Büld 1978). It appeared that the media preferred to focus on novelty reggae adopted by established musicians like Eric Clapton's version of 'I Shot the Sheriff' (1974), the Beatles' 'Ob-la-do-ob-la-da' (1968), and the Rolling Stones' cover version of Eric Donaldson's 'Cherry, Oh Baby' (1976). These white mainstream artists would make the music appeal to the audience by modifying the lyrics and music, and by maintaining their pop-like vocals (Alleyne 2000, 18). Nevertheless, there was a market for reggae music despite not being represented by the media. Underground venues and specialist record shops, in inner cities, constantly developed to cater for their audiences; therefore, musicians and deejays did not need to rely on national radio stations and major retail record stores to hear and have access to the latest sounds (Bradley 2000, 373). Having direct access to reggae music was due to imports, word of mouth, and the arrival of the second wave of migrants (Bradley 2000, 380; Partridge 2010, 110).

With this direct access, other musical practices and styles began to spread in Britain such as sound system culture and dub, from Jamaica, from the late 1960s. As well as consuming the music in homes, house parties, halls, blues parties and so on, the music was also associated with established venues such as 007 in East London and Ram Jam in Brixton. The music brought communities together to take pride in their identities, and to innocently voice their frustration about their treatment in British society. For example, there were further social issues to consider: the youth were facing discrimination (in education and society), unemployment, racism and police brutality. To conquer their battles and fears in British society, the youth indulged in their cultural heritage and music. Here, home-grown crews and groups emerged (the likes of Jah Shaka, The Cimarons, Matumbi, Aswad, Steel Pulse, Saxon Sound System, Fatman and Sir Coxsone). These crews and groups expressed their frustration with British society, racism and inequality issues. These views are justified by musicians such as Brinsley Forde of Aswad who critiques: 'We were born here and we should have been receiving all the benefits our white schoolmates were receiving, but this wasn't so. There were no jobs, [we had] bad housing and pressure in the streets' (Owusu 2000, 9). Forde neatly stated the bleak reality that British Caribbeans had to face in society. Despite the Race Relations Act being in place in 1976, which was intended to prevent racial discrimination in Britain, there were still tensions and unresolved issues in society (not forgetting the infamous Enoch Powell 1968 'Rivers of Blood' speech and race riots), particularly when the late Baroness Margaret Thatcher became prime minister – institutionalized racism was still active in Britain – which was the reason the media were not overly active in representing British Caribbean music. To demonstrate this point further, the following section discusses how the music was promoted in Britain.

THE MEDIA AND MUSICAL CROSSOVERS IN BRITAIN

The promotion of music was represented through selected media channels such as specialized press with the monthly magazines *Black Music* and *Black Echoes*, and regional radio stations (Radio Luxembourg, Capital Radio, Radio London) that would showcase Caribbean music at unsociable hours (Gilroy 2002, 221–23; Veal 2007, 226). In 1972 however, the national media displayed an interest in Bob Marley and the Wailers' music after they were signed to Chris Blackwell's Island Records. It was the overdub mixing of rock elements and increase of tempo on the *Catch a Fire* album (edited in London) rather than the roots reggae and sociocultural lyrical content (recorded in Kingston) that appealed to the British media (Moskowitz 2007, 21). Although the added elements of genre blending in reggae was showing signs of 'pop' music (Alleyne 2009, 83), reggae started to gain more attention. For instance, after the arrival of Bob Marley and the Wailers' music, reggae music composed in Britain seldom made the charts unless the bass was not too heavy in texture and timbre, and the music carried a pop flavour, with Janet Kay's *Silly Games* (1979) and selected music of Matumbi as examples.

With this in mind, it appeared that race relations among musicians were flourishing and were proving to have a positive impact in society (mainly with the British youth). This was also achieved with the formation of multi-racial groups which, as observed by Paul Gilroy, 'have intermittently created a 'two-tone' sensibility which celebrates its hybrid origins and has provided a significant opposition to 'common sense' racialism' (1993, 35). 'Two-tone' referred to the second wave of ska music, in Britain, in the late 1970s. British ska and multi-racial groups such as The Specials wanted to promote racial interaction and unity in Britain. The influence of two-tone inspired other genres emerging such as punk. British punk experienced a musical crossover with reggae such as Lee 'Scratch' Perry's production of 'Punky Reggae Party' (1977) which was sung by Bob Marley. The song was a homage to the British punk group, The Clash, who covered Junior Murvin's 'Police and Thieves' (1976). These musical connections and crossover of genres proved to strengthen the relationship between the artists who also shared similar views on British society and oppression from the government. Evidence of sociocultural and musical elements of reggae that were heard in punk and ska were played by multi-racial groups such as Basement 5 and The Specials. Their songs which addressed racism were not well received socially and by the media. Consequently, groups such as Basement 5 and The Specials were short lived, but their music has maintained longevity with their communities and fan bases. It is interesting however, that white British fronted ska and reggae groups such as Madness and UB40 were commercially successful from the 1980s (due to their pop musical elements). The 1990s saw a rise of multi-cultural groups in Britain but was again overlooked by the media because of a significant genre – Britpop.

Britpop

Britpop was, at first, a musical reaction to grunge, which had originated from the United States and dominated British popular culture in the early 1990s. Britpop had originally been perceived as a musical genre, but expanded into British culture, society and politics. The music was a revival of early British popular music (such as music hall, 1960s pop and rock), which addressed 'everyday Britain' themes (from greenery landscapes to working class culture). It was thought that Britpop music had to sound 'British' and sing themes on Britain, after all, it was supposed to be a reaction to grunge music – or so it seemed. It was considered that Britain celebrated unity through music, fashion, arts and sport. It had also aimed to celebrate British identity through people, values, traditions, history and scenery. David Hesmondhalgh noted that:

> Britpop echoed anxieties elsewhere, amongst educationalists, political leaders, and public commentators, about the fragmentation of national identity. But precisely because it came from within the realm of alternative popular culture, Britpop discourse arguably had a more powerful effect in reaffirming nationalism than the tired complaints of more respectable public figures (Hesmondhalgh 2001, 277).

Naturally, the term Britpop resulted in misleading connotations. While advocates of Britpop wanted to celebrate British identity (with musicians Brett Anderson of Suede and Damon Albarn of Blur as prime examples), it became a signal for the right-wing political supporters to use Britpop as an excuse to reuse Enoch Powell's 'River of Blood' speech. For instance, right-wing supporters used the Union Jack flag as a symbol to undermine the idea that Britain is a multi-cultural nation, after all, as stated by Paul Gilroy, *There Ain't No Black in the Union Jack* (Whiteley 2010, 57). Signs of Britishness appeared on the revival of 1960s British rock and pop music, and excluded British composed music such as reggae and ska. The views on British society represented by Britpop proved to be more overpowering than the views that were constantly voiced by British Caribbean and multi-racial groups. In other words, the British Caribbean's struggle for identity and acceptance faced a setback as white British social groups were also yearning for British identity. This is observed by Martin Cloonan who argues, 'as far as England is concerned, the fact remains that while black English-born (or resident) artists have, inevitably, commented about the state of England, they have seldom been identified with it' (Cloonan 1997, 59). Therefore, Britpop was perhaps intended to seclude British (English) nationals from other ethnic minorities in the hope for the nation to become a 'dangerously nostalgic zone, a fantasy of Britain pre-immigration, pre-EU, pre-US dominance' (Lloyd and Rambarran 2013).

Musically, it cannot be ignored that at the same time British popular culture was recovering from the rave and Manchester scenes, and underground electronica (jungle, trip hop) in inner city areas were beginning to develop, though these musical styles could not nationally compete with Britpop. Genre blended music flourished in cities such as London, Bristol and Manchester due to its cultural diversity. Manchester, the third largest city in Britain, in particular (where Audioweb were based), could not be pinned to one particular musical style due to the exposure of music from various multi-cultural, historical and musical backgrounds (Tony Wilson, BME). In particular, Manchester-based musicians and their audiences were open to all genres of popular music as demonstrated in the famous night club, the Haçienda. The club owners, the late Tony Wilson and members of Joy Division/New Order encouraged deejays, groups and performers to showcase their music regardless of genre. This musical exposure resulted in the formation of local groups such as The Stone Roses and The Happy Mondays. The 1990s genre-blended popular music in Manchester and elsewhere, however, were ignored by the white male dominated genre of Britpop as 'mainstream characterizations of Britpop tend to overlook questions of region, gender, and race' (Rambarran 2013, 136). This was evident with British Jamaican musician, Martin 'Sugar' Merchant, who experienced a brief musical success with Manchester-based dub-reggae-electronica-rock group, Audioweb, the main study of this article.

Audioweb

Audioweb were formed in 1991 in Manchester. Originally known as 'The Sugar Merchants', the band consisted of Martin 'Sugar' Merchant from Moss Side, an inner city area in Manchester; Robert 'Maxi' Maxfield, a drummer from Salford, Greater Manchester; and two southern English musicians who wanted to be part of the Manchester music scene, Robin File (guitarist) and Sean McCann (bassist). The Sugar Merchants were signed to Elektra records. As the group's recording deal did not work out with Elektra, the group renamed themselves as 'Audioweb' and were discovered by Irish rockers, U2, and were signed on their record label, Mother Records in 1995. Between 1995 and 1996, Audioweb released three singles,

'Sleeper', 'Yeah' and 'Into My World', and the group gained media interest with the help of fellow Mancunians, broadcasters Chris Evans, Terry Christian, Pete Mitchell and singer, Ian Brown, from The Stone Roses. For example, Audioweb appeared on television shows such as 'TFI Friday' and on several radio stations. Despite the television exposure and radio plugs, their early singles barely made the Top 40 in the British music charts. The group carried on regardless and collaborated with British producers, Jonathan Quarmby and Kevin Bacon on their self-titled debut album. Audioweb were musically attracted to Bacon and Quarmby for their dub and techno background, and for their work with Ziggy Marley and Finley Quaye. After remaking some of the songs, 'Sleeper' was re-issued and their album was released in 1996. Here, they received some positive recognition from the music press. In 1997, their cover version of The Clash's 'Bankrobber' led to musical success (it reached number 19 in the Top 40).

What had also contributed to their success was when Ian Brown declared in his press statement on the Stone Roses break up that he would 'kickback and listen to the new Audioweb album' (Republic of Audioweb 2005). The musical success was followed by the song, 'Policeman Skank', which would feature on their second album, *Fireworks City* (1998). This time, Audioweb collaborated with music producer, Steve Lironi on their second album. Although for promotional purposes, the group claimed that the making of the album was easier than the first (*The Ozone* 1998), in reality, it was the beginning of the end of the group. Despite the fans choosing *Fireworks City* as their favourite Audioweb album, and critiquing sociocultural issues in their lyrics (such as the British police force in 'Policeman Skank'), it was claimed that the group were not satisfied with how the album was produced. As Audioweb were not happy with the overall sound of *Fireworks City*, their disappointment put a strain on the band's relationship with each other. The deteriorating relationship of Audioweb deepened when the media were no longer interested in the group, and this resulted in three failed singles and the cancellation of their North American tour. After receiving setbacks from their record label, media and each other, Audioweb split up in 1999. Although Audioweb received short-term musical recognition, they were not as successful as Britpop groups, and were quickly turned away by the media. Was the failure of the 'second album syndrome' really to blame? What really went wrong? We need to focus on the lead singer.

'THE VOICE OF A GIRL, AND THE BODY OF A GLADIATOR' (MERCHANT)

Martin 'Sugar' Merchant was heavily influenced by reggae and dub music thanks to his Jamaican heritage. Although he musically grew up in sound system culture and at his father's blues parties, Merchant was also very open minded to different genres of popular music. He was after all, in a city famously known for its musical diversity. Merchant began his music career as a toaster and deejay for the Maverick Sound System, before working with the likes of Tippa Irie, Maxi Priest and the Saxon Sound System (Odell 1996). When Audioweb formed, Merchant presented his singjaying skills fused with reggae, electronica, dance, and rock music. The fusion of genres confused the media and the music press such as the *New Musical Express* paper, who believed that Audioweb were fronted by two lead singers: one who sounded feminine; the other an aggressive toaster – when in fact, both voices were projected by Merchant. Also, the media preferred to focus on the 'incompatibility' of a British Caribbean person, with a dub and reggae musical background, singing 'rock' about which Merchant argues:

> I don't think [Audioweb] got a fair press at all...the press was very racist but we knew it would be a problem...Manchester is a multicultural place but the music of the 1990s did not reflect it at all which was a shame. The rock and pop press like it when there are 4 or 5 white guys in a band! (Marco On The Bass 2010)

Merchant was arguing that the media preferred to focus on Britpop and its domination of white male musicians – they were not interested in a black singer in a 'rock' band. Merchant stresses that the media found 'it hard to sell a black face in England...a black guy in a guitar band? Do something different and the press can't handle it' (Mason 2007). Robert Maxfield (drummer) agrees: 'we had a black singer and let's be honest, if you're not a rapper from America, you've got no chance of gracing the pages of NME' (Retreat Store 2011).

Maxfield continues: 'the UK marketplace and the music press… were racist. We heard reports of NME…exec[utives] not wanting us in papers because they had Black Grape in, and they didn't want to confuse the readers by having two multi-racial bands' (Mason 2007). Or, to put it bluntly in Merchant's words: 'the readers would get confused if they had two bands with black members in the same issues' (Moran 1996). Black Grape was a multi-racial group with ex-members of The Happy Mondays. The two front singers were Shaun Ryder and British Caribbean Paul 'Kermit' Leveridge. The media favoured Black Grape because of one of the singers, Shaun Ryder, was a white British celebrity and former lead singer of famous group, the Happy Mondays.

Therefore, having that connection with Shaun Ryder was an advantage for Leveridge, as Ryder was an established musician and a popular figure in Britain. With Black Grape aside, another media-related issue that concerned Audioweb was their music. As Merchant states: 'I don't think the…writers got the reggae part of it. It wasn't dance enough to go into the dance tent. It wasn't rock enough to go into the rock tent, but, you know, it was our sound…' (Mason 2007). The guitarist Robin File supported this statement by claiming that 'people aren't used to it. They think just because we're doing something different they shouldn't be able to understand it' (Moody 1997, 22). The musical sound of Audioweb was ahead of its time (the fusion of dub, reggae, electronica and rock) as opposed to the Britpop sound which was going back in time (by recycling past British musical genres). Audioweb gracefully accepted the negative reaction from the press for the sake of the group's reputation and for the love of their music. There were, however, some occasions when Merchant would release his frustration by either exchanging explicit words or fighting with members of the audience – all because they could not understand the music of Audioweb (Barber 1997; O'Reilly 1996; Mason 2007). Merchant even admitted the lack of support at a gig in London when he announced, 'we're not everyone's cup of tea, but then we drink f**king coffee' (Kelso 1996). The timing of their music did not benefit Audioweb either as Sean McCann (bassist) claims that 'Britpop…didn't do us any favours…' (Mason 2007).

Trying to compete with Britpop culture was difficult. The group was made to wear suits and was portrayed as a 'cool' rock band. In reality, their dress style was laidback compared to their on-screen images: such as casual rock, sports, hip-hop and street gear. Their videos were mainly performance-based, therefore it was unlikely for the audience to search for visual connotations of their music – as you would find with Britpop videos, which would normally contain elements of British scenery (London, green pastures) and national identity (London buses, the Queen, the Union Jack Flag etc.) – which firmly cemented Britpop as an exclusion zone for ethnic minorities. However, while Audioweb were calm about the backlash they received from the media, there was one song that discreetly presented their views on the media and Britpop. The track *Faker* (1997) focuses on the struggle of accepting one's own identity. This could also be an indirect response to Britpop outfit Oasis, and their song *Supersonic* (1994), as it makes references on how it is hard to stay true to one's self. To understand the song, a musical analysis will now be discussed.

'Faker'

Faker begins with a solo Hammond organ that plays a quick blues introduction and is responded to with a thin textured electric guitar riff. In the background, static noise and high pitch frequency sounds can be heard. This quick introduction is followed by thick textured, multi-layered and manipulated distorted guitar sounds that play a crescendo and ascending scale. The timbre appears to represent a dramatic form of noise such as a rev jet engine sound. This brief climax leads to the main introduction of the song where Merchant toasts over the bass and guitar. Merchant's vocals are accompanied by a counter-melodic guitar part. When verse one begins, Merchant sings in an angelic tone and addresses escapism from everyday life with the aid of drinking alcohol ('breaking it back for another day'). The verse is accompanied with a thin texture of the drums, bass and a distant rhythm guitar sound (which is manipulated with effects). Elements of roots reggae is heard with a deep bass groove and drums that use the one drop technique. In the bridge, Merchant offers advice in an attempt for the character in question to know themselves ('Hope for you is not hope for me baby…what can I do what can I say to make you know yourself'). The music starts to build in texture which is supported with a double tracked guitar and is simply providing the riffs. When the chorus enters, the music repeats the main introduction and the lead guitar riff is decorated with record scratching which enhances the chorus. It is of course Merchant's words that sets the main hook of the song ('when will you know you've made it, when will you know you faker?') Here, Merchant's vocals are still soft until he sings 'Faker' in a stressed and forced tone. After the second round of verse and chorus, the music changes direction with a break. Here, Merchant drops his voice to a low and assertive tone and begins to toast. In this section, it appears that Merchant is plugging himself as genuine as he makes references to himself as a 'supersonic singer'. Merchant appears to be presenting two oppositional characters in the song in which one is the faker and the other is genuine. The rest of the song ends with a round of choruses.

The song's theme is visually supported by the music video. Unlike other Audioweb videos, which are performance-based, this one reveals signs that are related to the song's theme and the period it was filmed. The group is mainly shot in black and white, which is matched by their modern rude boy sharp suits, which suggests they are representing a modern two-tone culture, when in reality, racial unity is dismissed due to Britpop. In the video introduction there is a long shot view of the group, which gradually closes in on Merchant. The purpose of the long shot is to set the scene: for the viewer to identify the group and to take note of the surroundings. The surroundings consist of blown up pictures that pay homage to Merchant's musical identity in Britain. These images consist of sound systems, percussion and microphones. The images of the microphones are significant as Merchant always uses two different microphones in live performances. The two blown up images of the microphones, which are presented in a mirrored style, are clearly held by Merchant, which may either signify the 'black salute', or Northern Soul's 'Keep the Faith' motto. Indeed, Merchant could be representing both signs which signify his cultural heritage and musical sideline job as a Northern Soul deejay. Throughout the song, a lot of attention is focused on Merchant. The combination of the medium and close-up shots of Merchant allows the audience to switch from being the observer to being close with the singer. The lighting in the black and white video is a contrast of light and dark almost in a Chiaroscuro style as certain areas are illuminated. Here, it is Merchant's face that is illuminated. The binaries of light and dark, or black and white, again suggest the modern two-tone culture and racial unity. The mood of the lighting may also signal that the subject of the video is melancholic, which suits the theme of the song.

There are however, fast passing long shots of grainy colourful images of Audioweb which may suggest the 'real' Audioweb outside their performance zone. Here, the group is wearing their casual attire as you would expect to see in their live shows. More significantly, they are also surrounded by the Jamaican flag which opposes the infamous slogan 'there ain't no black on the Union Jack.' As before, these signs are paying homage to Merchant's heritage and also the identity of Audioweb as a multi-racial group. The fast grainy shots of the 'real' Audioweb are not placed in significant sections of the song, but instead are flashed randomly to the viewer. When studying these particular images and video closely and in slow motion, the Jamaican flag appears to stand out in the scene with the aid of the back light which enables the flag to 'glow'. This creates an allure effect. The prominent feature of the Jamaican flag becomes the visual subject, or a hook, which signifies the multi-racial group and Merchant's identity. The alluring sign makes the other subjects in the scene appear darker. The dark and what appears to be semi-concealed images of Audioweb, who are freely moving in front of the Jamaican Jack flag and carrying an 'in your face' attitude, reveal that the group are actually wearing masks of themselves. The concealed identities of Audioweb send out a message that they will not change their identities and music for the sake of gaining a place in Britpop culture. If they did conform, they too would be 'fakers' and the images of their real identities (the black salute, flag) would be meaningless. The concealed identities of Audioweb present an indirect action and silent protest to the media and Britpop.

The importance of the fast, unpredicted and randomness shots of the Jamaican Jack flag and masked group are powerful images, because it sets the theme of the song and video, and the sociocultural context of Audioweb. In reality, Britpop was an attempt to shield British identity by focusing on signs of Britishness. The isolation of Audioweb in Britpop and the British media was silently demonstrated in the music video through their two-tone nature, disguised identities and the display of the Jamaican Jack. To confirm then, Audioweb's attitude and their disguised (or indeed 'faked') identities displayed a silent protest as a way to protect their group, their music and their dissatisfaction with the media.

CONCLUSION

The track 'Faker' made it at number 70 on the UK charts. The poor sales of the single were due to the lack of support from the media (there were no song or video reviews). Not to their surprise, the response of the group's silent protest in the music video of 'Faker' went unnoticed by the media – just like their music. The inadequate media attention of the group and Merchant originates in the treatment of Caribbean music in Britain, which dates back to the earlier twentieth century. As a reminder, the chapter discussed the two stages of early Caribbean music in Britain. Despite the fact that the first stage of Caribbean music mainly consisted of jazz, it could not publicly compete with British jazz. Therefore, performers were restricted to certain venues and found it difficult to earn a living. The second stage of Caribbean music developed after the Second World War, and mainly consisted of traditional Jamaican folk songs. Here, the music appealed to the disillusioned migrants, where they could immerse in their culture and escape from reality. From the 1960s onwards, ska and reggae consisted of novelty hits, and the genres were reworked and overridden by established white British musicians. Although various artists and multi-racial groups emerged during the 1970s and 1980s, the array of talented musicians was not always appreciated nationally. This concept continued into the 1990s, where this challenging decade was ruled by Britpop culture that segregated British Caribbean music even more. For example, underground electronica developed (jungle), and punk-rock groups emerged with the likes of Dub War, Skunk Anasie, and Audioweb. Here, Audioweb was discussed to demonstrate the ongoing struggle of finding acceptance in the British media. Regardless of receiving support from broadcasters, musicians, and U2, Audioweb struggled to maintain public recognition because the media would not support them.

It was only at the time of Audioweb's cover version of 'Bankrobber' that the media paid attention – for a short period – as their attention reverted back to Britpop. Audioweb could not compete or receive the same recognition as Britpop artists. The frustration was observed in 'Faker', a music video which presented the celebration of Merchant's heritage, but yet at the same time silently communicated to the viewer in Audioweb's struggle to gain acceptance in British society. The music video that addressed Audioweb's displacement in British society was unnoticed by the media. In 1999, the frustration of gaining recognition ended after the release of their second album, and their decision to split as a group.

Although it was claimed that the second album led to the demise of Audioweb in 1999, it was more likely that they faded because they did not receive the support from the British media. Although there are no concrete findings from the media to confirm the reasons for why Audioweb did not receive support (are they likely ever to reveal why?), the closest and most convincing comment is offered by the journalist, Michael Odell, who, having wrongly predicted high hopes for Audioweb, correctly remarked that the media 'is still baffled by pluralism' (1996).

There still appears to be some lack of recognition of Caribbean music in current British society. Although styles such as jungle and dubstep have turned commercial, its identity is lost, and the sociocultural context of the music remains unrecognized. There have been attempts to nationally recognize achievers of other ethnic backgrounds but they only appeal to selected communities and creative industries; therefore, the sense of gaining public acknowledgement is still in question. For example, the Music of Black Origin (MOBO) awards used to celebrate music of black origin in Britain, but over the last few years, it has lost its identity as it has become transatlantic-based. There are worthy events that celebrate black British culture and music ('Celebration of life' which is organized by the Metropolitan Black Police Association), but again, it does not receive the national recognition it truly deserves. It seems that there will not be a consistent progression of media support for the achievements and works of British Caribbeans or other races, as demonstrated in this article and in its case study of Audioweb. As Rupa

Huq notes, 'it is village green versus concrete jungle and we know where we would rather be' (Huq 2006, 207). Although this comment appears persuasive, regrettably, the village green may be favoured in Britain as groups from the concrete jungle, like Audioweb, are out of sight, and are definitely out of the media's minds. Still, to this day (and despite the struggle that Audioweb had encountered) Merchant is not resentful and is proud of the group and their music. He fondly states 'we believed we were creating something special' (in an email correspondence to the author, 2013).

References

Alleyne, Mike. 2000. White Reggae: Cultural Dilution in the Record Industry. *Popular Music and Society* 24, no. 1:15–30.

———. 2009. Globalization and Commercialisation of Caribbean Music. *Helenski Collegium for Advanced Studies*, 76–101.

———. 2012. *The Encyclopedia of Reggae: The Golden Age of Roots Reggae*. New York: Sterling.

Audioweb. 1997. *Faker*. MUMCD 91, Mother Records. CD single.

———. n.d. *Faker*. Video. Retrieved on December 7, 2012 from http://www.muzu.tv/audioweb/faker-music-video/234818/.

———. 1998. Interview by The Ozone. BBC. Retrieved January 8, 2013 from http://www.youtube.com/watch?v=wONR_6t9WwE.

Barber, Nicholas. 1997. These feet are made for shuffling. *The Independent*, February 16.

Bennett, Andy and Jon Stratton, eds. 2010. *Britpop and the English Music Tradition*. Farnham, UK: Ashgate.

Bradley, Lloyd. 2000. *This is Reggae Music: The Story of Jamaica's Music*. New York, NY: Grove Press.

Büld, Wolfgand. 1978. *Reggae in a Babylon*. DVD. Germany: Stein Film.

Centre for Contemporary Cultural Studies. 1982. *The Empire Strikes Back*. London, UK: Hutchinson.

Cloonan, Martin. 1997. State of the Nation: "Englishness," Pop, and Politics in the mid-1990s.*Popular Music and Society* 21, no. 2:47–70.

Cowley, John. 1985. West Indian Gramophone Records in Britain: 1927–1950. *ESRC Occasional Papers in Ethnic Relations*, no 1.

———. 1990. London is the Place: Caribbean Music in the context of Empire 1900–60. In *Black Music in Britain: Essays on the Afro African Contribution to Popular Music*, edited by Paul Oliver. Milton Keynes: Open University Press.

Gilroy, Paul. 1993. *Small Acts: Thoughts on the Politics of Black Cultures*. London, UK: Serpent's Tail.

———. 2002. *There Ain't No Black in the Union Jack*. [orig. 1992] London, UK: Routledge.

Hebdige, Dick. 1979. *Subculture: The Meaning of Style*. London, UK: Routledge.

———. 1987. *Cut 'n' Mix*. London, UK: Comedia.

Hesmondhalgh, David. 2001. British Popular Music and National Identity. In *British Cultural Studies*, edited by David Morley and Kevin Robins. Oxford and New York: Oxford University Press.

Huq, Rupa. 2006. Asian Kool?: Bhangra and Beyond. In *The Popular Music Studies Reader*, edited by Andy Bennett, Barry Shank and Jason Toynbee. London and New York: Routledge.

Kelso, Paul. 1996. Music: This week's Pop CD releases. *The Guardian*, December 6.

Levine, Joshua. 2006. *Forgotten Voices of the Blitz and the Battle for Britain: A New History in the Words of the Men and Women on Both Sides*. Reading, UK: Ebury Press.

Lloyd, Christian and Shara Rambarran. 2013. Brand New You're Retro: Tricky as Engpop Dissident. Paper presented at the Mad Dogs conference at St Mary's University College, London.

Marco on the Bass. 2010. Interview with Martin 'Sugar' Merchant of Audioweb/Supajamma. Retrieved December 5, 2012 from http://marcoonthebass.blogspot.co.uk/.

Mason, Martin. 2010. The Republic of Audioweb. Retrieved December 5, 2012, from http://www.republicofaudioweb.com/.

Merchant, Martin. 2013. Email correspondence with Shara Rambarran, September 11.

Moody, Paul. 1997. The Boast Man's Call. *New Musical Express*, May 10.

Morley, David, and Kevin Robins, eds. 2001. *British Cultural Studies*. Oxford and New York: Oxford University Press.

Moran, Caitlin. 1996. Back to the graze days of variety – Pop. *The Times*, February 9.

Moskowitz, David V. 2007. *Bob Marley: A Biography*. Westport: Greenwood.

Odell, Michael. 1996. Playing the race chord. *The Guardian*, April 5.

O'Reilly, John. 1996. Music: With no Brit in it. *The Guardian*, December 27.

Owusu, Kwesi, ed. 2000. *Black British Culture and Society: A Text Reader*. London and New York: Routledge.

Partridge, Christopher. 2010. *Dub in Babylon*. Oakville: Equinox.

Rambarran, Shara. 2013. Britpop and the English Music Tradition. Book review. *Popular Music and Society* 36, no.1:134–36.

Retreat Brand. 2011. Rob 'Maxi' Maxfield Interview. Retrieved January 10, 2013 from http://www.blog.retreatstore.com/2011/03/rob-maxi-maxfield-interview.html

Veal, Michael E. 2007. *Dub: Soundscapes and Shattered Songs in Jamaican Reggae.* Middletown: Wesleyan University Press.

Whiteley, Sheila. 2010. Trainspotting: The Gendered History of Britpop. In *Britpop and the English Music Tradition,* edited by Andy Bennett and Jon Stratton. Farnham: Ashgate.

Wilson, Tony. n.d. Interview. Video footage. British Musical Experience, London.

Section 3
DISCURSIVE PATHWAYS IN JAMAICAN POPULAR MUSIC

Freedom Sound:
Music of Jamaica's Independence

Heather Augustyn

Upside-down plastic pennants on a string connect rooftop to rooftop through every street in downtown Kingston in anticipation of the arrival of Princess Margaret, representing the Queen of England, and her husband, the Earl of Snowdon. At the National Stadium, in a demure voice full of grace and dignity, she tells the audience that the youth are the future of Jamaica. As midnight approaches, the spotlight on the Union Jack goes out and re-illuminates on the Jamaican flag. Fireworks proclaim to all around, this is an independent Jamaica. Things are different now. Three hundred years of British reign are over. It is an age of progress and prosperity. Out of many, one people. It was a time for celebration, but the music that Jamaicans composed in honour of their new independence did not represent one people. Popular music in Jamaica represented two very distinct groups – uptown and downtown. Despite this class separation, the music did finally come together through the orchestrated work of musicians, producers and even politicians.

On August 6, 1962, Jamaica finally became independent from Britain and Jamaican music reflected the feelings of freedom, jubilation and promise. Upbeat ska tempos and tunes mirrored the people's hopes and aspirations, for the country and for themselves. There was a call for celebrations that represented the new national identity. *Jamaica Gleaner* Editor-in-Chief, Theodore Sealy, in his article, 'Independence – how to celebrate it!' makes the appeal, 'Let the people sing.' He writes,

> Some people want lavish pageants. Others want prayer. Some think Jamaica should try to outdo and outspend everything that Africa and India has attempted or done – just to show how great we in Jamaica are. Others feel that

the mood that should be left after the first Independence Day is not a mood of glory but a mood of gratitude at having lived to see the day. All these ideas and many more are now being talked about in the home, at clubs, in sunshacks, in yam fields, in bars, on the pavements, what should the government do? What should the people do? (Sealy 1962).

What the government did, and what the people did, were two very different things. The establishment and the people had two separate celebrations. This occurred, in part, because Jamaican society was, and still is to a large degree, stratified into upper and lower classes. The Institute of Social and Economic Research has found in their *Class, Race, and Political Behaviour* report that 'Urban Kingston and St. Andrew consist of a highly class-stratified population in which most residential areas are class homogenous', (Stone 1973, 34). Similarly, popular music during the time of Jamaica's independence fell into two categories, a reflection of Jamaican society – uptown and downtown. Dr Basil Waine Kong writes,

> We were told that if we didn't want to be second class, we had to speak and dress Western style, learn English manners, poetry, history and music, dance the quadrille, adopt Christian names, use your knife and fork correctly, deny your own being and transform yourself into an Englishman. Only then could you be worthy of respect. While Jamaica was granted Independence in 1962, Britannia continues to rule. I wish we would disavow classism (Kong 2009).

Despite the attempt to bring together one people, there were two very different cultures represented in Jamaican music, a tale of two cities, an 'ism schism', and so I divide my chapter between these two groups and will conclude with a post-independence examination of how Jamaican music has truly become representative of one people.

UPTOWN MUSIC

Before 1964, there was no mention at all in the *Daily Gleaner* of ska. There was simply no coverage, other than advertisements. No editorial whatsoever. This is because ska was seen as lowbrow music, music of the downtown, music of the streets. Instead of ska, organized independence celebrations included parades with floats and school or military bands. Schools themselves hosted ceremonies with speakers and sacred music and dancing the quadrille. Public performances for independence included classical music with vocal programmes, such as one featuring Jamaican Tenor, Rudolf Comacho, which was attended by government dignitaries, including Alexander Bustamante. An independence programme at the Myrtle Bank Hotel included an array of musical entertainers, including a 'late soiree' featuring Lennie Hibbert and His Combo, and the Alpha Boys Band who played, 'while tea is served', (Myrtle 1962). The Independence Arts Celebrations which took place over the entire month of August, featured plenty of dancers and theatre, and when it came to music, that too was a proper offering. The Festival Orchestra performed 'under Carlos Malcolm's baton', (Jamaican Life *Daily Gleaner* 1962). 'Original music for many of the ballets is composed by Carlos Malcolm and Oswald Russell with Malcolm doing the scoring', read the article while going on to list other credits for lighting, choreography, and guest dancers. There were choral concerts from school groups and men and women's groups at the State Theatre and plenty of sacred concerts.

Military parades, marches, and band performances took place in towns and villages all over the country. The national anthem was first publicly performed by the Jamaica Military Band at the Lyndhurst Methodist Church Hall just a few weeks before the independence ceremonies. The song's words were written by Father Hugh Sherlock and the music was composed by Mapletoft Poulle and his wife, Christine Alison Poulle, although many accounts have Robert Lightbourne involved in the composition as well and the confusion over the true composer comes down to politics (Seaga 2012).

Federal Recording Studios Engineer, Graeme Goodall, recalls recording the national anthem. He says that Captain Ted Wade, who was in charge of the Jamaica Military Band, brought the band to the studios in army trucks. 'I told him, no problem, we'll record them in the parking lot', said Goodall since they couldn't all fit in the studio. As Goodall began running microphones to the lot and then taking sound levels back in the control room, he noticed a problem. 'There was traffic outside on Four Shore Road, Marcus Garvey Drive', he says. But Wade radioed the military who responded by blocking off each end of the road and the recording went off without a hitch. They recorded the up tempo march version for the A side and a slower vocal version for the B side and worked all night to press 100 copies, complete with a label printed with the new Jamaican flag. The records appeared on each parliament member's desk the next morning by 9:00 a.m., as well as a copy for Radio Jamaica Redifussion (RJR) and Jamaica Broadcasting Corporation (JBC).

Music was important to help Jamaicans bridge their identity as part of the British Commonwealth into something that was all their own. But the music of the people, the music that was in the clubs and sound systems and studios, was very different from the music played at these celebrations. In 1962, ska was in full swing, much to the dismay of the uptown genteel classes. Even years later, people writing letters to the editor in the *Daily Gleaner* would call ska,

> Primitive rock with a heavy accent on the off-beat, depending on its monotony for its excitement. The words are indistinct and are usually about animals or parents or children, rather than love and romance. I nickname it the 'Bilious Beat,' says one writer, Ainsley Wilson of Spanish Town (Wilson 1964).

Others, like Yvette Bedway of Williamsfield in Manchester, wrote that 'the ska is raging too much on radio in Jamaica. In the early mornings more services would be welcomed. It gives one a healthier feeling to begin the day with divine service than with the ska tunes', (Bedway 1965). These were not isolated comments. The clubs where ska played were either frequented by the lower and middle classes, or tourists. Others that were high-class clubs, the ones up on Cross Roads, played a more refined orchestral version of ska from the likes of the Eric Deans Orchestra. Many of these clubs, like the Glass Bucket Club when it was operated by Don Soisson, were once even racially segregated. It is no wonder then that ska did not factor into any of the country's official independence celebrations.

DOWNTOWN MUSIC

Music had always been a part of Jamaican everyday life. The ring game songs, nine-night songs, work songs or digging songs, all had a function. So too did ska music, especially during the days surrounding the independence. Ska began in the late 1950s and by the time independence came around, ska was firmly established. Were there not the audio record and oral histories of this fact, one might not even know that ska existed around the time of the independence, since government musical programmes were without any representation from ska bands.

But there were plenty of independence celebrations that featured ska music, as advertisements reveal. The Hotel Flamingo hosted Sonny Bradshaw & His Combo for 'exciting music for dancing' to 'celebrate independence at the poolside terrace', (Hotel Flamingo, *Gleaner* 1962). The Carib Theatre hosted the 'Independence Showcase' with such ska musicians as The Blues Busters, Byron Lee & the Dragonaires, Keith 'N' Enid, Derrick Morgan; Derrick Harriott, Jimmy Cliff, and Hortense Ellis, among others (Independence Showcase, *Gleaner* 1962). The Deluxe Theatre was host to the 'Independence Ska-Ta-Rama' with the Skatalites, Derrick Harriott, Lord Creator, and lucky ticket holders even won 'free cases of Red Stripe Beer' – quite a juxtaposition to the tea served at the uptown celebrations.

Ska musicians and bands embraced the promise of independence, just as everyone else did. Independence gave people hope, opportunity, and freedom, especially in the poor and working-class neighbourhoods, and so singers commemorated that perception in their songs, such as Lord Creator's classic 'Independent Jamaica'. Lord Creator, a native of Trinidad and Tobago, says that Vincent 'Randy' Chin approached him to write the song. 'It was January, but Chin asked me to make an Independence song for him in tribute to the independent referendum that was approved by the people. I did the song, then I left Jamaica to complete my tour'. When he returned, Chin informed him that the song had been selling faster than 'hot bread' (Mills 1998). Chin asked him to write more songs for him, so Lord Creator followed up with other independence songs – *Welcome Princess Margaret* and *Freedom Song*.

The lyrics to 'Independent Jamaica', a calypso-flavoured tune, chronicle the story of securing independence and it is actually a decent recount of the events:

> Manley went up to England to seek for Independence
> and although Busta was late he still attended the conference,
> although from two different parties it was very good to see
> how these two politicians were shaking hands when they gained victory.

But the lyrics do more than just tell the tale. They also offer a tone of optimism and hope and foretell the benefits for the future. 'Independence is good for young and the old, also for me and you, Independence is good for the whole population including our children too.' Derrick Morgan also wrote a song in commemoration of the independence. Morgan says,

> In 1962 now, I made this one, when Jamaica was getting independent, I wrote a song called 'Forward March,' getting to the independence, and it was a big sell out. It was a boom. And on the Independence, we on the truck [sound system] going around singing that song 'Forward March' (Morgan 1997).

This song also has a tone of excitement and optimism and equally acknowledges both parties involved in the process. It is both a narrative as well as a statement of the buoyant mood of the people during this time. It is patriotic, it is spiritual, and it is in direct contrast to the songs in future years, future decades, that lamented the crime and poverty of the people. This song was a hymn to the vision for the nation:

> Gather together, be brothers and sisters, we're independent!
> Join hands to hands, children started to dance, we're independent!
> Don't be sad and blue, the Lord is still with you
> Because your time has come
> When you can have your fun so people run!
>
> Brothers and sisters give joy and praise to Sir Alexander
> Brothers and sisters, give joy and praise to Mr Manley.
> Don't be sad and blue, the Lord is still with you
> Because your time has come
> When you can have your fun so people run!

Jimmy Cliff's 'Miss Jamaica' embraced the national identity while acknowledging the troubles the country faced. The act of 'crowning' is both an act of establishing the prize, independence, as well as a reference to the British Commonwealth, the Crown, which has now been taken back by the Jamaican people and is only theirs to give – they now have the power. Cliff accepts his nation, as it is, problems and all, and is proud to call it his own.

> You're my Miss Jamaica
> My Miss Jamaica
> You're my Miss Jamaica

> I'm crowning you myself
> Although you may not have such a fabulous shape
> To suit the rest of the world
> But you do suit me and that's all I want to know
> I need not know nothing more

Al T. Joe's 'Rise Jamaica – Independence Time is Here' is a Fats Domino-style tune with cheerleader lyrics assigning aspects of Jamaican independence to each letter of the word 'independence', like nation, democracy, economics, progress, and equality. Joe also references the problems of Jamaica, perhaps British colonial rule, but he asks his people to overcome these problems by moving on, again with a tone of optimism and excitement:

> Rise Jamaica rise
> And let us celebrate
> Let's forget the past
> Independence time is here.

Joe White and Chuck offered their 'One Nation' in the spirit of independence. The lyrics are also positive, hopeful, and stress the unity of one people, both men and women. The words literally ask, as did Derrick Morgan's tune, for the nation to join hands and become one entity.

> We are all one nation,
> One nation we are,
> Independence celebration
> We all should jump for joy,
> Let's join hands together
> To celebrate the day
> Escorting to the festival
> That comes each time each year.
> Brothers we are marching on
> Sisters we are marching on
> Brothers we are marching on
> We are marching on to independence.

There was also The Skatalites' 'Independence Anniversary Ska', originally named 'I Should Have Known Better', a cover of a Beatles tune, which the Skatalites performed in the independence parade in August 1965 on the Cable & Wireless Float. This song had no lyrics, but was still written in the same spirit of celebration because of the title it was given, and because of the location where it was performed. It was a song that they performed for this special occasion, to commemorate independence. All lyrics aside, the fact that Jamaica had its own music, ska, required no lyrics to express the independence of the new nation. Ska music, like the Jamaican people themselves, was a blend, a collective, of other forms, yet it was original and very distinctly Jamaican. The fact that ska gave rise to rocksteady, reggae, dub, and dancehall in future years, also demonstrates how the people's identity as one nation is reflected in the creation of a national music. Writer Sonjah Stanley Niaah has said,

> Poor people went to the dancehalls. The dance provided physical, ideological, and spiritual shelter for a generation of lower-class Jamaicans, a generation mature enough by the time of independence when the music ska became popular. They asserted a new sense of self, a sense of freedom that was reflected in the beat and tempo of the music and dance (Stanley Niaah 2006, 14).

TWO SKAS CLASH

It is fairly well known that ska music first began organically in Kingston as a music of the people, in the schools, the studios, the streets, the dancehalls, the sound systems, and the hills. But there was also an orchestrated push to use this music as a way to develop Jamaica's tourist industry, which coincided with the days just after independence. It came from the same spirit, to establish Jamaica as its own country with its own identity and appeal. Most know how then Minister of Culture, Edward Seaga, selected the band he had managed, Byron Lee & the Dragonaires, to attend the World's Fair in New York in 1964, just two years after independence, but many may not realize how much more was involved and it is important to discuss because it is a continuation of the uptown music that existed during independence, and in a way, it merged the uptown with the downtown.

Seaga states in the liner notes to his *Reggae Golden Jubilee: Origins of Jamaican Music* box set:

> I took Byron Lee, leader of the top uptown dance band, the Dragonaires, to Chocomo Lawn in Denham Town where a session with The Techniques was in progress. Chocomo Lawn had been one of the original sound system dancehalls where dances were held almost every Sunday night. In 1963 it became my political

headquarters. The Techniques were performing with lead vocalist Slim Smith...Byron was hearing the ska beat live for the first time. He was in awe. He carefully analysed the instrumentation and took it uptown to his band. Byron Lee could now play the ska uptown. That helped to move ska from strictly downtown music to music that was accepted nationally. To attempt to penetrate the American market, I sent a team of ska artistes to perform at the New York World's Fair in 1964: Byron Lee and the Dragonaires, Jimmy Cliff, Delroy Wilson, Desmond Dekker, Roy Shirley, Ken Boothe and others, including a team of dancers. They drew crowds when they played at the World's Fair... (Seaga 2012).

Ronnie Nasralla confirms that the plan to use ska to bridge the social divide between uptown and downtown and spread its wealth to the rest of the world was an orchestrated move from Edward Seaga, childhood friend of Nasralla. He explains how he came to showcase the ska with his friends Eddie Seaga and Byron Lee:

Let me tell you how it started. One day, Eddie Seaga, who was my close friend, called me. Eddie Seaga was friends with my sister. He was my sister's boyfriend and he used to come by my house and I help him with his political campaign. Advertising was my forte. So I did all the advertising for the government, Eddie Seaga at that time. I help him with all his promotion. He told me he heard a music that was breaking out in Western Kingston called ska and he asked if I could promote it for him, so I said, 'Well, I'd like to learn about [it].' And we organized and I said, 'well Byron Lee is the best person to promote it.' So we get together with Byron Lee down in Western Kingston and I learned the ska music. Eddie organized a dance at the Chocomo Lawn in Western Kingston – it's an outdoor nightclub. And Byron played there and all the ska artists performed with Byron and it was a sensation. He [Seaga] said to me, 'Ronnie, move around the crowd and see what they are doing on the dance floor and see if you can come up with a brochure about how to dance the ska. So I did that, saw the people dancing around and came up with a brochure about a week after, how to dance the ska, give them different steps in the ska, and something that they could use to promote ska worldwide. That brochure was used by the government, they put it in all the record albums and it was sent all over the world and I was asked to go to the states and promote the ska with somebody and I got Jannette Phillips to dance with me. Jannette was a dancer, a belly dancer, a friend of my sister. We took pictures doing the different steps and the brochure was produced and given to the government and it was put in all the ska albums (Nasralla 2013).

The ska, as presented at the World's Fair, was as far from the downtown musicians who created the sound as possible. Not only were the downtown musicians overlooked in representing Jamaica at the fair, perhaps for their association with Rastafarianism, but the World's Fair events where ska was unveiled were far from the sound system yards. Instead, these events were sophisticated, stylish, and socially exclusive. In US newspaper articles covering the World's Fair, dignitaries and the noble class were photographed 'doing the ska' with the Jamaican dancers flown in for the occasion. In one article from the *New York Amsterdam News* on May 2, 1964, one such dignitary is shown kicking up his heels in his suit and tie while seated onlookers smile. 'When Arthur Murray takes a dancing lesson, that's news! Here the famed dance instructor catches on fast as he learned the "Jamaica SKA," newest dance sensation to hit New York', reads the photo caption, noting that the dancers introduced the craze to the 'jet set' during an event at Shepheard's at the Hotel Drake on Park Avenue in Manhattan (Learning to Dance! *New York Amsterdam News* 1964).

Another article at the end of that month found in Cathy White's posh 'Personally and Socially' column notes,

> Oom...ska oom...ska! Oom...ska! That's the sound of the 'up' beat on the bass guitar where the latest dance craze, the Jamaica Ska, gets its name. We headed for Shepheard's and to L'Interdit [a private club, subterranean in what was then the Gotham Hotel at 55th and Fifth Ave.] t'other evening and found Park Avenue gyrating all over the place. Leaving our inhibitions in the 'tent' we joined the fun. Believe me, if you can Twist, you can Ska!' (White 1964).

The World's Fair Singer Bowl also played host to a 'Jamaica ska party' in August, 1964 when Byron Lee and his 12-piece orchestra, Millie Small, Jimmy Cliff, and others performed for 'youths from an assortment of nations' who 'twisted, bounced, wiggled, and shook to the rhythmic beats of the Caribbean dance craze known as the Jamaica Ska' (*New York Amsterdam News*).

Even after the World's Fair ended, Seaga continued to send his well-connected musicians to the US to promote tourism to his country. By October, 1965 the *Pittsburgh Courier* claimed that Ronnie Nasralla had 'made four promotion trips to the U.S. spreading ska', not only at the World's Fair but subsequently at clubs in New York like the Peppermint Lounge, on TV shows, and at night spots in Miami Beach. They described Nasralla, not as a dark-skinned Jamaican with dreadlocks, as the Jamaican government tried to hide and squelch, since Nasralla certainly was not, but as

> A long, lean chap, currently in training as a fencer for the Eighth British Empire and Commonwealth Game scheduled for Kingston next August. An all-around athlete, Ronnie has had quite a career in his 35 years as an actor, dancer, school teacher, and salesman. He is now a partner in McMillan Advertising and an account executive for Red Stripe, the island's famous beer. Ska anyone? (*Pittsburgh Courier* 1966)

Nasralla was not only one of the iconic ska dancers sent to the World's Fair with Jannette Phillips, but by this time he was also manager of Byron Lee & the Dragonaires.

In July 1966, Byron Lee & the Dragonaires entertained 'the huge throng' which watched a ceremony on the Avenues of the Americas to unveil Jamaica's coat of arms. The formal procedure involved ministers from Jamaica, New York City's Mayor, John Lindsay, and business dignitaries from the US (*New York Amsterdam News*). In August 1966, Byron Lee returned to promote the ska with his band and the Blues Busters at an event in Manhattan's Riverside Plaza in recognition of Jamaica's anniversary of independence. In October 1966, Ronnie Nasralla travelled to the states with the Caribs to promote the country via 'the ska – the big sound and dance in Jamaica that rivals the Frug, Wobble, Jerk and other discotheque dances', courtesy of the Jamaica Tourist Board (*Pittsburgh Courier* 1966).

Ska had to be presented a certain way in order to cross over the class divide. Years later, Patricia Ann Spence would opine in her article, 'The Roots of Reggae' for the *New York Amsterdam News*,

> Ska was essentially a people's music, 'roots' music—conceived, played, and listened to by the poor. The middle and upper classed Jamaicans avoided it like a plague. And after labelling its 'gutbucket quality as vulgar, they banned it from the island's only radio station, RJR (1976).

Of course Seaga's intention was to market the country, to encourage tourism, and although he can be perplexing at times, supporting the music of the people one minute and bulldozing

Back O' Wall without notice the next minute, but love or hate him, the result was that he helped to bridge the gap between uptown and downtown. He helped to bring ska to the world.

Seaga's support of ska was not exactly met with widespread support. Seaga had to fight to encourage ska's survival, a testament to his passion for the music. William Strong in his 'You Can Quote Me…' column for the *Daily Gleaner* criticized Seaga for backing ska:

> Development Minister Eddie Seaga has spent a lot of good public money promoting this outrageous dance called ska into a national teenage craze, and trying to revive dead dances which this generation of adults will never go for and the over-60s are much too weighted down with economic troubles and rheumatism to enjoy much dancing. Our ears are bombarded round the clock from every corner of the island with ska music and the idiotic "Sammy Dead." And the right of a roomful of young people doing ska is more reminiscent of souls in Dante's Inferno than of civilized humans dancing. If this is how to spend money to promote culture in a country with money troubles and serious social problems, then Seaga has the inside track to ruin us…Sure, let's bring the common people into the national picture. Let's infuse and imbue them with the national spirit. But let's move them up from out of the gutter. Ska is gutter-level. It appeals to the lowest instincts (Strong 1964).

Senator Dudley Thompson in June 1964 also denounced Seaga for his excessive expenditures promoting ska. He said that the Government had failed to meet up to some of the challenges of independence, such as the inculcation of a national spirit. Senator Thompson said that over £50,000 had been spent to promote the Ska. He said that when the word was properly spelled out it would be 'scandal'.

> Still, Seaga fought on with a deliberate strategy because he saw that ska was connected to the newly independent Jamaica and the nation's cultural identity. He founded the Jamaica Independence Festival, a showcase of Jamaican arts, which included an all-island ska and mento competition. At the first annual festival, Byron Lee & the Dragonaires performed, of course, and the festival was hosted and funded by the Ministry of Development & Welfare (*Gleaner* 1964, Jamaica Festival). The first festival began in 1962 to celebrate and coincide with independence. Seaga continued the festival each year after and in 1966, brought the Popular Song Competition into the offerings. Seaga's meetings of

the Parish Festival Committee were broadcast on JBC and RJR so the public was aware of his agenda to promote ska. And he was photographed and appeared in the newspaper as he cut checks to artists like Prince Buster for their help in promoting ska (*Daily Gleaner* 1964). His recording studio, West Indies Records Ltd (WIRL) produced souvenir records with ska called 'I'll Remember Jamaica' from Byron Lee & the Dragonaires so you could 'Take Jamaica Home with you!' as the advertisements read (*Daily Gleaner* 1966).

We know now, with decades of hindsight, that ska did successfully develop a national identity, leading to the career of Bob Marley, Jamaican icon and world star, and reggae music as a whole. We know now that ska helped to bridge the gap between classes as the sounds of the orchestras mixed with the sounds of the dancehalls and powerful politicians like Edward Seaga got behind the vision. The success of ska came because of two distinct forces – the uptown and the downtown. The downtown was more organic, came from the people, simmered up through the people. It came to the airwaves through Treasure Isle time. It spread through producers at RJR. It crossed oceans with West Indian immigrants and spread seeds of its own. Still, having a champion with money to throw behind it in the name of independence, even if the vision was to turn ska into a commodity, was another component that helped to bridge the gap between the two skas. Byron Lee & the Dragonaires, the band that spread the sound of ska to the United States and the uptown crowds, was essential in bridging this gap. Sheila Khouri Lee, widow of Byron Lee says, 'Eddie sent them [to the World's Fair], not because they were better musicians, not because they created the music, but because they could sell it. They could sell it to the general public. They understood that' (Lee 2014). Ken Stewart, long-time manager for the Skatalites says,

> Byron Lee was the uptown band who played ska but not with the soul and vigour that Skatalites had. Certainly the Skatalites was the more popular band but the downtown band and [was] known for ganja smoking and all kinds of debauchery. I can see why the government was concerned. Having seen various members of Skatalites act out in public over the years, these were valid concerns. Nobody knew what some of these guys would pull next, especially the drinkers like Tanamo and Jackie (Stewart 2011).

Ska music was a source of pride, albeit not for everyone. And for those who saw its potential, and those who lived with it and relished it and performed it, ska was an uplifting music full of promise. It was a reflection of the promise that independence itself held. It belonged to the people and it gave the people belonging. Jamaica's many forms of music – classical, choral, folk, ska, rocksteady, dub, dancehall – are all part of one Jamaica, whether overtly promoted as an attraction to the island, or simply heard on a transistor in the street.

References

Bedway, Yvette. 1965. Too Much Ska. *Daily Gleaner,* November 21.
Goodall, Graeme. 2013. Interview by author, February 8.
Hotel Flamingo. 1962. Advertisement in *Daily Gleaner,* August 3.
Independence Showcase. 1962. Advertisement in *Daily Gleaner*, August 3.
Jamaica Festival. 1964. Advertisement in *Daily Gleaner*, July 25.
Jamaican Life will be shown in Dance. 1962. *Daily Gleaner,* July 19.
Jamaica's Shield Hoisted. 1966. *New York Amsterdam News*, July 23.
Kong, Dr Basil Waine. 2009. Racism and Classism in Jamaica. *Jamaicachapter*. Retrieved on January 14, 2013 from jamaicachapter.blogspot.com/2009/07/racism-and-classism-in-jamaica.html.
Khouri Lee, Sheila. 2014. Interview by author, April 9.
Learning To Dance...! 1964. *New York Amsterdam News,* May 2.
Mills, Claude. 1998. Lord Creator has a passion for ballads. *Sunday Gleaner,* April 12.
Minister of Development and Welfare. 1964. *Daily Gleaner*, May 22.
Morgan, Derrick. 1997. Interview by author, June 5.
Myrtle Bank Hotel Announces Its Independence Programme. 1962. *Daily Gleaner*, August 3.
Nasralla, Ronnie. 2013. Interview by author, August, 16.
Photo stand alone. *New York Amsterdam News*, August 29. 1964.
Photo Stand Alone. *Pittsburgh Courier,* October 8, 1966.
Seaga, Edward. From colony to Independence Pt. 1. 2012. *Jamaica Gleaner*, July 15.
———. 2012. Reggae Golden Jubilee: Origins of Jamaican Music [CD booklet]. New York: VP Records.
Sealy, Theodore. 1962. Independence – how to celebrate it! *Sunday Gleaner,* February 18.
'Ska', Jamaica's Dance Rivals the Jerk, Frug. 1965. *Pittsburgh Courier*, October 30.

Spence, Patricia Ann. 1976. The Roots of Reggae. *New York Amsterdam News,* May 1.

Stanley Niaah, Sonjah. 2006. Kingston's Dancehall Spaces. *Jamaica Journal* 29, no.3 (December 2005– April 2006).

Stewart, Ken. 2011. Interview by author, May 20.

Stone, Carl. 1973. *Class, Race, and Political Behaviour in Urban Jamaica.* Institute of Social and Economic Research. University of the West Indies, Jamaica.

Strong, William. 1964. You Can Quote Me…. *Daily Gleaner,* August 10.

Take Jamaica Home with you! 1966. Advertisement in *Daily Gleaner,* August 13.

Senator Thompson charges Govt. with discriminatory, repressive practices. 1964. *Jamaica Gleaner,* June 27.

White, Cathy. 1964. Personally and Socially: The Jamaica Ska Takes Over! *New York Amsterdam News,* May 30.

Wilson, Ainsley. 1964. The Ska. *The Daily Gleaner,* April 16.

Your Name A Mention: Media Coverage of Clashes/Feuds in Jamaican Popular Music 1970–2010

Donna P. Hope and Livingston A. White

> *From ah your name a mention,*
> *Nuh badda fret nor worry yuh intention*
> (Mega Banton 1993)

INTRODUCTION

Dancehall music and culture have become significantly renowned for their propensity to encourage, generate, and promote feuds or clashes. However, feuds and clashes within Jamaican popular music predate dancehall's rise to dominance, even while these activities become more visible and popular towards the end of the twentieth century, and into the new millennium. The explosive Gaza/Gully clash between rival dancehall artistes Vybz Kartel and Mavado, and their followers, precipitated in 2006, and which took centrestage during 2009 and 2010 in Jamaica, stands as a high point or watershed moment in the development of this phenomenon. This musical feud or clash holds a record for its strong resonance within the Jamaican media landscape and amongst the populace. It sparked multiple and varied activities both within and outside dancehall culture. These included on- and off-stage musical volleys, violent interaction with sound system operators and fans of one rival artiste, a wave of Gaza and Gully graffiti across many communities in Jamaica and combative activities among schoolchildren who supported one or the other. The intense and very public activities that characterized this musical feud/clash resulted in intervention from the highest levels of the state when then Prime Minister Bruce Golding and several other government ministers called a meeting with both artistes, in December 2009, in an attempt to stem what was perceived as a tidal wave of violent activities precipitated by their Gaza/Gully feud/clash. Thus, the Kartel/Mavado infarction seemed radically differentiated from the usual artiste-artiste musical feud or clash because of these multiple and various activities of the artistes and their supporters, and also based on the intense attention from Jamaica's traditional electronic and print media houses, for a significant period of time spanning almost five years, from 2006–2010. For many observers, this intense and extended media focus arguably bordered on agenda-setting. Yet, the role of a liberalized and highly competitive Jamaican print and electronic media sector, and their involvement in and propensity to expand visibility for popular music clashes/feud in this era, remains significantly elided in discussions and research.

In an effort to unearth underlying themes and provide critical and necessary data regarding popular music feuds or clashes, this chapter presents key preliminary findings of a research that explored media coverage of popular music feuds/clashes in Jamaica during the period 1970–2010. In so doing, the work initiates a necessary process of closing the gaps in the research on this recurrent facet of Jamaican music culture by engaging with the historical themes to provide valuable information on the characteristics of this facet. Hopefully, the information garnered can also aid in the creation of relevant strategies towards resolution.

This chapter focuses on the results of a content analysis of over 700 newspaper articles on musical feuds/clashes, which examines, among other variables, the nature of the stories, the relative frequency of coverage, and the visual support associated with the text presented in the articles. In addition to highlighting challenges associated with a study of this nature, this work also makes a case for the development of a research instrument which can be applied to the analysis of current and past media coverage of popular music feuds or clashes, and also be replicated to enhance our understanding of feuds or clashes which are yet to occur. As such, it provides a useful template for analysis of future musical duels. A brief historical discussion of Jamaican popular music clashes or feuds is also offered.

RELATED ENGAGEMENTS WITH DANCEHALL MUSIC AND CULTURE

While the chapter focuses on Jamaican popular music, it is more clearly related to Jamaican dancehall music and culture as the phenomenon of musical feuds or clashes operated as a crucial component of the development of this genre over several decades from the early 1980s to 2010 and beyond. In Jamaica, the early and primary component of analyses of dancehall culture first emanated from journalistic endeavours in the print and electronic media, for example, in newspaper columns, letters to the editor in the daily and weekly Jamaican newspapers, in particular, the *Daily* and *Sunday Gleaner*, the *Daily* and *Sunday Observer* and the *Star* newspaper. Other newspapers such as the Observer's *Chat*, a short-lived foray into the entertainment tabloid format (as a competitor to the longstanding *Star*, from the Gleaner Company), the *Herald* and the *X-News* are also critical in this framework. Consequently, journalistic endeavours in the Jamaican newspapers predate formal academic inquiry into this arena, and continue to provide raw data, as well as valuable analytical planks, for continuing academic work. They remain valuable resources for academic research on social and political responses to, and perceptions of, Jamaican music, but specifically dancehall music and culture in Jamaica. A growing body of critical inquiry in the academy after the late 1990s spawned burgeoning academic work that provides critical analysis of dancehall music and culture. (cf. Cooper 2004; Hope 2006 and 2010; Stanley-Niaah 2004 and 2010; Stewart 2002; Stolzoff 2000). The work on Jamaican musical feuds or clashes, and dancehall's seminal clash culture is an emerging component of this debate.

In this regard, journalist Kavelle Anglin-Christie (2006) in an article in the Jamaican *Star* titled, 'Feuding the Fire in Dancehall', locates the origin of the discourse of Reggae/Dancehall feuds in the 1950s, beginning with Duke Reid versus Clement Dodd and Derrick Morgan versus Prince Buster. Her discussion moves to the post-millennial example of Vybz Kartel and Mavado, where Reggae/Dancehall feuds are used to crown and cement lyrical heroes within this space. Anglin-Christie temporally contrasts Jamaican popular music feuds of the 1950s and 1960s with contemporary manifestations (since Sting 2003) where feuds are not just lyrical but also become physical.

In the wake of Kartel/Mavado's Gaza vs. Gully clash/feud in the dancehall, Michael Barnett (2010), Annie Paul (2010), Kim-Marie Spence (2010) and Sonjah Stanley-Niaah's (2010) presentations at the UWI's International Reggae Conference in 2010 waded into this debate. Their deliberations underscored the notion that the dominance of the clash motif in Jamaican popular music predates its centrality in dancehall music and culture. For example, as with Anglin-Christie's article, Barnett highlighted the intense rivalry and ongoing clash between two prominent Jamaican artistes, Prince Buster and Derrick Morgan during the 1960s. Noting this as Jamaica's first musical clash between two recording artistes and stating this also provided these two Ska giants with both intense publicity and financial rewards, for Barnett, this war of words was both personal and political, having at its centre notions of black nationalism, black economics and black consciousness.

Stanley-Niaah (2010) identifies the origin of musical feuds or clashes in black popular cultures in continental Africa, as a component of her discussion on 'black performance cultures' with trans-Atlantic umbilical cords in, for example, some West African musical traditions such as that of the Anlo-Ewe of Ghana (Avorgbedor 1994, 112). Within these groups, musical clashes are as much about talent as they are about lyrical/musical prowess. In a related vein, John Constantinides (2002), in quoting Norman Stolzoff (2010), states that 'for the Ewe as much as the Jamaicans, musical clashes are a good way to establish power relations within the musical community as determined by the tastes of the crowd'(10). Indeed, in an analysis of 'Beef, Media and Rap Music in the USA', E. Sweet (2005) also highlights this propensity towards musical challenges and clashes in hip hop culture, a black performance form that is aligned to Jamaican dancehall culture. For Sweet, 'beef is a type of conflict between rappers, most clearly manifested in songs degrading one another' while 'on actuality however, beef is something much more subtle and complex...it is a discourse between people and composed of an assemblage of texts – texts that are often mistaken for the beef itself' (2).

Clashes or feuds within Jamaican popular music are said to have their origins in the period of the late 1940s–1950s, with the emergence of the sound system phenomenon. Stolzoff (2000) notes that sound system operators, at the time, used their equipment to not only 'drown out' their rivals, but also competed with getting 'exclusive' North American R&B records to 'kill' another sound. The two primary sound system rivals of the time were Duke Reid's *The Trojan* and Coxsone Dodd's *Sir Coxsone's Downbeat*. Clashes between these sounds playing at different venues initially were based on the sound that could attract the largest audience using loud volume. Separate venues were changed to a single venue where each sound would play against each other showcasing 'exclusive' records, and either appointed judges or the crowd would determine the winner of the clash. During that era, when R&B records became difficult to obtain, sound system operators produced their own records, which were not released to the public. These records would become arsenals for upcoming clashes (Stolzoff 2000).

In this framework, the discourse of Jamaican musical feuds or clashes are also power-laden debates and, as Carolyn Cooper (2004) acknowledges, (border) clash in Jamaican defines a broad range of issues, including the clash between English language and Jamaican; clashes between Culture proper and Culture improper; class clashes; the politician versus the ghetto youth; clash of the brown pigment versus the black pigment; and clashes between and among Christians and Rastafari. Here, Donna Hope contends that verbal clashes remain an important part of the thematic dialogue that ordinary Jamaicans have with respect and power based on one's dexterity with the spoken word. As such, if you are able to level your opponent lyrically you are superordinate. This underlies the desire of many dancehall adherents who attend stage shows like Sting to celebrate lyrical prowess (Hope 2011a).

The popular, annual dancehall stage show, Sting, held annually on December 26 every year since 1983, can be described as a crowning glory of dancehall's clash culture, where the lyrical gladiator of dancehall of the year is crowned. Sting developed as a critical component of the dancehall space and place peopled by hardcore dancehall fans who attend the event to be entertained by their lyrical king/s and to signify their support for their dancehall heroes. The proliferation of newspaper articles and interviews and discussions on entertainment programmes on local television (e.g.,

Entertainment Report and Intense on Television Jamaica [TVJ] and On Stage and DWRAP on CVM TV) around the staging of Sting each year, underscores the seminal role that this annual event plays on Jamaican's entertainment calendar as well as in the celebration and development of dancehall clash culture.[1] Where Sting and its clash culture is concerned, Hope (2004) noted in the wake of the lyrical and physical clash between Kartel and Ninja Man at Sting 2003, that artistes likes Vybz Kartel represent a new generation of dancehall artistes who have 'now come of age and [are] demanding a space in the front rows of dancehall culture' at the clash kingdom because Sting is where 'cultural Kings are dethroned and new ones crowned.'

As a component of more contemporary debates on gender and sexuality in Jamaican popular music, Annie Paul (2010) specifically examined the Gaza/Gully feud's facilitation of a public discussion in the print and electronic media about sexuality and alternative lifestyles, as well as the clash of DJ culture versus the gender-bender Shebada.[2] For Paul, this served to further expose transitions in Jamaica's response to male homosexuality, where 'social and political responses from the mass media have been critical at best and condemnatory at the very least and dancehall artists are blamed for Jamaica's social pathologies.'

In a renewed vein of debate, Kim-Marie Spence (2010) examined this traditional element of the musical feuds or clash as a possible market-savvy move in a music and world culture in which, for her, 'distinction is something conferred as much by one's own notoriety as by any expensive marketing campaign.' Thus, she argues that clashing or lyrical warfare in dancehall (and hip hop) is business and has been used to launch successful careers for artists such as Beenie Man, Bounty Killa and Vybz Kartel; and also to sustain careers, especially in the absence of new musical hits, such as the case with veteran dancehall artiste, Ninja Man. Positing that 'the seismic-like, rapid change and demand in global music cultures and markets for albums/records has been on the decline due to the introduction of the social media outlets such as Napster and iTunes which introduced digital downloads', Spence suggested that digital downloads helped to democratize demand and access of individual consumers of music cultures and shifted the focus to the individual song or performance of the individual artist. She argues, convincingly, that it is this global transformation that impacted on the demand in Jamaica's popular musical landscape, particularly since Jamaicans do not usually buy albums, but instead access music from various free or cheap sources. As such, Spence (2010) underscored the notion that this new wave of digital media (in the form of MySpace, Youtube, etc.) should be and can be used as self-marketing tools. This point of analysis is reflected in Sweet's (2005) analysis of a similar phenomenon, 'beef' in rap music and hip hop culture and its convergence with media and marketing in the USA where Sweet (2005) examines the role of different and related texts in creating, disseminating and promoting/marketing 'beef' and its related products.

Tomekha McCarthy's (2011) pilot study on the coverage of the Kartel/Mavado feud in Jamaica's mainstream dailies concluded, in part, that

> the positioning of the stories, the amount of space given to the stories, the headlines used in conjunction with the stories, the images that accompanied the stories, the words used in reference to the feud and simple the fact that the feud was discussed in that public forum may have however, aided in giving the feud more prominence in the minds of their readers (33).

Here, she suggests that the media is critical in this process of development and promotion of the feuds.

This current study on Jamaican popular music feuds and clashes, draws from the foregoing and other earlier work and research on Jamaican music in general and dancehall music and culture in particular to engage a larger scope of work and deploys several theoretical frames to provide a wider frame of reference for conclusions made herein.

The analysis of the media's role within this popular music framework work was guided by the media's agenda-setting function as a framework for analysis and discussion. Maxwell E. McCombs and Donald L. Shaw (1993) note that while the opening phases of agenda setting research focused on 'who sets the public agenda – and under what conditions,' more recent research has shifted attention to the question 'who sets the media agenda?' For this work, a content analysis is used to determine the prominent issues in the media. One critical aspect of the agenda setting perspective worth noting here is the distinction between first- and second-level agenda setting. First-level deals with issue salience and the second-level deals with attribute salience; in other words, first-level agenda setting underscores the media's role in telling audiences what issues to think about, while second-level agenda setting focuses on the media's role in telling audiences how to think about issues.

YOUR NAME A MENTION: **FINDINGS AND ANALYTICAL OVERVIEW**

Both the title, and first line of Mega Banton's 1990s dancehall hit, 'Your Name A Mention', suggests that once you are being 'mentioned' or made known then you should not be worried thus '*From A your name a mention, no badda fret nor worry yuh intention*' [*Once your name is being mentioned (made public) then do not worry or fret*]. In short, no publicity is bad publicity, or rather, any publicity is a good thing, within or beyond the frame of Jamaica's popular music arena. Its choice as epitaph and title for this work is brokered specifically on this meaning.

As previously noted, a content analysis was conducted on the coverage of popular music feuds/clashes in Jamaican newspapers during 1970 to 2010, which allowed the researchers to detect multiple examples of how Jamaican media report on confrontations between performing artistes.

Where Jamaican popular music and dancehall is concerned, a content analysis is also of particular import because, as mentioned earlier, the journalistic endeavours in Jamaican newspapers pre-date any systematic academic documentation or inquiry on Jamaican popular music and culture, and so provide/d a critical cache of raw data and analytical ruminations on this social and cultural phenomenon that far pre-dates and often outweighs the forays and incursions made by electronic and new media in the contemporary era.

Subsequent to a three-month newspaper archive search during summer 2012 at the National Library of Jamaica, approximately 700 articles regarding Jamaican musical clashes or feuds were located in all archived daily Jamaican newspapers available at the Library – *Chat*, the *Gleaner*, the *Herald*, the *Jamaica Observer*, the *Star* and *X-News*. While several of these newspapers (e.g., *Chat*, *Herald*, and

X-News) are no longer in circulation, they were included in the study to ensure that a wide range of articles were examined.

A code sheet developed for the study, categorized into four main sections which structured the coding of content as follows: (1) Medium; (2) Newspaper Headline Text; (3) Newspaper Visuals and (4) Newspaper Body Text. The patterns herein provide an opportunity to expand our understanding of the nature of the newspaper's coverage of popular music clashes or feuds. The following sections provide some key findings and analysis of same.

THE MEDIUM

The majority of stories on popular music feuds appeared in the *Star* with just over 65 per cent of the stories analysed found in that newspaper. The *X-News* featured the second largest number of stories on clashes or feuds, with 11.2 per cent of the stories analysed appearing in that publication. Table 6.1 below shows the distribution of stories across each newspaper.

In this Jamaican case, it is not surprising that the majority of the stories appeared in the *Star*, the longstanding Gleaner Company Ltd's tabloid-size newspaper that covers topics such as crime, sports, and entertainment, with a consistent focus on popular Jamaican personalities. The *Star's* 'Starbiz' section, which focuses explicitly on entertainment, would have captured multiple happenings regarding popular music clashes or feuds over many years. In addition, the *Herald, Chat* and *X-News* newspapers were relatively short-lived publications – a key reason for their lower frequency of coverage of music feuds/clashes during the period under examination, than the *Star* which, to date, is still in circulation. Where coverage per week is concerned, stories on popular music clashes or feuds appeared mostly on Tuesdays and Fridays as shown in table 6.2.

One possible explanation for the recurrence of Tuesdays and Fridays as the two most popular days of the week for stories on musical clashes or feuds is that stories appearing on Tuesdays would document various entertainment shows that usually occur during the previous weekend, while the Friday stories would highlight upcoming shows, as well as cover or pre-empt issues regarding upcoming weekend entertainment events.

Table 6.1: Number of Stories Appearing in Each Newspaper

Newspaper	Number of Stories about Popular Music Feuds	Percentage (%)
Chat	32	4.8
Gleaner	47	7.2
Herald	13	2.0
Observer	63	9.6
Star	427	65.2
X-News	73	11.2
Total	**655**	**100**

Table 6.2: Number of Stories Appearing Each Day of the Week

Day of Week	Number of Stories about Popular Music Feuds	Percentage (%)
Monday	64	12.0
Tuesday	102	19.2
Wednesday	73	13.7
Thursday	74	13.9
Friday	150	28.2
Saturday	45	8.5
Sunday	24	4.5
Total	**532**	**100**

Nonetheless, coverage of musical clashes or feuds was still present throughout the entire week with most stories appearing Mondays to Fridays as shown in table 6.2 above. This could result from the fact that most of these newspapers had daily sections focusing on lifestyle and entertainment, of which the actors and activities within dancehall music and culture form a critical and significant component.

While the period covered by this content analysis was 1970 to 2010, stories on musical clashes or feuds mainly appeared in newspapers from 1982 to 2010. And, in 1985, 1986 and 1990, no stories about feuds appeared in the newspapers. Additionally, before 1995, only a few stories appeared about feuds; with the number of stories appearing prior to 1995 ranging from three to seven stories per year. The highest number of stories (117) appeared in 2009 with the next highest appearing in 2010 (60 stories) followed by 56 stories in 2006.

Where this annual coverage is concerned, 1980 has been noted as a significant moment in the rise of dancehall music and culture, with the release of Wayne Smith's song, 'Under Mi Sleng Teng', on the *Sleng Teng* rhythm. In addition, several key dancehall activities, including the musical clash arena of stage shows, heralded by the first staging of Sting, in 1983, at the Cinema 2 venue in New Kingston, mark the early 1980s as a transition in the form and format of the Jamaican musical genre, and its attendant, very visible and popular facets – to include the seminal aspect of clash culture, that becomes solidified in this genre. Thus, it is arguable that a growing recognition of the role of popular music forms as valuable local entertainment, as well as an appreciation of the value and role of feuds in helping to promote artistes and the stage show events, backed by their strong appeal (whether in assent or dissent) and their obvious propensity to boost newspaper sales, could account for the increase in the coverage since 1995. The liberalization of the Jamaican media landscape in the mid-1990s resulted in increased competition for audience share and ratings among local media houses. The *Jamaica Observer*, for example, began circulation in January 1993 and is still in operation. The *X-News* began in February 1993 but ceased operations in early 2010. The *Jamaica Herald*, which started as a daily publication called *Jamaica Record* in 1987 became known as the *Herald* in 1992, and eventually transformed to a weekly publication, the *Sunday Herald* which was inconsistent in its circulation. Arguably, the increase in the newspaper coverage of musical clashes and feuds, particularly in the dancehall, can be directly linked to the increase in the number of newspapers in circulation since the mid-1990s, with the more liberal scope of publication topics. In this regard, while overlooking the print media, Hope (2006) identifies media liberalization as an important plank in dancehall's evolution, noting that 'the development of Jamaica's media landscape from the late 1980s through the 1990s aided in the spread of dancehall…' (15)…'with some stations like IRIE FM and RETV being developed with an exclusive focus on Jamaican music and entertainment, with dancehall music and culture representing more than 80 per cent of their output' (16). This symbiotic relationship between the liberalization of Jamaican media and the rise of dancehall music creates a critical media platform upon which activities within and/or related to dancehall music and culture continue to enjoy prime time media coverage in all forms of print, electronic and new media to date.

Musical feud/clash stories appeared in various sections throughout the newspapers but most notably in sections devoted to either entertainment or lifestyle news. For example, 110 stories (20 per cent of the stories analysed) about music feuds appeared on page 11. The *Star* had a section regarding entertainment news called 'Starbiz' which featured content mainly on page 11 of the newspaper. Only 11 stories or 1.6 per cent of the entire sample of over 700 stories appeared on the front page of any newspaper or any of its major entertainment sections. For example, the story headlined, 'Bounty Killer seeks peace' appeared on page 1C of the *Daily Gleaner* on Friday, December 15, 2000. The *Gleaner* is usually divided into sections and page 1C indicates that the story appeared on the first page (or headline page) of section C, which at that time was devoted to entertainment news and called 'Showtime'. A similar pattern could be observed in the *Observer* where the story titled, 'It wasn't me– Bounty Killer' appeared on the first page of the January 2, 2004 issue of the 'Splash', the *Weekend Observer's* pullout on entertainment. These stories appeared on the first page of the section in the newspaper and not on the main front page. This is not to suggest that no story about feuds ever appeared on the main front page of a newspaper. The December 28, 2003 issue of the *Sunday Gleaner* had its lead story headlined, 'Terror at Sting'. However, in general, stories on music feuds/clashes appeared in sections that focused on entertainment news. It is clear from this placement that media houses, as well as their journalists and editors, continue to perceive the activities from within the popular musical landscape as mainly 'entertainment'.

This does not dismiss attempts to engage with the discourse in more in-depth opinion pieces from regular or guest columnists (or radio and television talk shows and panel discussions).

NEWSPAPER HEADLINE TEXT

In terms of the type of headline used to caption these stories, 73.8 per cent of the stories had only headlines while 25.2 per cent had a subheading (or kicker) along with the main headline. The headlines' relative font size in relation to the rest of the text was judged by the coders to be big (70 per cent); medium (23.2 per cent) and small (6.8 per cent). The subheadlines' relative sizes were judged as big (6.1 per cent); medium (60.2 per cent) and small (33.7 per cent). Regarding the weight of the headline, coders assessed 95 per cent of the headlines to be bold and 87 per cent of subheadlines to be bold. The number of words per headline ranged from one to 15 with an average of five words per headline.

Artiste-artiste musical feuds or clashes make the headlines of stories in newspapers, as well as on the radio and television stations, where they are sensationalized and given special attention (the *Sunday Gleaner*, July 23, 2006). Indeed, the role of the media in the Kartel/Mavado debacle was questioned in one *Jamaican Star* article headlined, 'Media pushing Kartel Mavado War?' (Henry 2008). It was admitted in this article that the media oftentimes hyped the Kartel/Mavado feud for their (the media's) benefit. In the same article, Anthony Miller, the producer of Entertainment Report (ER), a very popular entertainment programme broadcast on TVJ, offered the caveat that media shows such as his, broadcast what they think the public is interested in. Wading in on this debate within the mass media, Carolyn Cooper (2009) makes the point that dancehall music and culture get a lot of press only when it is something considered negative by traditional Jamaica where the usual labels 'filthy sexual politics, the deadly gun talk, the quarter-naked women' and the more recent (at that time), 'Kartel/Mavado clash' are regurgitated.

NEWSPAPER VISUALS

As the most contemporary form of Jamaican popular music, dancehall music culture is renowned for its flashiness, colourful nature and high visibility (Cooper 2004; Hope 2006 and 2010; Stanley-Niaah 2010; Stolzoff 2000). Consequently, the terrain of popular music clashes or feuds also presents spectacular and highly visible phenomenon ranging from fabulous and fantastic costumes, eye-grabbing props, and stunning lyrical interaction, among others, that positions this popular cultural genre as a crucial and organic component of the life and times of Jamaica's underclasses. Thus, it was not surprising that the majority (81.8 per cent) of news stories analysed included some visual element that included cartoons or photographs which were either presented singly or as montages.

Most pictures (94 per cent) appeared as single photographs and these pictures depicted either various shot sizes (head shot, mid shot or full body shot) of the artistes, or scenes from performances on stage or audiences' reactions to performances. The captions for the photographs either stated the name of the artiste featured or described elements of the performance conveyed in the image.

Most images (58.5 per cent) accompanying stories were photographs on file while another 28.6 per cent were taken by named photographers,[3] many of whom gained significant renown from their work in documenting the graphic activities of this popular music form and showcasing same for many within and outside Jamaica who are unable (or unwilling) to be physically present at these venues.

Where both photographs and headlines are concerned, Sunil Saxena (2006) argues that photographs, graphics and headlines are three news elements that arrest eye movement on a newspaper page (24). Headlines help readers to assess the relative importance of a news report by manipulating the length of the headline, its font size and width (Saxena 2006). Most of the headlines regarding dancehall feuds were coded as bold and followed the tenets of journalism in ensuring that they were written concisely. This suggests that the newspapers attempted to emphasize the importance of popular music feuds or clashes for its readers. This is debatably a form of first-level agenda setting where the media establish issue salience by helping audiences to think about certain issues. The second-level agenda setting function (attribute salience) of the media could be exemplified in this study as the use of war-related language in news stories about feuds that help in telling the audiences how to think about feuds. One cannot ignore the fact that hardly any of the stories analysed appeared on the main front page of a newspaper. The article on the front page (not entertainment section) of the December 28, 2003 issue of the *Sunday Gleaner* appeared in that position not only because it was about a feud/clash but because of the newsworthiness of the negative outcomes associated with the feud/clash. Thus, the story about dancehall culture moved beyond the category of entertainment to become 'prime time' news, headlined on the day that the *Gleaner* enjoys its highest circulation and readership. Here, the consistent twinning of activities in dancehall culture with the criminal and reprehensible elements of Jamaican society is a critical component of many media narratives around dancehall, which ostensibly promote 'entertainment' or, in this instance 'entertainment as news.' The story headlined, 'Terror at Sting' emphasized the negative elements of the event in its opening paragraphs:

> The ugly face of the mob ruled Sting 2003 at the Jamworld Entertainment Centre in Portmore, St. Catherine, as bottles, stones and gunshots peppered the air to bring a premature, terror-filled end to the annual dancehall show on Boxing Day. The police say seven persons were injured, including a CVM employee, during the ensuing melee and mini-stampedes in the venue as people bolted for safety, seconds after it was announced that deejay Bounty Killer would not be appearing on the show (2003).

This story and others framed in a similar manner, no doubt, help to shape how readers think about musical feuds and dancehall clashes and feed into the social and cultural condemnation of a popular cultural form that emanates from the lower socio-economic spaces of Jamaica. Here, dancehall theorists and activists continue to argue that dancehall's positioning in a subject category, is polarized against other forms of 'accepted' Jamaican cultural forms in the high culture versus low culture dichotomy. In this dichotomous placement, dancehall, as a popular cultural form is rejected by high society as a form of 'slackness' while Eurocentric forms, or those selectively identified as bearing historical cultural markers (heritage culture) are elevated as true forms of accepted and traditional 'culture.'

Additionally, the visual elements, such as the use of graphic and colour photographs in the media also function to elevate the feuds/

clashes in the minds of the audience is a form of second-level agenda setting. More particularly, the type of photographs selected and the positioning of individuals in these photographs impute Jamaican musical feuds/clashes as high drama, war-like and inflammatory. Many pre-clash and post-clash photographs position artistes facing each other, often with a microphone in hand. The use of head shots or upper body shots in many of these instances project a large and often menacing image of the artistes 'at work' on the clash battlefield. Other photographs highlight the spectacular costumes and graphic props that are used to impute violence. For example, the inflammatory and highly popularised clash at Sting 2008 between Vybz Kartel and Mavado was rendered multiple times showcasing Kartel in full army fatigues, complete with helmet, bulletproof vest, and 'weaponry', and Mavado facing him in his full black 'assassin' garb, complete with flowing cape, gloves, ski-mask and requisite armament. Other photographs used in these stories include visuals of the audience, for example, the 'Terror at Sting' story discussed above was captioned with a Carlington Wilmot photograph of a patron lying on a stretcher bearing the following caption:

> This injured woman lies on a stretcher, which is being taken into an ambulance, after a bottle-throwing melee at the Sting 2008 concert at the Jamworld Entertainment Centre on Boxing Day.

Here, readers are left in no doubt as to the enormity of the 'terror' that unfolded both on and off the Sting 2008 stage; thus, adding to the persistent notion that Sting, and other dancehall events, are a haven for war, crime, potential injury and 'terror'. Indeed, ongoing research on dancehall continues to showcase this 'terror' that many feel when dancehall events are mentioned, to the extent that many persons shy away from these events out of a fear for their personal safety.

Other headlines worth mentioning include some around the then growing Gaza/Gully musical feud such as, 'Media pushing Kartel, Mavado war?' in the *Jamaica Star,* November 11, 2008 (Krista Henry); and in the *Gleaner*: 'One love on Gaza Street' in the *Sunday Gleaner,* November 22, 2009 (Carolyn Cooper); 'Calling Gully and Gaza' in the *Daily Gleaner,* November 14, 2009 (Anthony Hamilton); editorial titled 'Mr Golding's dancehall summit' in the *Daily Gleaner,* December 9, 2009 and 'Gully vs. Gaza Bruce vs. Portia' in the *Daily*

Gleaner, December 12, 2009. As Brian Brooks and Janus Pinson (2009) have noted, these visual elements are indeed content and an important part of content too (227) where, from their research, about 90 per cent of readers enter pages through large photos, artwork or display type (such as headlines and promos). Running a visual element with text makes it three times more likely that at least some of the text will be read and headlines are more likely to be read when a photo is nearby.

The fact that 81.8 per cent of the stories analysed included photographs indicate that media's treatment of the stories on musical feuds or clashes are designed to attract the reader to the story, help the reader focus on the story, and think about its content in a specific fashion. Authors argue that the vividness of news reports and the positioning of stories help to prime audiences or draw their attention to some aspects of news content at the expense of others (Baran and Davis, 2000). Indeed, as McCarthy (2011) argues in her work, others were drawn into the Gaza/Gully debate,

> …evidenced by the fact that on numerous occasions, the letters to the editor were responses to articles that had previously been published about the feud – a section of society which would not have normally discussed the feud openly or at all, was drawn into the discourse as the feud had become a major talking point in their daily source of news (33).

Likewise, Barnett (2009 and 2010) is of the view that,

> …had it not been for the media attention, the issue involving supporters of dancehall stars Adidja 'Vybz Kartel' Palmer and David 'Mavado' Brooks, would have long petered out…At what point have we decided that these people are so important to us that everything they do is to be on the front pages of the paper?

For dancehall feuds and clashes, this thought process, is often negative and inflammatory, as directed by the headlines and the photographs. The role of the text, within the body of the stories is also critical herein.

NEWSPAPER BODY TEXT

Various elements of the body text of the news stories were also analysed to provide a description of the characteristics of popular music feuds and the majority of stories on musical clashes or feuds were either presented as news (61.8 per cent) or features (19.5 per cent). Fewer stories appeared as opinion pieces (12.7 per cent), editorials (1.5 per cent) or letters to the editor (3 per cent). A smaller number coded as 'other' (1.5 per cent) appeared in the gossip column of the newspaper or as vox pops.

Almost half of the stories (49.7 per cent) had a clear byline; other stories were either contributed (18.3 per cent) or did not have any stated byline (32 per cent). Of the stories with a clear byline, several individuals were identified as the story's writer.[4] Of this group of writers, Howard McGowan, Krista Henry, Mel Cooke, Sadeke Brooks and Teino Evans produced an average of 30 stories each on music feuds in the newspapers examined. While a majority of the individuals were titled as staff reporter or writer, senior reporter or editor, stories were also done by freelance writers or reporters, columnists and contributors who would usually provide a service in documenting coverage of musical feuds or clashes to the newspapers. What becomes clear is that this documentation stands as a historical cache of the life's work of specific journalists and simultaneously represent their perceptions, (subject to editorial approval) that colours the sociocultural meanings that are represented within and projected through these stories.

In keeping with Potter et al.'s (1999) notion of coding latent projective content, 27.7 per cent of the stories were deemed to be sensationalized and 56.7 per cent were not. While the overall tone of most stories (54.2 per cent) was perceived as neutral, more stories were seen as negative in tone (17.5 per cent) compared to stories deemed to have a positive tone (13.5 per cent), and 14.75 per cent of these stories were deemed both negative and positive. The selective language used in the newspaper stories is obviously responsible for this, as a wide range of words and phrases in English and Jamaican Creole, associated with war, violence, chaos and combat were used in the various stories. The research highlighted over 330 words which occurred in various articles several times as examples of language suggestive of war, violence, chaos and combat used in writing stories on musical feuds. A sample of these highly suggestive words include:

> Aggression, abuse, army, battles, blood, bomb, combat, confront, chaos, danger, dead, dismantle, erupt, enemy, expletives, face-off, fracas, funeral, gang, gladiator, gunshot, hate, hit, hurt, incident,

injury, insult, jab, kill, knife, lash, lethal, lynch, madness, melee, missile, nasty, nemesis, negative, obscenity, odds, opponent, pain, pandemonium, punch, quarrelsome, rebellion, retaliate, revenge, slaughter, square-off, suicidal, tension, threaten, tribalism, vengeance, victims, violation, and war, weapon, wound.

The articles also utilized over 130 phrases indicative of war, violence, chaos and combat that included:

At each other's throats; blood thirsty fans; cass-cass;[5] dancing war; feuded fierce rivalry; fight against; going at it; heated words; heinous murder; kick down; killer instinct; lashed out; lyrical onslaught; lyrical funeral; making duppy;[6] musical massacre; nursing a wound; orgy of violence; periodical animosity; personal vendetta; rising tension; show down; stage struggle; street war.

The selective and explicit use of this inflammatory and violent language (words and phrases) in the newspaper stories during the period of 1970–2010 clearly indicates a deliberate media bias towards positioning dancehall music and culture in general, and popular music feuds or clashes in particular, as negative elements of Jamaican popular music and culture. Words and phrases which consistently impute war, strife, violence and combat, position dancehall culture and its musical feuds/clashes as more than lyrical sparring and verbal wordplay. They impute social and cultural meanings about dancehall music and culture, and about musical feuds or clashes as negative, violent, dangerous and criminal. Indeed, the negative tone of many stories also highlights a clear risk of personal harm and danger to potential or actual fans and audiences for dancehall's staged output. Nonetheless, the fact that events like the hardcore, annual staging of Sting and Reggae Sumfest's annual Dancehall Night on Thursdays continue to attract thousands of local and international and longstanding patrons/supporters is important to this debate. These patrons/supporters and their willingness to participate in the communal rituals of musical feuds/clashes, also underlines the existence of individuals for whom the symbols parlayed operate as entertainment, while simultaneously generating critical meanings on life, status and mechanisms for self-elevation and mobility.

CONCLUDING THOUGHTS

The clash/feud motif, a historical component of Jamaican popular music, resonates throughout dancehall music and culture, growing in intensity as dancehall evolves. It emerged with growing force in the early 1990s propelled by a liberalized media landscape, based on the high levels of competition and its resultant benefits to multiple players. Based on the foregoing, it is arguable that the musical or dancehall clash/feud motif gains visibility in Jamaica's traditional media forms in the early 1990s, through a symbiotic relationship between entertainment/dancehall, audience/consumers and the need to grab attention and readership for higher ratings which translate into greater rewards for different parties. For media houses, these rewards include better advertising revenues and higher sales overall. In an artiste-to-artiste clash, the artiste who emerges the winner benefits materially, in terms of visibility, access to real resources, and access to publicity. In a similar vein, the dancer who wins a dance clash or the sound system who wins a sound system clash, benefits in terms of recognition, visibility and material rewards. An example of this symbiotic relationship of rewards in the electronic media, oriented around the motif, is the Guinness Sounds of Greatness, a televised sound system clash competition (aired on TVJ) that begun in Jamaica in 2008. This TV programme is an organic end product of dancehall's sound system clash culture in a rewarding marriage with traditional media and a 'big name' advertiser to provide a contemporary form of televised popular culture competitions that offers its winners J$1M in prize money, and provides entrants with intense media visibility and publicity over the duration of each competition. Here, everyone is a winner since 'no publicity is bad publicity'.

Thus, Jamaica's print and electronic media devoted intense and particular attention to the Gaza/Gully or Kartel/Mavado feud/clash, arguably fuelling it beyond the dancehall space and into the wider social spaces of Jamaica, generating intense social and cultural debates and discussion. Here, McCombs and Shaw's (1972) argument that the mass media set the agenda of and for public discussion is relevant as they argue that,

> [I]n choosing and displaying news, editors, newsroom staff, and broadcasters play an important part in shaping political reality. [Listeners and viewers] ...learn not only about a given issue, but also how much importance to attach to that issue from the amount of information in a news story and its position (36).

This agenda-setting in mass media was a significant point of reference for the sensational headlines that formed part of the Jamaican media's response to the Gaza/Gully phenomenon, including articles with inflammatory and suggestive headlines, graphic and inflammatory language, and bearing graphic and suggestive pictures with similar captions. This was also evidenced in the growing numbers of annual stories that peaked in 2009 at 117 stories, at the culmination of this musical feud or clash. In this regard, the Jamaican media played a dual first- and second-level agenda setting role (McCombs and Shaw, 1993) by telling audiences *which* feuds or clashes to think about, and, more critically, by using select placement, pictures and inflammatory language to also tell audiences *how* to perceive these clashes or feuds; that is, as negative, violent, bad, warlike, and so on.

In its holistic form and/or individual facets, the media – in this instance newspapers, and their actors, photographers, reports, journalists, opinion writers, and letters to the editor writers – act as both consumers and creators of dancehall culture, as per Hope's 2006 conceptualization of Affectors and Affectees who simultaneously create and consume the cultural form (28–35). Thus, the role of the media moves beyond reportage to re-create and project symbolic meanings about popular music feuds or clashes within and beyond the Jamaican body politic and outwards to international and diasporic spaces. As a seminal agent of socialization, its hegemonic meaning-making facet is heightened with the persistent and pervasive focus on specific aspects of Jamaican music culture, and dancehall's culture of clash with a consistent underscoring of these facets as negative, criminal, warlike and inflammatory, under the guise of 'entertainment', with a smattering of 'news' and opinion pieces. The authoritative role of the media is a critical component of the value placed on its treatises in Jamaica where many were raised with the mantra 'if it in di Gleana, is true' (if it is in the *Gleaner*, then it is true). Its longstanding position as Jamaica's premier newspaper since 1834 means that the term 'Gleana', or Gleaner, has become a stand-in for all forms of Jamaican newspapers in popular language discourse. This dominant hegemonic placement of the 'Gleana'/newspapers in Jamaica suggests that the veracity of stories, whether news, editorial, opinion, entertainment, letters to the editor or otherwise in newspapers, is often unquestioned by many. Additionally, the promotion of an aspect or component of Jamaican popular music (or dancehall music and culture) as important, critical or timely – in a negative or positive sense – also falls within the hegemonic purview of the media as both a key agent of socialization, and a critical contributor to social, cultural and political debates and meaning-making. As with the intense and overwhelming volume of articles, report and other publications on the Gaza/Gully feud between 2006 and 2009, this is achieved by maintaining a steady and consistent deluge of output on the subject matter, using carefully written and placed headlines, photographs and other visuals, and selective and inflammatory language.

In the final analysis, the media plays a critical role in shaping public opinion on the form and content of Jamaican popular music in general, and dancehall music and culture in particular. The research also suggests that alternative placement, positioning, use of visuals, and language could result in a renewed or different perception of popular music forms. This includes the aspect of musical feuds/clashes that play a significant role in providing a platform for the promotion of artistes through a display of lyrical prowess, thus guaranteeing their hold on economic and social rewards.

This work focused specifically on newspapers as a critical component of the Jamaican media landscape. However, as the media landscape evolves to incorporate social media, the nature of the agenda-setting role played by traditional media will also change. Jack Rosenberry and Lauren Vicker (2009), note that bloggers, citizen journalists and independent media are all providing additional and diverse voices that help to shape the agenda in society (155). This trend has implications for future approaches to an analysis of the media's coverage of any issue in society and will form part of future research on Jamaican popular music. In its current form, this work provides a critical understanding of the nature of musical/dancehall clashes or feuds; and the role of traditional media in projecting and manipulating popular perceptions of this phenomenon that is/has been part and parcel of the mechanisms operationalized by ordinary people within the frame of popular culture, to make meanings of and negotiate the powered and status-ridden spaces that coalesce around their lives in Jamaica.

Authors' Note: *This paper forms part of a larger book-length work that is forthcoming on the role of media in popular music discourse.*

Notes

1. See, for example, Bartley 1993, 1994 and 1995; Boyne 2004; Henry 2008 and 2009; Hope 2004; Johnson 2009; McGowan 1988 and 1992; Mills 2003 and 2006; Walters 2001, and Wray 1995, 1996, 1997 and 2000.
2. Keith 'Shebada' Ramsay rose to national prominence in Jamaica during the first season of the popular, televised, comedy series, *Comedy Buss* in 2006, copping third place at the end of the competition. Shebada entered the world of popular Jamaican theatre in the 2006 Stages Production, *Bashment Granny*. He has become renowned for his popular gender-bending activities, and his 'borderline' incarnations of identity. See Hope's (2013) discussion on Borderline Constructions of Jamaican Masculinity.
3. These included Adrian Foster, Alan Lewin, Bryan Cummings, Carlington Wilmot, Claire Clark, Claudine Housen, Colin Hamilton, Fabian Ledgister, Garfield Robinson, Herbert McKenzie, Ian Allen, Ingrid Brown, Jermaine Barnaby, Joseph Wellington, Karl McCarty, Krista Henry, Lionel Rookwood JT, Marlon Myrie, Michael Gordon, Michael Sloley, Nathaniel Stewart, Nicketa Thomas, Noel Thompson, Peta-Gaye Clachar, Ricardo Bailey, Ricardo Makyn, Roxroy McLean, Rudolph Brown, Winston Burke and Winston Sill.
4. These included Adrian Frater, Adrian Nelson, Balford Henry, Basil Walters, Christine Hewitt, Claude Mills, Clyde McKenzie, Conroy Walker, David Dunkley, Dennis Howard, Daraine Luton, Dwayne Gordon, Dwayne McLeod, Eugene Pitter, Fabian Ledgister, Francine Black, G. Fitz Bartley, Garvin Davis, Germaine Smith, Hillary Lannaman, Horace Hinds, Howard Campbell, Howard McGowan, Ian Boyne, Ingrid Brown, Jermaine Lannaman, Karil Wright, Karl Vernon, Karyl Walker, Kavelle Anglin , Kesi Asher, Kim Gray, Krista Henry, Leighton Williams, Mel Cooke, Milton Wray, Nathaniel Steward, Patrick Roberts, Roland Burke, Roxroy McLean, Sadeke Brooks, Sharon Barnes, Sharon Leach, Sheena

Gail, Steven Jackson, Tieno Evans, Trevor 'Boots' Harris, Tyrone Reid, and Vinette Pryce.
5. *Cass-cass* is a Jamaican Creole term that means argument, strife or war as in 'Mi nuh wah inna nuh cass-cass wid yuh' (I do not wish to be in an argument or any strife with you).
6. *Making duppy* is a jamaican slang term that means to 'commit murder' or to 'kill someone'. It literally means 'making a dead'.

References

Anglin-Christie, Kavelle. 2006. Feuding the Fire in Dancehall. *Star*, September 22. Retrieved from http://jamaica-star.com/thestar/20060922/ent/ent7.html.

Baran, Stanley and Dennis Davis. 2000. *Mass Communication Theory– Foundations, Ferment and Future*. California: Wadsworth.

Barnett, Michael. 2010. Prince Buster vs. Derrick Morgan: The Original Dancehall Clash. Paper presented at the International Reggae Conference 2010, February 17–20, University of the West Indies, Mona. Retrieved from http://tv.mona.uwi.edu/dancehall-feuds-factions-and-fandom.

Bartley, G. Fitz. 1993. Prince Buster, Derrick Morgan Still have their Sting. *Jamaica Herald,* December 28.

———. 1994. An Incident Free Sting. *Jamaica Herald*, December 28.

———. 1995. Positive Vibes at Sting. *Jamaica Herald*, December 28, 1995.

Bilby, Kenneth et al. 2006. Jamaica. In *Caribbean Currents: Caribbean Music from Rhumba to Reggae*, by Peter Manuel. Philadelphia, PA: Temple University Press; Kingston: Ian Randle Publishers.

Boyne, Ian. 2004. 'Sting' A disgraced Institution. *Sunday Gleaner*, January 4. Retrieved from http://jamaica-gleaner.com/gleaner/20040104/focus/focus1.html.

Brooks, Brian and James Pinson. 2009. *The Art of Editing in the Age of Convergence*. 10th ed. Boston: Pearson Education Inc.

Campbell, Andrew C. 1997. Reggae Sound Systems. In *Reggae, Rasta, Revolution: Jamaican Music from Ska to Dub*, edited by Chris Potash. New York, NY: Schirmer Books.

Chang, Kevin O'Brien and Wayne Chen. 1998. *Reggae Routes: The Story of Jamaican Music*. Kingston: Ian Randle Publishers.

Constantinides, John. 2002. The Sound System: Contributions to Jamaican Music and the Montreal Dancehall Scene. Faculty of Music, department of Ethnomusicology Universite de Montreal. Retrieved from http://www.uvm.edu/~debate/dreadlibrary/constantinides2004.htm.

Cooper, Carolyn. 2004. *Sound Clash: Jamaican Dancehall Culture from Lady Saw to Dancehall Queen.* Basingstoke, UK: Palgrave Macmillan.

———. 2009. One love on Gaza Street. *Daily Gleaner*, November 22. Retrieved from http://jamaica-gleaner.com/gleaner/20091122/cleisure/cleisure3.html.

Cooke, Mel and Krista Henry. 2009. Dancehall Rife With Feuds. *Jamaican Star*, November 12. Retrieved from http://jamaica-star.com/thestar/20091211/ent/ent2.html.

Davis, Stephen and Peter Simon. 1992. *Reggae Bloodlines: In Search of the Music and Culture of Jamaica.* New York, NY: Da Capo.

Forbes, Marcia. 2010. *Music, Media and Adolescent Sexuality in Jamaica.* Kingston: Arawak Publications.

Guinness Sounds of Greatness Massive Success. 2011. *Daily Gleaner*, November 24. Retrieved from http://jamaica-gleaner.com/gleaner/20111124/ent/ent2.html.

Gully vs Gaza and Bruce vs Portia. 2009. *Daily Gleaner*, December 12. Retrieved from http://jamaica-gleaner.com/gleaner/20091212/letters/letters1.html.

Hamilton, Anthony. 2009. Calling Gully and Gaza.' *Daily Gleaner*, November 14. Retrieved from http://jamaica-gleaner.com/gleaner/20091114/letters/letters1.html.

Henry, Krista. 2011. Guinness Sounds of Greatness launched. *Star*, August 25. Retrieved from http://jamaica-star.com/thestar/20110825/ent/ent6.html.

———. 2008. Hours After Clash, Kartel Records Sting Song. *Star*, December 29. Retrieved from http://jamaica-star.com/thestar/20081229/ent/ent2.html.

———. 2008. Media pushing Kartel, Mavado war? *Jamaica Star*, November 11. Retrieved from http://jamaica-star.com/thestar/20081111/ent/.

Hope, Donna P. 2013. *Pon di Borderline*: Exploring Constructions of Jamaican Masculinity in Dancehall and Roots Theatre. *Journal of West Indian Literature*, Vol. 21, No. 1 & 2 (November 2012/April 2013).

———. 2011. Dancehall: Origins, History, Future.' *Groundings*, Issue 26 (July 2011): 7–28.

———. 2011. Popular Music and Strategic Culture in Jamaica. Presented at the Jamaica Strategic Culture Workshop, Florida International University's Applied Research Center/Latin American and Caribbean Center, Miami, Florida, July 7.

———. 2010. *Man Vibes: Masculinities in the Jamaican Dancehall.* Kingston, Jamaica: Ian Randle Publishers.

———. 2006. *Inna di Dancehall: Popular Culture and the Politics of Identity in Jamaica*. Kingston: UWI Press.

———. 2004. Sting 2003 – Performing Violence and Social Commentary. *Sunday Gleaner*, January 4, A10-A11. Retrieved from http://www.jamaica-gleaner.com/gleaner/20040104/cleisure/cleisure5.html.

Johnson, Richard. 2009. Sting 2009: A Mixed Bag. *Observer*, December 28, 2009.

King, Stephen, et. al. 2002. *Reggae, Rastafari, and The Rhetoric of Social Control*. Mississippi: University Press of Mississippi.

McCarthy, Tomekha. 2011. Jamaica's Media: A Look at the Gully-Gaza Feud. Unpublished BA Thesis. Kingston: University of the West Indies.

McCombs, Maxwell, E. and Shaw, Donald L. 1972. The Agenda-Setting Function of Mass Media. *Public Opinion Quarterly*, Vol. 36, Issue 2:176–87.

———. 1993. The Evolution of Agenda-setting Research: Twenty-five Years in the Market Place of Ideas. *Journal of Communication*. Vol. 43, No. 2: 58–67.

McGowan, Howard. 1988. Who Will Win the 4-the-hard-way Clashes? *Star*, December 16.

———. 1992. Who will come out on top at Sting? *Sunday Gleaner*, December 20.

McLeod, Erin and Joshua Chamberlain. 2012. Sound Clash Resurrection. *Cluster Mag Online*, April 8. Retrieved from http://theclustermag.com/blog/2012/04/sound-clash-ressurection/.

Mills, Claude. 2003. Terror at Sting. *Daily Gleaner*, December 28. Retrieved from http://jamaica-gleaner.com/gleaner/20031228/lead/lead1.html

———. 2006. War! *X News*, December 13.

Mr Golding's dancehall summit. 2009. *Daily Gleaner*, December 9. Retrieved from http://jamaica-gleaner.com/gleaner/20091209/cleisure/cleisure1.html.

Paul, Annie. 2010. Eyeless in Gaza and Gully: —Mi deh pon di borderline. Paper presented at the International Reggae Conference 2010, February 17-20, University of the West Indies, Mona. Retrieved from http://tv.mona.uwi.edu/dancehall-feuds-factions-and-fandom.

Rosenberry, Jack and Lauren Vicker. 2009. *Applied Mass Communication Theory–A Guide for Media Practitioners*. Boston, MA: Pearson Education Inc.

Saxena, Sunil. 2006. *Headline Writing*. New Dehli, India: Sage Publications India Pvt Ltd.

Seaga, Edward. 2010. *The Origins of Jamaican Popular Music.* Booklet with CD. Kingston.

Spence, Kim-Marie. 2010. Clash! – Jamaican Artistes in a New Digital Music Market. Paper presented at the International Reggae Conference 2010, February 17-20, University of the West Indies, Mona. Retrieved from http://tv.mona.uwi.edu/dancehall-feuds-factions-and-fandom.

Stanley-Niaah, Sonjah. 2010. Gully vs. Gaza?: Feuds, Factions and Fuelling Fandom in Jamaican Dancehall Performance. Paper presented at the International Reggae Conference 2010, February 17–20, University of the West Indies, Mona. Retrieved from http://tv.mona.uwi.edu/dancehall-feuds-factions-and-fandom.

———. 2004. Kingston's Dancehall: A Story of Space and Celebration. *Space and Culture*, Vol. 7, No. 1 (February): 102–118.

Stewart, Kingsley. 2002. 'So Wha, Mi Nuh Fi Live To?': Interpreting Violence in Jamaica Through the Dancehall Culture.' *IDEAZ*, Vol. 1 No. 1, University of the West Indies, Mona (May):17–28.

Stolzoff, Norman. 2000. *Wake the Town: Dancehall Culture in Jamaica.* Durham and London: Duke University Press.

Sweet, E. 2005. *Bullet on the charts: Beef, the Media Industry and Rap Music in America.* Haverford College. Retrieved from http://thesis.haverford.edu/dspace/bitstream/10066/1123/1/2005SweetE.pdf.

Walters, Basil. 2001. Bounty Returns to Sting 'To Save Dancehall.' *Observer*, December 8.

Wimmer, Roger and Joseph Dominick. 2003. *Mass Media Research–An Introduction.* 9th ed. California: Wadsworth.

Wray, Milton. 1995. Sting '95 an Anticlimax. *Jamaica Herald*, December 29.

———. 1996. No San, Ninja Clash at Sting. *Star*, December 24.

———. 1997. War, War and More War. *Star*, January 14.

Wu, D. and R. Coleman. 2009. Advancing Agenda-setting theory: The comparative strength and new contingent conditions of the two levels of agenda setting effects. *Journalism and Mass Communication Quarterly* 85, no. 4:775–89.

From Dub Plate to Dancehall: Versioning as an Analogue Template for Digital Reggae

Brent Hagerman

This project stems from research I conducted between 2007 and 2010 among music industry professionals in Kingston, Jamaica, for my dissertation, which was an ethnography of dancehall artist, Yellowman. Part of this research found me going to several Kingston studios with Yellowman to observe him recording dubplates for sound systems around the world.[1]

Modern dubplate producers have computer databases of thousands of popular rhythms ('riddims') and have hundreds of global sound system clients who order these exclusive recordings, or 'specials'. As I watched Yellowman and several other artists voicing dubplates in various studios, I thought about the slim technological distance between the roots of this practice – a studio producing a test acetate of a band's instrumental recording – and its current iteration – a digital file of a popular riddim recycled countless times by countless singers and deejays. Despite the fact that the genre of music and medium of recording had changed drastically since its inception in the 1960s, the mode of recording seemed to me to remain unchanged. With this in mind, I began to consider the process of reggae music creation and production over and against John Culkin's (1967) idea that 'we shape our tools and thereafter our tools shape us.' As such, this chapter looks at the creation, arrangement and recording of Jamaican reggae music during the shift from analogue to digital production between the 1970s and 1980s, and focuses on the practice of versioning.

In popular music discourse, analogue recording refers to music recorded to magnetic tape whereas digital recording involves converting an analogue wave to a digital format (a sequence of 1s and 0s) such as an audio file like WAV or AIFF.

In other words, recording music on a 24-track tape machine would be an example of analogue recording whereas using a digital audio platform such as Pro Tools would result in digitally recorded music. In reggae, however, the term digital signifies something different. The terms digital reggae, computerized reggae and ragga arose in the 1980s to refer to dancehall that was recorded with the assistance of electronic drum kits, drum machines and digital synthesizers such as the Casio MT-40.[2] The actual recording of the songs, however, was still done using analogue tape technology. The term digital reggae can refer to the use of digital instrumentation, the mode of production where these digital instruments partially or completely replaced studio musicians, and the aesthetic of the subsequent music produced; the music sounded robotic, computerized or digital. When I use the phrase 'reggae's digital revolution' I am referring to the shift towards the use of digital technology by artists like Sly Dunbar and producers like King Jammy. Jammy, particularly, helped change the industry's focus from acoustic and electric instruments played by studio musicians when he began using electronically generated sounds. The song that instigated this digital revolution in dancehall was the King Jammy-produced 'Sleng Teng' sung by Wayne Smith in 1985. Following this, I use the term analogue reggae to refer to music produced before the digital reggae era using session musicians instead of digital instrumentation.

I will now briefly turn to a description of the pre-digital Jamaican music industry and demonstrate how its focus on collaboration and the reuse and sharing of content directly influenced the way reggae songs were written.

I draw on the work of Peter Manual and Wayne Marshall (2006) who have offered a musicological framework for looking at the history of what they call 'riddim-plus-voicing' production and have argued that this Jamaican music production system is influential to music production in the digital age. But unlike their work, I apply new media theory and see analogue versioning as a pre-digital template for what media theorists (O'Reilly 2007; Flew 2008; Lessig 2008) have come to term Web 2.0 culture. I ask how did the tools and technology of reggae production in the 1960s and 1970s determine how reggae was created in the digital era. I argue that the participatory nature of the versioning in the 1960s and 1970s meant that the reggae industry was an early adopter of digital technology and that despite digital technology making it faster, easier and cheaper for producers to create reggae without studio musicians, reggae's digital revolution could not sever the industry's reliance on versioning because its participatory nature suited the new digital world characterized by collaboration and the reuse and sharing of content. In short, the new possibilities in production instigated by the digital era dovetailed with reggae culture's unique practice of collective authorship. Versioning was a product of the analogue studio culture and that technology determined how reggae songs were written, but because it was participatory in nature it was already inclined towards the values of the digital age. Essentially, the characteristics media scholars associate with the digital age were already in existence in the Jamaican music industry as far back as the 1960s.

I also employ the work of Mark Katz (2010) LM113 who has studied how music technology – the technology used to create, record, reproduce and listen to music – affects the way we compose, perform and listen to and even think about music. Katz suggests that the relationship between the technology and the user determines the end product. And this influence is not simply a one way flow; users transform technologies to meet their needs at the same time as those technologies determine and influence the scope and sound of a musical project.

Mostly, however, my analysis is informed by both the new media and alternative media theorists (Atton 2002; Flew 2008; Lessig 2001, 2008; Waltz 2006) that have characterized their objects of study with similar traits, and I find those helpful when looking at the Jamaican music practice of versioning. These include Web 2.0 attributes such as the use of open access technology, the expectation for evolution and change over time, and digital media that are collectively created, user-focused, participatory, and decentralized in terms of control (Flew 2008, 21). Similarly, alternative media have been theorized as media which are counter-hegemonic, non-hierarchically structured and participatory. Whereas the mass communication paradigm generally rests on the assumption of a one way flow of information – or 'Read/Only culture' as Lawrence Lessig (2008) has dubbed it –

participatory media is characterized by a flow between the user and the creator, or what Lessig characterizes as 'Read/Write culture'. My research suggests that the versioning practice in Jamaica shares many of the qualities of Read/Write culture and that these are helpful theoretical frames for thinking about the creation and function of reggae music.

As Manual and Marshall (2006) have shown, starting in the late 1960s and early 1970s, studios such as Studio One and Treasure Island began recycling older riddims by enlisting vocalists to write new melodies and lyrics over preexisting backing tracks. This practice of releasing a new version of an older song became known as 'versioning.' For example, in 1968 both Toots and the Maytals and Marcia Griffiths had hit songs ('54-46' and 'Feel Like Jumping' respectively) based on the Ethiopians' 1967 classic 'Train to Skaville'. The riddim was revived by Supercat in 1986 for his massive hit 'Boops'. The song was so popular that the riddim is now usually known as 'Boops' instead of its original title, and new versions of the riddim are released every year. Riddim database Jamrid.com lists 91 versions of the riddim. Like 'Boops', many riddims have over 100 iterations that may run across several genres of Jamaican music such as ska, rocksteady, reggae, dub and dancehall. A reggae fan may never hear the original iteration of a riddim such as 'Full Up' – one of the most versioned foundational riddims in existence but they will know several versions of the riddim.

Versioning and riddims are the essential tools of this art form in the studio. Since its inception versioning has dictated the mode of creation of reggae songs so that it is standard practice for a singer or deejay to write a new song using a pre-recorded backing track, or a riddim, as opposed to writing an autonomous stand-alone composition.

This may not seem exceptional to Jamaicans, but as Manual and Marshall (2006) point out, it stands in contrast to how most Western popular music has been created and produced. Take, for instance, mainstream American popular music in the mid-twentieth century: the Tin Pan Alley model of the 1930s and 1940s or the Brill Building model of the 1960s. Both these models employed professional songwriters who wrote songs that were then recorded by a professional class of singers and musicians. Motown adopted this model by having songwriting teams (Holland–Dozier–Holland), an in-house studio band (The Funk Brothers) and professional singers (Supremes, Temptations). Stax, Muscle Shoals and Atlantic also had similar models.

Reggae's model of original songs first recorded by professional studio bands, then recycled as riddims for generations to come – evolving musically in the process as new producers and bands recorded new versions or 'relicks' – is exceptional. Riddims of the 1960s and 1970s were recorded to reel to reel tape using studio musicians with the standard practice being that the instruments would be recorded to one track and the vocals to the other. With the advent of four-track systems, three tracks could hold the riddim (usually one for drums, two for other instruments, one for vocals). One track was always left open by producers like Lee Perry so that he could rerecord new vocal tracks over the instrumental riddim. When you add the fact that singers and deejays use these riddims to write entirely new melodies and lyrics over a pre-existing song, thereby creating a new one, this model of creation and production was highly original in the pre-remix era of music production. Indeed, the Jamaican practice of versioning is an early example of the remix.

This also accounts for why music critics more used to listening to rock, pop, classical or country have argued that reggae sounds derivative, unimaginative, imitative, and even plagiarized – the 'it all sounds the same' critique. Certainly some of the students in my rock 'n' roll history classes say this sort of thing about genres that are based on what Lessig (2008) calls 'remix culture', Aram Sinnreich (2010) calls 'configurable culture', or what John Oswald (1985) has dubbed 'plunderphonics'. All these terms effectively allude to taking an existing audio recording and altering it in some way to make a new composition.

While the versioning practice is exceptional, it is not entirely unique. Hebdige (2003) argues that it is at the heart of all Afro-American and Caribbean musics, including jazz, blues, rap, R&B, reggae, calypso, soca, salsa, and Afro-Cuban. Think, for instance, of how blues songs interchanged common licks, lyrics, chord progressions and rhythms, or how rap popularized the use of sampling older songs.

What I'm getting at here is that reggae creation and production has a long history of collective authorship. Unlike the songwriting models mentioned above, new reggae songs have often been constructed by a series of actors such as studio bands, producers, deejays and singers that each added something new to their iteration of a riddim. There is tremendous room for evolution and modification of older riddims. New versions or relicks can be recorded by rival studio bands who might develop the old riddim by adding a new riff or melody, change the arrangement, key, tempo, or chord progression or alter the drum beat or bass line. In addition, a singer might alter the lyrics to an older song or write a new song on a previous theme, such as Yellowman's 'Me Kill Barnie' which was an answer to Lone Ranger's 'Barnabas Collins', both recorded using the 'My Conversation' riddim. The result is that reggae songs are created as part of a genealogy of riddims, themes and lyrics. Manual and Marshall (2006) suggest that, by 1983, it was unusual to have a Jamaican hit employing an original riddim.

What interests me about the practice of versioning for the purposes of this chapter is that it allows new artists to create new art using old media. In addition, it means that the majority of reggae music is created collectively with new artists and producers building on the work of their forebears. The production of reggae music, then, is the recurring negotiation between past and present elements, choosing what to keep, what to alter, what to tear apart, and what to build anew. It is, at the same time, deconstructing and paying homage to the past. Versioning is integral to reggae. It respects and protects the roots of the music, ensuring they are not lost, yet expects and therefore promotes vibrant creativity from an endless stream of new artists. It sets in motion a continuous and ever-evolving revival of past music traditions and fads where an artist may use both a mento song from the 1940s and the previous year's dancehall hit to generate a new song. While versions are part of the Jamaican musical tradition artists are free to deconstruct the riddims in their attempt to give the riddim a new stamp of originality. Each artist is free to offer their version of a riddim, including lyrics, themes, musical motifs and bass lines from previous songs and are often quick to point out to their audience how original their treatment is.[3]

Yellowman's songs, like all dancehall deejays in his day, were voiced over existing riddims provided for him by either a record producer or, in the case of live dancehall performances, selectors working the turntables. Yellowman often introduces his versions as 'a counteraction', meaning a response to a previous iteration of the song. For instance, he announces at the beginning of 'Herbman Smuggling' that this is a 'counteraction for satisfaction'; on 'Shorties' he says: 'now here come the counteraction'; and on 'Natty Sat Upon a Rock', his introduction is extended, ensuring the audience that his counteraction is guaranteed to bring them pleasure:

> Now here comes counteraction for satisfaction
> Ya, someone come fe rock the nation
> Give you like a medicine injection, you know?
>   [Yellowman, introduction to 'Natty Sat Upon a Rock']

The implication is that the deejayed version is a more boisterous counteraction to the sung version, as riddims in the 1960s and 1970s often started their life as a hit for a singer and were then used as backing tracks for deejays. This was especially true in live dancehall shows where the selector might play the sung version first, then replay just the instrumental dubplate for the deejay to improvise over. The counteraction lyric is a common riff for Yellowman, used to introduce many songs, but it also demonstrates the trend in dancehall reggae to add a new voice to an old song, or use a previous idea in a novel way. Yellowman's counteractions are often commentaries on the songs to which he is responding.[4]

To provide an example of the way the versioning of analogue riddims provided a template for digital riddims of the 1980s, I will use Vin Gordon's (aka Don Drummond Jr.) song, 'Heavenless', recorded at Studio One in 1968. The riddim of the song has become one of Jamaica's foundational riddims with over 300 versions and growing. While Studio One used the original backing track to record other artists in the '70s, other producers like Joe Gibbs (1983), King Jammy (1985) and George Phang (1985) recorded relicks of it using the new digital technology. Part of the digital aesthetic that became popular in reggae was the sound of a keyboard bass instead of bass guitar and a computer-generated drum machine instead of an acoustic drum kit played by a professional studio drummer.

Producers like King Jammy fundamentally altered the sound and business of reggae with the advent of digital reggae but they did not alter the way reggae songs were created and produced. Take, for example, Wayne Smith's famous riddim, 'Sleng Teng', which was recorded using a Casio MT-40, by King Jammy, in 1984. In an intensely competitive industry where success was built on fresh new songs, the digital 'Sleng Teng' riddim touched off a massive revolution in reggae music that fundamentally changed its sound but not its production techniques. Because of 'Sleng Teng's' unique sound and massive success, everybody wanted that digital sound. Artists and producers very quickly adapted to the new paradigm and produced new songs using the digital aesthetic. However, significantly, they still relied on the versioning paradigm first minted in the 1960s.

Roy Shuker (2002) has observed that new sound technologies have democratized the industry. In Jamaica the significance of the versioning format was multiple. Versioning meant that producers could audition new singers over existing riddims without paying a studio band (Manuel and Marshall 2006). They were free to release the song if they wanted, but had very little investment tied up in it if they did not. With the advent of electronic instruments that could be programmed by singers and producers, as in the case of 'Sleng Teng', very little equipment or personnel was needed to record a song. Small producers such as King Jammy could now record backing tracks in his tiny bedroom studio in Waterhouse, Kingston, even though it could barely hold two musicians and a mixer (Lesser 2002). This really did not happen in the rest of the world until over a decade later. And this allowed Jammy to go on and become one of the dominant producers in the early digital era, displacing the hit-making studios of the 1960s and 1970s.

The advent of digital versioning also meant that the professionalization of the industry was drastically reduced. While there was still a degree of professionalization on the part of the producers, the industry became far more accessible and interactive than it had been before. Producers did not have to rely on musicians to create riddims. They could do it themselves. In the 1960s, the person listed as 'producer' on a Jamaican record could merely have been the financer of the session or owner of the studio. In many cases, the song would be actually recorded by a hired engineer. The digital revolution allowed a few enterprising musicians like Sly and Robbie or Steelie and Clevie to record and produce their own riddims, then hire singers and deejays to voice over them. The digital era of versioning furthered levelled the playing field and made what was once a participatory culture for professionals and semi-professionals into a participatory culture for amateurs. Bassist, Dennis Bovell, has argued that versioning in the digital era became little different from karaoke:

> When computers came in, that's when the amateurs took over. The Japanese got stuck into reggae and they made it so easy that any man could go down the road there and buy an ordinary little synthesizer that's even got one beat already in it called reggae. You didn't need a band, you could do it at home on a four-track and release it – just press up a couple of hundred copies and sell it (Bradley 2000, 501).

Jamaican music production predates the values of the digital age. This is partly because Jamaican producers had a long tradition of being early adopters of technology – the use of echo machines in dub reggae for example. Combined with the already entrenched versioning practice, this meant that Jamaican producers and artists already shared the core values of the digital era. As such, there was no reason to get rid of the versioning practice because it dovetailed so well with digital values.

I find it interesting that after King Jammy's success with 'Sleng Teng', he still continued to version older foundational riddims like 'Heavenless'. The tools were in his hands now to produce new riddims cheaply, or even allow singers (like Wayne Smith) to write their own riddims for each new song. Digitization could have led to the end of the versioning practice, but instead it accelerated it by giving the means of production to anyone with a Casio keyboard and a mixer.

This brings me back to the concept of Web 2.0, which has at its heart collective ingenuity. Terry Flew describes it as how the quality of participation on the Internet increases as the number of participating users increases (2011). The practice of versioning fits into the Web 2.0 paradigm in many ways.

First, it shares the principles of collective creation because a new song is the product of several artists – the original riddim plus multiple relicks and vocalists – and is part of a genealogy of music production involving previous versions. Second, there is the expectation for evolution and encouragement of modification. Reggae audiences love it when a foundational riddim is versioned in a new way, given a modern relick. Modification is encouraged because it gives a new artist or producer a competitive edge. Jammy's modification of the 'Heavenless' riddim into a keyboard bass line was rewarded not only by its popularity among reggae fans, but also by the fact that subsequent digital versions were recorded by rival producers. Third, versions are an example of open access technology because anyone can record a relick of a foundational riddim. Copyright issues mean that this is more difficult today, but traditionally the way one studio would get around not paying for the use of a riddim was to record their own version of it. Fourth, versioning is user-focused: the professionalization of the industry was drastically altered by digital versioning. Amateur producers and musicians could now drive production whereas previously riddim production was in the hands of middle-class studio owners and professional studio bands. This is a form of decentralized control of the industry.

In conclusion, even though digital production altered musical tastes and created a new genre of digital dancehall, the reggae industry continued to rely on the pre-digital model of versioning. Despite digital technology making it faster, easier and cheaper for producers to create their own new riddims, reggae's digital revolution could not sever the industry's reliance on versioning existing riddims because its participatory nature suited the new digital world characterized by collaboration and the reuse and sharing of content. The tools of reggae production, then, first forged during the 1960s using studio bands, analogue tape recorders, and versions of earlier songs, shaped how Jamaican artists would create music in the digital age.

Notes

1. Chamberlain differentiates between 'dub plate' – a one-off recording on an acetate made by Jamaican studios for the sole purpose of testing out a new song at a sound system, and therefore not for public consumption – and a 'dubplate' – 'the re-recording of an existing song in order to create a special, personalized song for a particular radio deejay or sound system selector' (Chamberlain 2010, 20). Veal traces how the use of dub plates in live dances led to the popularity of riddims and instrumental versions of popular songs, which evolved into commercially released 'rhythm versions' and the sub-genre of dub (Veal 2007, 51–55). I use 'Dub Plate' in the title of this chapter to invoke the practice of studios recording an instrumental 'version' to be used as a backing track for their subsequent releases.
2. I use the term dancehall here as a sub-genre of reggae that came to prominence in the late 1970s and early 1980s and was characterized, initially, by deejays and singers voicing over riddims played by a sound system at a live dance. The term is often used in opposition to roots reggae, though in reality there are several points of overlap between the two styles. Whereas dancehall is often associated with the digital era of reggae, dancehall originated previous to reggae's digital revolution so the terms dancehall and digital reggae should not be seen as synonymous.
3. In an interview with dancehall photographer and historian Beth Lesser, Lesser described for me how an artist may change one lyric in a song and then tout it as 'original'. The word original here does not mean independently generated but rather refashioned in a novel way.
4. My thinking on this topic was greatly assisted by Joshua Chamberlain's work on dub plates, dubplates, versioning and counteractions. I based my questions to Yellowman on this topic on an unpublished interview Chamberlain conducted with Yellowman in January, 2007.

References

Atton, Chris. 2002. *Alternative Media.* London: Sage Publications.

Bradley, Lloyd. 2000. *This is Reggae Music: The Story of Jamaica's Music.* New York: Grove Press.

Chamberlain, Joshua. n.d. Interview with Yellowman. Unpublished.

———. 2010. So Special, So Special, So Special: The Evolution of the Jamaican 'Dubplate.' *Jamaica Journal* 33, no. 1–2:20–28.

Culkin, John M. 1967. A Schoolman's Guide to Marshall McLuhan. *Saturday Review* (March 18).

Flew, Terry. 2008. *New Media: An Introduction.* 3rd ed. South Melbourne, Vic.: Oxford University Press.

Hebdige, Dick. 2003. *Cut 'n' Mix: Culture, Identity and Caribbean Music.* London, UK: Comedia.

Katz, Mark. 2004. *Capturing Sound: How Technology Has Changed Music.* Berkeley, CA: University of California Press.

Lesser, Beth. 2009. Interview by author.

Lessig, Lawrence. 2001. *The Future of Ideas: The Fate of the Commons in a Connected World.* 1st ed. New York: Random House.

———. 2008. *Remix: Making Art and Commerce Thrive in the Hybrid Economy.* New York, NY: Penguin Books.

Manuel, Peter and Wayne Marshall. 2006. The Riddim Method: Aesthetics, Practice, and Ownership in Jamaican dancehall. *Popular Music* 25 no. 3:447–70.

O'Reilly, Tim. 2007. What is Web 2.0: Design Patterns and Business Models for the Next Generation of Software. *Communications & Strategies* 65:17.

Oswald, John. 1985. Plunderphonics, or Audio Piracy as a Compositional Prerogative. Paper presented at the Wired Society Electro-Acoustic Conference, Toronto, ON.

Sinnreich, Aram. 2010. *Mashed Up: Music, Technology, and the Rise of Configurable Culture.* Amherst, MA: University of Massachusetts Press.

Shuker, Roy. 2002. *Key Concepts in Popular Music.* New York, NY: Routledge.

Veal, Michael E. 2007. Dub: *Soundscapes and Shattered Songs in Jamaican Reggae.* Middletown, CT: Wesleyan University Press.

Waltz, Mitzi. 2006. *Alternative and Activist Media.* Edinburgh, Scotland: Edinburgh University Press.

Section 4
DANCEHALL MATTERS

Between 'Murder Music'[1] and 'Gay Propaganda'[2]: Policing Respectability in the Debate on Homophobic Dancehall

Patrick Helber

In the opening ceremony of the International Reggae Conference in February 2013, the Hon. Lisa Hanna, Jamaican Minister of Youth and Culture, emphasized in her speech at the University of the West Indies, Mona: 'It goes without saying that there is an urgent need for a social and cultural revolution in Jamaica. It is a revolution to restore sanity to our social relations, to the end of murder, the end of bloodshed, and the abuse of our children' (Hanna 2013). The speech, which urged the 'rebuilding of a national confidence through music' (Hanna 2013), contained typical elements and terms of a crisis discourse that constructs the Jamaican nation as sick or at least as lacking sanity in various layers of its society. This discourse is also visible in products of popular culture. Popular music is especially portrayed as symptom, reason and remedy for the social crisis of the country. The rastafari artiste, Queen Ifrica laments, for example, in her song, 'Times Like These' (2011), the absence of certain black Jamaican national heroes and their moral guidance for the society and its citizens. She paints a dark picture of the circumstances on the island, which becomes particularly clear in the first setting in the music video. The beginning of the clip portrays the artiste between rundown houses and smoking ruins, while masked young men are running in the background. In the lyrics of 'Times Like These', she states:

> They took away the voices, that gave the people pride
> Now we're plunging into darkness
> We all have to play our part, make a bold start,
> Every disc jock, tell every artiste
> Media houses, we notice you love support the slackness

> How so much alcohol inna we parties
> While the girls a broke out
> A the something weh she drink knock her out
> Now she nuh care where they prop her up.³

Queen Ifrica's lyrics, even more than Lisa Hanna's speech, evoke a critical image of Jamaica and promote a call to action. The image centres on violence, drug abuse and vulgarity, which, in the deejay's perspective, contribute to a lack of social values and morals. The absence of these aspects is held responsible for the advancing decay of Jamaican society. The symptoms of this crisis are also embodied in the gendered bodies of the young generation. In the lyrics, Jamaican young men become *shottas* and criminals whose only future perspectives are the jail or the graveyard:

> They breed up di shotta dem, now we have a lot of dem
> Prison pack up, now di grave dem ago pack up dead.⁴

The decay of young Jamaican women is described through their transgression of respectable norms of female behaviour and sexuality. The consumption of alcohol and the participation in sexually explicit dancing to dancehall music are highlighted by the deejay and criticized as 'slackness'.⁵ Various statements related to an ongoing social crisis are also embodied in the controversy on homosexuality and Dancehall music in the Jamaican press.

This chapter elaborates on the example of the media controversy on homophobic Dancehall lyrics in 2004 and how a certain discourse of crisis is articulated, mainly through voices of the Jamaican middle class in the Jamaican press, and how based on this 'crisis talk' (Thomas 2011) notions of respectable citizenship are reinforced. Furthermore, the work contextualizes the international discussion on Jamaican anti-homosexual Dancehall lyrics within practices of othering in a (post)colonial situation and demonstrates how images of Jamaican 'Hate singers' (Tatchell 2013) function to maintain a racist dichotomy between normative whiteness and deviant blackness.⁶ Finally, the chapter points out that the need for respectability is entangled with the ambition to gain recognition from the former colonizer. I will demonstrate how this recognition is denied and how colonial practices of othering continue and centre on the issue of homophobia as an important marker for alterity in the twenty-first century. Frantz Fanon's psychoanalytic work, *Black Skin, White Masks* (1952), which focuses on the effect of colonialism and racism on the 'collective unconsciousness' of black people, is used to support and contextualize this hypothesis.

Since the early 1990s, Jamaican Dancehall music has been constantly criticized both locally and internationally for promoting homophobia as well as inciting violence and encouraging vulgar behaviour. Initially, the offending object was Buju Banton's anti-homosexual song 'Boom Bye-Bye' (1993), which brought to attention the homophobic attitudes in Jamaican Dancehall music and caused protests from LGBTI-organizations (Lesbian, Gay, Bi-Sexual, Transsexual and Intersexual) in the United States and the United Kingdom.

After the turn of the millennium, when several violent homophobic incidents occurred in Jamaica, and reports from Amnesty International and Human Rights Watch pointed out the dangerous conditions in which homosexuals lived on the island, a broader campaign against homophobic Dancehall music was launched. The project started in 2004 and was organized by the British-based LGBTI-group *Outrage!* and it's Jamaican equivalent J-FLAG (Jamaican Forum for Lesbians, All-Sexuals and Gays). Peter Tatchell, a British human rights activist and spokesman of *Outrage!*, stated that, in 2004, the organization received a request from J-FLAG to start a campaign against Jamaican homophobic Dancehall lyrics and therefore lobbied Human Rights Watch and Amnesty International to publish reports about the precarious life circumstances of the LGBTI-community in Jamaica.[7]

The international alliance, created to expose the violence sexual minorities face in Jamaica, labelled Dancehall Music 'Murder Music' leading to various boycotts and concert cancellations in North America and Europe. The campaign and the protests affected, in particular, the US and European tours of Jamaican Dancehall artistes Buju Banton, Elephant Man, Beenie Man, Bounty Killer, Vybz Kartel, Capleton and Sizzla, who were all internationally known for having anti-homosexual lyrics in their repertoire.

The term 'Murder Music' expresses the assumed connection between violent homophobic incidents in Jamaica and the anti-homosexual Dancehall lyrics. It suggests that there is a connection between the murders of Jamaican homosexuals and anti-gay lyrics in the Dancehall, which is underlined by Tatchell's reading of the lyrics as direct 'incitements and glorifications of violence and murder' of members of the Jamaican LGBTI-community.[8]

Alternative readings of anti-homosexual Dancehall lyrics are articulated by Carolyn Cooper and Donna Hope. Cooper considers violent lyrics as mainly metaphorical, while Hope sees the role of anti-gay lyrics as an enhancing of the artistes' own heterosexual masculinity through the devaluation of the male homosexual.[9]

In the campaign of 2004, the white British gay-activist, Peter Tatchell, soon became the international face of the protests against homophobic Dancehall artistes. Tatchell and *Outrage!* dominated the public perception not only in the international but also in the Jamaican media, while Jamaican, Jamaican-American and Jamaican-Canadian homosexuals only appeared in letters to the editor. An alternative LGBTI-campaign, called *No More Murder Music* and driven by Caribbean migrants in the US, only led to a few actions and could not reach the same international audience as *Outrage!*, who could build on Tatchell's international popularity as a well-known LGBTI- and human rights activist (Larcher 2009).

This development led to two major problems: first, it supported the perception that the pressure on Jamaican artistes was mainly carried out through white activists from Europe and North America who had the intention to ruin their careers; second, it almost muted the interests of black sexual minorities, not only in Jamaica but also in the international scene. After the murder of J-FLAG's spokesperson, Brian Williamson, in June 2004, homosexual Jamaicans lacked representative on the international level and had to stay in the background because of the existing dangers they were confronted with in the Jamaican public sphere. The campaign's momentum in many countries further centered on stereotypical depictions of, per se, homophobic Jamaicans and ignored black homosexuals who agreed with the protests against anti-homosexual lyrics, but criticized the campaign because of its ignorance of the intersections of racism and homophobia and the marginal influence of Caribbean homosexuals (Larcher 2009).

The heavy reactions of the international LGBTI-communities and their supporters reflected the issue of anti-homosexual contents in Jamaican popular music back to the island and resulted in a huge media controversy. The boycotts and concert cancellations affected the income of the artistes immensely while the international media coverage of Jamaican homophobia had a very negative effect on the country's international reputation, which was explosive, because one of the country's main sources of income is tourism. All these factors led to a discussion among Jamaicans and members of the Jamaican diaspora communities. The controversy, which focused on homophobic and violence-inciting lyrics, was mainly battled in the *Jamaica Gleaner*, the *Jamaica Observer* and the *Star*. There, it provided the ground for a large discussion about the negotiation of Jamaican cultural identity forged between postcoloniality and transnationality.

This chapter underlines the important role of popular culture in the process of shaping a collective Jamaican cultural identity in the twenty-first century. It further highlights the importance of respectability and outlines how crucial elements of the 'respectable state' are in crisis because of a variety of social, cultural, political and economic changes, which occurred in the second half of the twentieth century (Thomas 2004).

On the political level, P.J. Patterson's administration, which began in 1992, enacted variety of changes, which eroded the hegemony of the creole multi-racial state. Patterson's claim of 'Black man time now' led to numerous actions and discussions about blackness, culture, sexuality, nationality and commemorative culture (Zahl 2002). The most famous controversy followed the uncovering of the 'Redemption Song' monument in the Emancipation Park in New Kingston, displaying a black heterosexual couple. Different opinions about nudity, posture, and size of the genitals of the statues led to a broad public discussion, in which notions of sexuality, race, class and gender were articulated by Jamaicans at home and in the diaspora. [10]

The emergence of a black bourgeoisie also led to notable changes on the economic level (Robotham 2000). The influence of neoliberal politics did not only create precarious conditions for many Jamaicans, but also provided sections of the lower strata of the society with new social mobility and power 'to define cultural citizenship on their own terms' (Thomas 2011). The structural changes affected the creole multi-racial state and its paternalistic elements. This lack of control by the old elites opened the door for popular culture from the urban working class, which started to redefine the 'national imaginaries' (Thomas 2011).

These diverse changes and tensions in the social fabric of Jamaica resulted in the ascendency of a crisis discourse that the culture anthropologist Deborah A. Thomas describes as follows: '[...] when the hegemony of the respectable state has been threatened, what often emerges is a discourse that foregrounds a sense of crisis rather than one that acknowledges or celebrates a particular kind of liberation' (Thomas 2004). In the following section, I argue what exactly is threatened.

THE RESPECTABLE JAMAICAN STATE UNDER THREAT

Deborah Thomas's quote emphasizes the 'hegemony of the respectable' state under threat. She refers to the long dominant concept of the Jamaican creole multi-racial state, which has been challenged through what Thomas describes as 'Modern Blackness'. She defines 'modern blackness' as 'urban, migratory, based in youth-oriented popular culture and influenced by African American popular style, individualist', 'radically consumerist', and 'ghetto feminist' (Thomas 2004). Thomas further points out a struggle for 'public representational power' between Dancehall music, the strongest element of popular culture, and what she calls the 'respectable state'(Thomas 2004).

However, these two concepts of Jamaican cultural identity, blackness versus creole multi-racial nationalism, have always been negotiated in the area of tension between national and racial approaches (Thomas 2004). An example for this are pre-independence, anti-colonialist nationalist movements, like the Jamaica Progressive League in New York or the famous pan-Africanist, Marcus Garvey.

The origin of the respectable state lies in the unification of the 'two Jamaicas' in need of a common cultural identity on the way to the country's independence in 1962 (Sherlock 1998). Between the years 1655 and 1940, the British colony was divided into two groups based on race, colour and the access to political power (Sherlock 1998). The overcoming of this division is emblematized in the Jamaican national coat of arms and its slogan, 'Out Of Many, One People.'

The concept of respectability played a very important role in the formation process of the creole multi-racial state and its cultural identity. It links the ideas of modern Christianity, nuclear family, traditional gender roles of men as breadwinners and women as housewives, and education as necessary elements to gain progress, upward mobility, and access to modernity (Thomas 2004). Its maintenance further plays an important role in the argumentation against homosexuality and other practices considered as sexually deviant. Because the nation state is challenged by a variety of socioeconomic developments at the beginning of the twenty-first century, the emphasis of heterosexual citizenship and its safeguarding through legislative measures, is a common practice (Alexander 1994). Jacqui Alexander points out how the image of the citizen is connected to notions of heterosexuality and heteromasculinity (Alexander 1994). In addition, she demonstrates that the assumed nature of heterosexuality is not only interlinked with respectability, but also with black masculinity and nationalism (Alexander 1994).

The policing of respectability in Jamaica and other countries in the Caribbean have a long history, which goes back to colonialism and plantation slavery. Throughout the colonial period the difference between colonizers and colonized was maintained through sexual control (Stoler 1989). On the other hand, respectability was also adopted by the lower strata of the Jamaican society to criticize immorality, sexual excesses and misbehaviour on the side of the elite (LaFont 2001). Also, respectability was shaped like the sexual mores in a 'complex dialectic between elites and Afro-Jamaicans involving racial, political, economic, religious, and moral forces' (LaFont 2001). It remains until today, an important 'mechanism for policing social difference' and is a significant aspect, which helps in shaping a Jamaican cultural identity (Thomas 2004).

THE THREATENING TRANSNATIONAL, INTERNATIONAL AND LOCAL INFLUENCES

The 'hegemony of the respectable' state feels mainly threatened through the intersection of transnational, international and local influences. The transnational support for civil society organizations and the constant movement of people and products of popular culture between Jamaica, North America, and the UK can be considered as an example, which eroded borders and opened the Jamaican national state more and more to what is perceived by many Jamaicans as dangerous foreign influences.

The strong campaign against homophobia in Jamaica, carried out mainly by US- and British-based LGBTI-organizations together with Human Rights Watch and Amnesty International, is one of these threatening transnational aspects. Worries among Jamaicans related to an increasing appearance of homosexuals and a stronger presence of homosexuals in Jamaica underline Jaqui Alexander's argument that the rejection of the 'heterosexual imperative of citizenship' is perceived as endangering the survival of the nation (Alexander 1994). The campaign was often perceived in Jamaica as an attempt and sometimes even, as a 'crusade' to turn the country by force 'into a nation of gay-loving people' (Levy 2004).

Mark Wignall (2004), for example, a columnist, talks in a commentary in the *Jamaica Observer* about homosexuals, who are '…forcing themselves into our collective consciousness and ultimately into our living rooms'. The availability of US-television and productions of popular culture from the US, in particular, are often perceived as vehicles that carry transgressions like homosexuality into the Jamaican society.

In articles and letters to the editor of the two big daily newspapers the *Jamaica Gleaner* and the *Jamaica Observer*, Jamaicans on the island and abroad turned against the campaign and asked Amnesty International, Human Rights Watch and *Outrage!* to 'stay out of their national business (as) we are mature enough to deal with it' (Reid 2004). The international campaigns were mainly seen as an attempt to force Jamaicans through economic and political pressure to accept sexual practices, which they did not perceive as a part of their national identity and culture: 'We have to let these people who represent the antithesis of the very existence of mankind into our homes, just because we need the money to pay our bills.'[11]

Besides foreign influences and homosexuality, the locally and transnationally influenced phenomena of Dancehall culture provides another serious challenge for the respectable state. Dancehall confronts the hegemony of the creole multi-racial state through 'urban popular expressions of Blackness that had been marginalized within the cultural policy designed at independence' (Thomas 2004). Dancehall culture creates a counter-cultural space (Thomas 2004) in which Black identity and solidarity (Stolzoff 2000) are practised and a female empowerment, carried out through what Carolyn Cooper (1994) describes as 'erotic maroonage'. Within the Dancehall space the concept of respectability is challenged. Instead, respect is paid to usually marginalized black working-class men and women. This is picked up by popular Dancehall artiste, Macka Diamond in her novel, *BUN HIM!!!* in describing the character Mitsie:

> She may've been thirty-five with three children, and had more baby-father drama than a soap opera, but Mitsie still considered herself to be the hottest thing since jerk chicken. Then again, it wasn't as if she was lying to herself, 'cause in all aspects, she was who she was, a bashment girl of the highest order.[12]

Looking at the quote, we can witness how Dancehall is able to redefine class, race and gender relations (Stolzoff 2000). Outside the Dancehall space, a woman like Mitsie transgresses the image of respectable femininity, but within the Dancehall, she is still 'of the highest order'.

Dancehall takes a very ambivalent position in the social, cultural and political struggles in Jamaica. On one hand, the music subverts the pillars that carried the creole multi-racial state through its provocative and vociferous celebration of urban blackness and explicit sexuality. On the other hand, it reinforces notions of respectability through what Denise Noble describes as the 'reproduction of compulsory heterosexuality as a key signifier of postcolonial Blackness' (Noble 2008).

THE ROLE OF INTERNATIONAL LGBTI-ORGANIZATIONS

In the context of dangerous foreign influences, not only Jamaicans perceived homosexuality as something completely 'un-Jamaican'. White LGBTI-activists also often constructed an image of black homosexuals as completely outside of their original culture, which was perceived as essentially homophobic and hostile, due to a lack of modernity. This is, for example, visible in a statement expressed by *Outrage!*'s voice, Peter Tatchell:

> In recent years, more than 30 gay men have been killed in Jamaica. They have died horrible, gruesome deaths at the hands of homophobic mobs. It is like Afghanistan under the Taliban. Queers are stoned to death, chopped up with machetes, beaten unconscious with sticks, dowsed with petrol and set ablaze, blasted in the head with shotguns and chased into the sea until they drown from exhaustion (Thatchell 2013).

Tatchell's attempt to display homophobia in the Jamaican society is a part of the discourse, which cultural scientist, Stuart Hall calls, 'The West and The Rest' (Hall 1992). Hall demonstrates to what extent this discourse is an important mechanism in the process of creating and re-creating a 'Western' self-identity:

> Thus, we argue, the West's sense of itself – its identity – was formed, not only by the international processes that gradually molded Western European countries into a distinct type of society, but also through European's sense of difference from other worlds – how it came to represent itself in relation to these 'others'(Hall 1992).

Hall also highlights the importance of sexuality in the processes of othering and identity formation: 'Sexuality was a powerful element in the fantasy which the "West" constructed, and the ideas of sexual innocence and experience, sexual domination and submissiveness, play out a complex dance in the discourse of "the West and the Rest"' (Hall 1992). Obioma Nnaemeka (2009) emphasizes that the '... inscription of criminality, immorality, abnormality, and threatening sexuality on the Black body has a long and enduring history.' Historically, the marker to label the black subject as the 'other' was articulated around the image of an insatiable black sexuality. The white colonial subject ensured its supremacy by portraying black bodies and sexuality as the absolute opposite to whiteness and therefore reassured the latter as the norm (Nnaemeka 2009). This intent took shape in the buggery laws of Jamaica, which until today provide the legislative ground for the social ostracism, especially of male homosexuals. The laws with a focus on anal intercourse were established by the colonialists during the Christianization of the slaves. Although sexual laws also existed in the colonial motherland, they were an essential component of colonialism. They were the excrescence of racist assumptions, which sexualized black people permanently and considered them as a threat to the 'civilized' sexuality of the colonizers. The laws had the function to protect the latter against deviation and to establish European derived heterosexuality as a social norm for the whole society.

At the beginning of the twenty-first century, a new marker of alterity comes into play. The (post)colonial subject is now additionally labelled as extraordinary homophobic and violent in comparison to an assumed white European subject, which appears as the complete opposite to the 'Black homophobic savage' and its embodiment in the 'Black Hate Singers' (Thatchell 2013). The dramatic expression of Tatchell's reproaches can be read in a neocolonial struggle, where attitudes like homophobia and sexism are perceived as essential aspects of the culture of the 'other'. Through comparing Jamaica with Afghanistan and later labelling the country as the 'most homophobic place on earth', discursive borders reassure the colonial division between modernity and backwardness (Padgett 2006).

Grada Kilomba (2008), in analysing processes of everyday racism, describes the effects on the individual that statements such as Tatchell's have:

> The combination of these two words, 'plantation' and 'memories,' describes everyday racism as not only the restaging of a colonial past, but also as a traumatic reality, which has been neglected. It is a violent shock that suddenly places the Black subject in a colonial scene, where as in a plantation scenario, one is imprisoned as the subordinate and exotic 'Other' (Kilomba 2008).

A letter to the editor in the *Jamaica Observer* criticizes the procedure of *Outrage!*: 'In dubbing Jamaica homophobic, our country is being stigmatized as abnormally intolerant towards gays without any real supporting evidence' (McKenzie 2004).

THE MANIFESTATION OF THE CRISIS DISCOURSE

The social, cultural, economic and political transformations within Jamaica produced 'doubts and uncertainties regarding the future' (Thomas 2011). The popular talk show host and *Gleaner* columnist, Ian Boyne, commented, in an article on the violence at the Dancehall festival, *Sting*, in December 2003: 'The degeneracy is from top to bottom. Sections of the capitalist classes are also irresponsible morally bankrupt and philosophically nihilistic' (Boyne 2004).

The uncertainties and transitions created a discourse in the public print media shaped around the central aspects of dissolution and deviance in several layers, not only of the Jamaican society, but also of the 'Western world'. An anonymous letter to the editor of the *Jamaica Observer* bemoans the 'blurring' of the borders between 'normality' and 'abnormality': 'We live in a world where there is an increasing tolerance of abnormal behavior. Such tolerance has got to the worrying extent where the lines between what is right and what is wrong have become seriously blurred.'[13] Another commentator in the *Star* argues:

> All of a sudden the world has become a lot more uncomfortable and it has nothing to do with terrorism or the war in Iraq. Change is inevitable but not all change must be about throwing away what is right for what has become socially acceptable (Levy 2004).

Then again, the decay of the 'Western World' is considered as a part of Jamaica's crisis, because transnational links are perceived as threatening influences, which enter Jamaican society and Jamaicans are characterized with a critical fascination for things which come from abroad:

> We still have a cargo cult mentality in this country where goodies are always expected to arrive from 'farrin'. And then, of course, when the goodies arrive, without testing for quality, it is taken as a given that the foreign fare is superior design and delivery (Wignall 2004).

Fears about the future are also articulated in an article from Betty Ann Blaine (2004) headlined with, 'The New Gay World Order' in the *Jamaica Observer*: 'I realize that what we are seeing is the ever-expanding borders of human degradation, where absolutely anything goes, and where people with a sense of decency are being goaded into silence.' Fears about the future and the decay of social and sexual morals are also articulated, when Jamaica is described as a new 'little San Francisco' (Stoddart 2004). The city of San Francisco stands internationally for an open presence of homosexuals and hosts one of the world's most famous LGBTI-marches. The public presence of homosexuals and their collective coming out of the closet is especially feared and therefore rejected by many Jamaicans.

In general, the crisis discourse creates a morbid picture of Jamaica, which is often drawn in articles targeting Dancehall and homosexuality. The Jamaican society and especially the inner-cities, are described as 'dysfunctional' (Boyne 2004), 'sick' (Boyne 2004) or even as a 'time bomb' (Wignall 2004).

THE EFFECT OF THE CRISIS DISCOURSE

The construction of the crisis bears the effect of a discursive reinforcement of respectability. The urge for respectability is emphasized in the discourse on popular culture and homosexuality. This happens through four different discourses: The first discourse puts a strong emphasis on the Christian Bible and the importance of Christian values for the Jamaican society. Its connection with the popular culture is obvious in the following quote:

> Buju Banton was right when he sang *Boom Bye Bye*, in spite of the uproar that caused him to refine or recant his original message. The lyrics might have been harsh, but clearly spoke figuratively about ridding Jamaica of the nasty sex habits. Buju was also right in his follow-up song that pointed to Leviticus as the Jamaican cultural standard on homosexuality (Stoddart 2004).

The plea for the Bible as a moral guideline is further inherent in the common figurative expression 'God mek Adam and Eve, not Adam and Steve', which appears in various articles (Mills 2004). Through reference to the biblical creation, the second discourse carries out the naturalization of heterosexuality. This discourse forges Jamaica as a strict heteronormative society and condemns homosexuality as an unacceptable moral transgression and a sin. A preacher is quoted in the *Gleaner* with the statement, 'don't let the devil fool you, you cannot be born that way' (Mills 2004). These statements contribute to the discourse on respectability, because they define a rigid idea of sexuality, which happens between a male and a female, figuratively expressed in the following commentary from the *Jamaica Observer*:

> Most importantly, we do not want a mountain of a crusade in our society acculturated into a belief that male/male sex is sinful, sick and alien to a nation of people who have bought into the idea that a vagina is a penis's best friend (Wignall 2004).

Sexuality is constructed as an activity, which is less linked to individual pleasure than to reproduction and to ensure the 'the survival of human civilization' (Gabbidon 2004). In this perception, 'to legalise gay activities is to say to your children that it is OK not to procreate and carry on the lifeline', as mentioned in a letter to the editor of the *Jamaica Observer* (Mitchell 2004).

The third aspect is the policing of respectability through the verbal condemnations or restrictions against vulgarity and sexually explicit practices in Dancehall culture. Ian Boyne (2004) labels the Dancehall show, *Sting*, as an 'annual vulgar orgy', where Jamaicans only go because they 'want to hear Lady Saw' and the 'bruk out, skin out female artistes who can best describe their anatomical make-up'. He also talks about Dancehall artists as promoters of 'anarchy and vulgarity' (Boyne 2004). Respectability is reinforced also, when criticisms target the 'objectification and demeaning of women' (Boyne 2004) and chastise artists because of their 'disrespect' towards 'women and girls' (Simms 2004). Glenda Simms (2004), executive director of the Bureau of Women's affairs, wrote in a commentary in the *Gleaner*:

> The mainstay of dancehall and related musical styles is the disrespect that is aimed at women and girls. The so-called 'slackness' that is the titillater of both genders is part and parcel of the content of artistes who produce some of the most disgusting lines about women's sexuality, their body parts, their undergarments and their age-related potential or lack thereof. The music that glamorizes date rape, the use of the penis as a weapon of pain and humiliation must be seen as violent hate-based music (Simms 2004).

In this context, argumentations which primary might target sexism, can also reinforce certain expectations of female respectability. It is further problematic that vulgarity in the Dancehall is mainly criticized when it comes to women or the depiction of heterosexual intercourse. Vulgar expressions of homophobia do not appear problematic to the critics of Dancehall from the middle class, although lyrics are often quoted with gaps in the explicit parts. Male authors especially, seem to enjoy jokes with innuendo and ambiguity about homosexuals, which ridicule them and the agenda of LGBTI-organizations.[14]

Fourth, respectability is maintained through a strict distinction between 'high' and 'low' culture, which constructs Dancehall generally as valueless and a threat to society. In this discursive strand, cultural practices of the working class, like Dancehall, are excluded, because they are neither presentable nor respectable. Mark Wignall (2004), for example, denies the cultural value of Dancehall and states:

> Brought up in a time when lyricists were royalty, Elvis was king, Sinatra was chairman of the 'bored', Nat King Cole was the smoothest and Jazz was the soul which kept them all alive, it is difficult for people like me to listen to even two minutes of American hip hop or 20 seconds of Elephant Man.

The quote demonstrates how Wignall excludes certain parts of black urban popular culture from what he perceives as valuable or respectable cultural products. It seems that only jazz or rock 'n' roll bear for him valuable intellectual content, which he argues, is lacking in Dancehall music and its supporters:

> Quite apart from the 'fact' that DJs have neither the brains nor the 'socially responsible' acumen to deal with criticisms such as mine, what galls me is that they insist that they are 'giving the people what they want'. What this means is, they feed the people crap... (Wignall 2004).

The lack of 'social responsibility' can also be considered as a lack of respectable behaviour, which is related to education and appropriate parlance, behaviour and style. Dancehall culture is perceived as an inferior cultural practice: instead of promoting respectability, it supports tendencies of dissolution through the propaganda of the wrong role models like dons, drug dealers or *shottas* (Wignall 2004).

CONCLUSION

The public debate on Dancehall music and homophobia provided a basis for a larger debate on Jamaican cultural identity. Within this debate, which was originally caused through transnational activities of LGBTI-organizations, Jamaicans on the island and in the diaspora expressed a discourse of crisis, which blamed the decay and dissolution of constitutional values and morals for the Jamaican society.

Respectability was reinforced through a medial discourse, which focused on four central aspects. First, the emphasis of Christian morals and values; second, the maintenance of heteronormativity through chastising homosexuality as biologically abnormal; third, the rejection of urban popular culture as vulgar and 'slack'; and fourth, the reinforcement of a dichotomy, which separates black urban popular culture like Dancehall from respectable cultural practices and maintains the division between 'high' and 'low' culture by excluding the urban working class, as it happened in the nation building process, which led to the formation of the creole multi-racial state in 1962.

Dancehall itself adopts a highly ambivalent position in this process. It subverts colonial and (post)colonial respectability through its glorification of 'slackness' and its empowerment of working-class blackness, but also reinforces heteronormativity, which forms a central part of respectable citizenship. The ambivalence within the Dancehall illustrates that notions of respectability are not only important for upper- and middle-class Jamaicans but also for Jamaicans from the lower stratum of society and their aspirations for social mobility.

The understanding of respectability in Jamaica is highly connected to the sexual morality of the population. These mores have been shaped in a dialectic process between the colonial oppressors, the slaves, and their offspring and contributed to a dialectic understanding of respectability. Patterns of behaviour, which have been demanded originally by the colonizer, have been modified but internalized and are now a part of the collective self-definition of many Jamaicans. The reinforcement of respectability functions in the media discourse as an important vehicle to reach or prove modernity and to present a certain level of 'civilization'. This attempt focuses not only on Jamaica but also on how the country is perceived on an international level. I read this as an attempt to get recognition by the former colonizing states. Arguably, it reproduces Fanon's theory about the dependency and inferiority complex, which characterizes the black subject in the colonial situation on the level of international affairs. Fanon mentions in his work, *Black Skin White Masks,* how 'the educated black man suddenly finds himself rejected by the civilization he has nevertheless assimilated' (Fanon 2008).

Transmitted onto the level of collective behaviour, this means that Jamaicans who attempt to gain recognition through respectability are pushed back and abashed by the European and North American reaction towards homophobia. Fanon writes about the black man: 'but if he forgets his place, if he thinks himself equal of the European, then the European becomes angry and rejects the upstart, who on this occasion and in this "exceptional instance" pays for his refusal to be dependent with an inferiority complex' (Fanon 2008).

The experience of being rejected and pushed back into colonial readings parallels Grada Kilomba's earlier-mentioned thesis of the permanent repetition of the *plantation memories*. 'White civilization and European culture have imposed an existential deviation on the black man. We shall demonstrate furthermore that what is called the black soul is a construction by white folk' (Fanon 2008). That means that attributes, which are assigned to the black colonized subject, are in reality part of a construction process through the white colonizer. As Fanon points out, 'It is the racist who creates the inferiorized' (Fanon 2008), and in this case, homophobia works as an aspect to highlight inferiority and lack of a certain level of civilization. Tatchell's depiction of the extraordinary homophobic violence in Jamaica therefore parallels pictures of cannibals used by the first colonizers to construct colonized subjects as the 'other'. It uses colonial discourses, which sexualize and racialise black men and portray them as the dangerous 'other'. Fanon (2008) mentions the necessity of the former colonizer to 'recall the age of cannibalism'. Tatchell's detailed description of the barbaric homophobic circumstances of the island echoes the racist image of the cannibal, who now does not eat the victim, but demonstrates through his gruesome treatment of homosexuals, the lack of 'civilization', which affords domestication through the hand of the 'West'. International interventions are further legitimized through the image of the 'Taliban'. This term became, after the terrorist attacks of September 11, 2001, an internationally known collective symbol for 'anti-Western' fundamentalism, backwardness, barbarism, and the threat of international terrorism. Further parallels to Tatchell's term of the 'Hate Singer' include the expression 'Hate Preacher', which gained popularity in islamophobic discourses in North America and Europe after September 11.

The modification of the colonial situation is that in the discussion on homosexuality and Jamaican popular culture, the main marker for the alterity of the black subject is an assumed extraordinary homophobia. On the international level, this functions to keep Jamaicans in their marginal space, and outside of 'Western modernity', which is defined by the guarantee of certain human rights. The construction of Jamaicans as homophobic 'others' provides white gay and human rights activists in North America and Europe simultaneously with the possibility to construct themselves as normative and 'modern'.

The goal of this chapter is not to modify and disguise violent homophobia in Jamaica, but to highlight how homophobia, the criticism of homophobia and racism intersect. 'Western' representations of homophobia in Jamaica are simultaneously used as self-representations for the 'West'. These images make it possible to criticize postcolonial countries while ignoring racist and homophobic discrimination in European and North American societies. Additionally, these representations create and maintain circumstances in which Jamaican and other non-white homosexuals have hardly a chance to articulate their own interests and political agendas. Such dynamics might have influenced J-FLAG's spokesperson Dane Lewis's decision to distance himself from international campaigns against homophobic Dancehall artists in 2012:

> I want to make it clear that J-FLAG is not directly involved and does not support these 'anti-murder music campaigns' anymore. That has sort of taken on a life of its own [...] we maintain that boycotts cannot be the first option as they prevent objective dialogue.[15]

Researches on homophobia in Jamaican popular culture therefore should always critically review common representations of 'otherness', include the voices and self-interest of black sexual minorities, and be careful not to reproduce Gayatri C. Spivak's (1994) famous thesis 'White men are saving brown women from brown men', which, applied to the Jamaican case, reads white homosexual men are saving black homosexuals from black heterosexual men.

Notes

1. *Star.* Aussie Paper Calls Reggae 'Murder Music'. September 6, 2004, 13.
2. Leighton Levy, Another Gay Propaganda. *Star,* November 26, 2004, 8.
3. Queen Ifrica. 'Times Like These', 2011. Retrieved from http://www.youtube.com/watch?v=0FsuA9WGGm0 (accessed June 20, 2013).
4. Ibid.
5. Carolyn Cooper points out the various readings of 'slackness' in the Dancehall: 'I argue that slackness, though often conceived and critiqued as an exclusively sexual and *politically* conservative discourse, can be much more permissively theorized as a radical, underground confrontation with the patriarchal gender ideology and the duplicitous morality of fundamentalist Jamaican society. Slackness is not mere sexual looseness, though it certainly is that. Slackness is a contestation of conventional definitions of law and order; an undermining of consensual standards of decency. At large, slackness is the antithesis of restrictive uppercase Culture.' Carolyn Cooper. *Sound Clash: Jamaican Dancehall Culture at Large* (New York Palgrave Macmillan, 2004) 3–4.
6. Obioma Nnaemeka, 'Bodies That Don't Matter: Black Bodies and the European Gaze,' in *Kritische Weißseinsforschung in Deutschland,* ed. Mauren M. Eggers, Grada Kilomba, Peggy Piesche and Susan Arndt, 90–104 (Münster: Unrast, 2009).
7. 'Yeah it was *Outrage!.* It wasn't me personal [...]. It was *Outrage!* and J-FLAG. In 2004, when the new wave of homophobic lyrics came out like you know Beenie Man, Elephant Man and so on (...) we got a request from J-FLAG to renew and step up the campaign.' Peter Tatchell, interview by Patrick Helber, Brussels, October 22, 2011.
8. 'I don't think most people regarded the origin of the music with much importance. It was simply these were shocking incitements and glorifications of violence and murder....' Peter Tatchell, interview by Patrick Helber, Brussels, October 22, 2011. Peter Tatchell, interview by Patrick Helber, Brussels, October 22, 2011. See also Peter Tatchell, 'Black Hate Singers Urge: Kill Queers. Why are reggae singers allowed to incite the murder of gay people?' http://www.petertatchell.net/a2/print_versions/441.htm (accessed June 20, 2013).
9. Carolyn Cooper reads the glorification of guns and gun violence as metaphors: 'A lyrical gun is the metaphorical equivalent of a literal gun. Words fly at the speed of bullets and the lyrics of the DJ hit hard. In this context, the word "lyrical", belonging to the domain of verbal play and fantasy, becomes a synonym of 'metaphorical'. Carolyn Cooper,

Sound Clash: Jamaican Dancehall Culture at Large (New York Palgrave Macmillan, 2004) 154. Donna P. Hope points out how Dancehall artistes assure their heterosexual masculinity through the performance of anti-homosexual lyrics: 'Dancehall culture's vocal and extreme anti-homosexual lyrics are a part of the wider terrain of Jamaica's hegemonic, patriarchal structure as its consistent and extreme invocations vocally and ritualistically empower the Jamaican male by any means…Thus, the discursive representation of the powerful, masculinized dancehall body is incarnated and elevated on the cadaver of the powerless, feminized male homosexual body.' Donna P. Hope, *Man Vibes. Masculinities in the Jamaican Dancehall* (Kingston: Ian Randle Publishers, 2010) 87–88.

10. For an analysis of the *Redemption Song* controversy see Winnifred Brown-Glaude, 'Size Matters: Figuring Gender in the (Black) Jamaican Nation.' *Meridians: feminism, race, transnationalism* 7, no. 1 (2006): 38–68.
11. Angry, Very. 'Homosexuals Blurring the Lines.' *Jamaica Observer*, October 17, 2004, 28.
12. Macka Diamond, *Bun Him!!! Jamaica's First Official Dancehall Novel* (Kingston: Pageturner Publishing House, 2007) 38.
13. Angry, Very. 'Homosexuals Blurring the Lines.' *Jamaica Observer*, October 17, 2004, 28.
14. Peter Tatchell's statements against homophobia are, for example, ridiculed as 'rectumphilia' in a commentary in the *Jamaica Gleaner*. Orville W. Taylor, 'Anti-Gay Stink.' *Jamaica Gleaner*, October 3, 2004, A9.
15. See Dane Lewis, 'No support for these anti-murder music campaigns'. Retrieved from http://www.migrazine.at/artikel/no-support-these-anti-murder-music-campaigns-english accessed June 20, 2013).

References

Alexander, Jacqui M. 1994. Not Just (Any) Body Can Be a Citizen. The Politics of Law, Sexuality and Postcoloniality in Trinidad and Tobago and the Bahamas. *Feminist Review* 48:5–23.

Angry, Very. 2004. Homosexuals Blurring the Lines. *Jamaica Observer*, October 17, 28.

Blaine, Betty Ann. 2004. The New Gay World Order. *Jamaica Observer*, November 23, 10.

Boyne, Ian. 2004. Boomerang. Dancehall's Chickens Come Home to Roost. *Jamaica Gleaner*, October 3, G1 and G6.

———. 2004. Dancehall: Good to Go? *Jamaica Gleaner*, October 24, G8.

———. 2004. 'Sting' a Disgraced Institution. *Jamaica Gleaner*, January 4, E7–8.

Brown-Glaude, Winnifred. 2006. Size Matters: Figuring Gender in the (Black) Jamaican Nation. *Meridians: Feminism, Race, Transnationalism* 7, 1:38–68.

Cooper, Carolyn. 1994. *Noises in the Blood : Orality, Gender and the 'Vulgar' Body of Jamaican Popular Culture* Warwick University Caribbean Studies. Reprint ed. London, UK: Macmillan.

———. 2004. *Sound Clash; Jamaican Dancehall Culture at Large.* New York, NY: Palgrave Macmillan.

Diamond, Macka. 2007. *Bun Him!!! Jamaica's First Official Dancehall Novel.* Kingston: Pageturner Publishing House.

Fanon, Frantz. 2008. *Black Skin, White Masks.* New York, NY: Grove Press.

Gabbidon, Newton. 2004. Gay Marriage Not a Human Rights Issue. *Jamaica Gleaner*, March 18, A5.

Hall, Stuart. 1992. The West and the Rest: Discourse and Power. In *Formations of Modernity: Understanding Modern Societies, An Introduction*, edited by Stuart Hall and Bram Gieben, 275–332. Cambridge: Polity Press.

Hannah, Lisa. 2013. International Reggae: Traditional and Emerging Themes in Popular Music. Speech at the Opening Ceremony of the International Reggae Conference, February 14, 2013. Retrieved from http://tv.mona.uwi.edu/international-reggae-conference-2013-openingceremony.

Hope, Donna P. 2010. *Man Vibes. Masculinities in the Jamaican Dancehall.* Kingston: Ian Randle Publishers.

Ifrica, Queen. n.d. Times Like These. Retrieved from http://www.youtube.com/watch?v=0FsuA9WGGm0.

Kilomba, Grada. 2008. *Plantation Memories. Episodes of Everyday Racism.* Münster: Unrast.

LaFont, Suzanne. 2001. Very Straight Sex: The Development of Sexual Morés in Jamaica. *Journal of Colonialism and Colonial History* 2, no. 3:1–71.

Larcher, Akim Ade, and Colin Robinson. 2009. Fighting 'Murder Music': Activist Reflections.*Caribbean Review of Gender Studies*, no. 3:1–12.

Levy, Leighton. 2004. Amnesty: How Dare You! *Star*, June 4, 10.

———. 2004. Another Gay Propaganda. *Star*, November 26, 8.

Lewis, Dane. n.d. No Support for These Anti-Murder Music Campaigns. Retrieved from http://www.migrazine.at/artikel/no-support-these-anti-murder-music-campaigns-english.

McKenzie, Clyde. 2004. What More Do You Want, Mr Maxwell. *Jamaica Observer*, August 15, 36–37.

Mills, Claude. 2004. Ex-Jesuites Ruffles Male Feathers. *Jamaica Gleaner*, May 30, A1 and A3.

———. 2004. Will 'Gay-Dar' Hurt Dancehall? *Jamaica Gleaner*, June 27, A2.

Mitchell, William. 2004. Jamaicans Should Not Be Forced by Anyone to Change Laws. *Jamaica Observer*, November 19, 9.

Nnaemeka, Obioma. 2009. Bodies That Don't Matter: Black Bodies and the European Gaze. In *Kritische Weißseinsforschung in Deutschland*, ed. by Mauren M. Eggers, et al. 90–104. Münster: Unrast.

Noble, Denise. 2008. Postcolonial Criticism, Transnational Identifications and the Hegemonies of Dancehall's Academic and Popular Performativities. *Feminist Review* 90:106–27.

Padgett, Tim. 2006. The Most Homophobic Place on Earth. *Time*, April 12.

Reid, Tyrone. 2004. Church Backs State! *Jamaica Gleaner*, November 21, A3.

Robotham, Don. 2000. Blackening the Jamaican Nation: The Travails of a Black Bourgeoisie in a Globalized World. *Identities* vol. 7, no. 1:1–37.

Sherlock, Philip, and Hazel Bennett. 1998. *The Story of the Jamaican People*. Kingston: Ian Randle Publishers.

Simms, Glenda. 2004. Unlikely Alliances. *Jamaica Gleaner*, October 10, G1 and G7.

Spivak, Gayatri C. 1994. Can the Subaltern Speak? In *Colonial Discourses and Post-Colonial Theory: A Reader*, ed. Patrick Williams and Laura Chrisman, 66–111. New York, NY: Columbia University Press.

Star. 2004. Aussie Paper Calls Reggae 'Murder Music.' September 6, 13.

Stoddart, Mervin. 2004. There Are Too Many Beautiful Women for Men to Fall into Homosexuality. *Jamaica Observer*, November 26.

Stoler, Ann L. 1989. Making Empire Respectable: The Politics of Race and Sexual Morality in the 20th-Century Colonial Cultures. *American Ethnologist* 16, 4:634–60.

Stolzoff, Norman C. 2000. *Wake the Town and Tell the People: Dancehall Culture in Jamaica*. Durham and London: Duke University Press.

Tatchell, Peter. n.d. Black Hate Singers Urge: Kill Queers. Retrieved from http://www.petertatchell.net/a2/print_versions/441.htm.

———. 2011. Interview 22.10. Brussels.

Taylor, Orville W. 2004. Anti-Gay Stink. *Jamaica Gleaner*, October 3, A9.

Thomas, Deborah A. 2011. *Exceptional Violence. Embodied Citizenship in Transnational Jamaica*. Durham and London: Duke University Press.

———. 2004. *Modern Blackness. Nationalism, Globalization, and the Politics of Culture in Jamaica*. London: Duke University Press.

Wignall, Mark. 2004. DJ Music: Creativity or Curse? *Jamaica Observer*, August 22, 14–15.

———. 2004. Those Flamin' Homosexuals. *Jamaica Observer*, July 17, 8.

———. 2004. What Do These Homosexual Activists Want? *Jamaica Observer*, November 21, 6 and 27.

Zahl, Peter Paul. 2002. *Jamaika*. München: C. H. Beck.

Good, Good Goodas Gyal: Deconstructing the Virtuous Woman in Dancehall

Anna Kasafi Perkins

> Who can find a virtuous woman? For her price is far above rubies. The heart of her husband doth safely trust in her, so that he shall have no need of spoil. She will do him good and not evil all the days of her life (Prov. 31:10–12; KJV).

> Good, good, good, good, Goodas Gyal/...Gyal wave yu han ca yu nuo se yu a goodas/...../Some gal no desire no good pon eart.
> (Good, good, good, good, Goodas Girl/.../Girl, wave your hand because you know you are a goodas/.../Some girls don't desire anything good on earth.)
>
> Harry Toddler, Dancehall artiste.

The Bible is an iconic reference in Jamaican society, which is predominantly Christian (Tafari Ama 2006; Census 2011). One of the best-loved Bible passages for Christian weddings in Jamaica is Proverbs 31:10–31. It is often used at weddings in Jamaica to describe the virtues or good characteristics of a woman who is an excellent wife – 'the Virtuous Woman'. According to the Book of Proverbs, this woman is trustworthy, faithful to and caring of her spouse, industrious and entrepreneurial, generous to the poor and needy, strong, worthy of honour and praise, wise and God-fearing, and has a well-respected husband. This well-known biblical image is clearly a source of influence in shaping the image of the ideal woman among many Jamaican Christians. For example, in a *Jamaica Gleaner* article featuring several men called, 'Christian Catches', one Christian young man, who is an engineer, described his ideal woman as: 'God-fearing, creative, talented, educated, ambitious and slim, dark-skinned, modest, physically well proportioned' (Christian Catches 2008). Another, who is a user-support technician desired:

> [A woman who is] ...attractive (look amazing in my eyes). The kind who I can share dreams and passions with. She has to be supportive and bears me up in prayer, loves children, and knows how to take care of her family (Christian Catches 2008).

There is another powerful discourse around the good woman, or 'wifey', which also has an important role in shaping Jamaican society and culture. This second image of the good woman emanates from the Dancehall, itself a powerful shaper of Jamaican life. This woman is referred to as a 'Goodas/Goodas Girl/Gyal'. This is the woman who is considered good enough to be the number one woman in a man's life. In the urban dictionary, 'Goodas' (also Goodaz) is used to describe a good girl who does not sleep around or cheat on her lover; she gets what she wants through hard work or talent (not by the use of her body). The Goodas is, in effect, the 'virtuous' woman in the Dancehall repertoire. The appellation itself bears this out as Goodas seems to connote: 'good as (gold)', 'as good as it gets' (the best), 'good as new' (fresh/new) and 'has the goods' (desirable physical and personal characteristics). The central idea is about goodness/ good qualities or actions of a woman as they are identified by the male connoisseur. The Goodas is often set against what I call the 'NotGoodas/ NoGoodas' in order to highlight her value. The similarity with the virtuous woman in Proverbs is striking as she herself is a foil for her rival, the Immoral Woman.

Using the description of the virtuous woman in Proverbs 31 as a kind of scaffolding, this chapter deconstructs the meaning of the virtuous woman in the Dancehall context (the Goodas Gyal) by doing an examination of the lyrics of three artistes, who extol the virtues of this woman. It approaches the question from the perspective of Christian or theological ethics, which foregrounds the perspective of the Christian faith and its role in shaping attitudes and practice in society; one of the questions that Christian ethics attempts to answer is, 'What is good character?' Goodness is about character, 'the core moral identity of an individual person, which is both unique and self-chosen' (Perkins 2013, 21). A person's character is shaped by the actions undertaken as well as the values held dear. Virtues are an essential part of character also; virtues are 'desirable lived out behaviour traits that contribute to and are essential for achieving happiness, getting along with others, and, in general, living well,' (Gini and Marcoux 2009, 8, quoted in Perkins 2013, 21). Virtues are self-chosen and become second nature by repetition and habits. In the case of the Virtuous Woman in Proverbs, the main virtues identified are prudence and temperance, which are important for the woman's well-being and that of the community in which she lives (Wilson 2011). Of course, individual character is shaped by the communities we live in as well as the actions we perform. Our character impacts our future actions and, at the same time, affects the evolving shape of our communities. We can gain insights into the goodness of our character and that of others by looking at patterns of behaviour, habits, values and attitudes.

The discussion attempts to answer the question, 'How it go?' as posed by Harry Toddler in his track 'Goodas Gyal' (the title for the chapter is taken from the bridge of that particular song). 'How it go?' is an oft-asked question by Jamaicans to demand an explanation. The chapter 'demands' answers to questions: 1) Why is the Goodas Gyal constructed as the total opposite to and/or rival of the NoGoodas/Sketel/Matey, as in Tony Matterhorn's 'Goodas Fi Dem?'; 2) How is her vaunted independence, as extolled in self-proclaimed King of the Dancehall, Beenie Man's *Goodas Gyal*, meaningful?; 3) How is the righteous/cultural path she is 'trodding' to be reconciled with the public wining and glamorous displays as in General Levy's 'Goodas Gyal'? It concludes that the Goodas' virtue may, in fact, be contradictory or illusory; the image of the Goodas is actually one that may simply re-inscribe the objectification of women as it defines women by the desires of men, not on their own terms. Further, it continues to set women up as rivals for male affection and resources, and projects a misleading idea of independence that may simply relieve the male of his responsibility.

THE MALE GAZE

Throughout the discussion, the male gaze, which encompasses, defines, describes, and controls this Goodas Gyal, is assumed to be at play. The idea of the male gaze was proposed by Laura Mulvey in her analysis of film in order to dissect the representation of women in culture, especially popular culture. The 'male gaze' speaks to the objectification of the female within a patriarchal culture for the pleasure of the male spectator, who has power to produce the very object he views. Women are viewed as functioning merely as objects of sexual pleasure and use by men.

The importance of wrestling with the male or patriarchal gaze in the Jamaican context is that it is central to understanding the role of women in society as influenced by Dancehall culture. The underlying assumption challenged by this discussion is that the women's place, role, and value in Jamaican society are based largely on her outward appearance. Ought that to be so? At the same time, the image of the 'Goodas', made central in many lyrical offerings in the Dancehall, is accompanied by other images in the print and visual media and the Dancehall lifestyle. 'Unnoticed and unreflected upon, these images suffuse our thoughts, speech, bodily reactions to others, judgements, and ordinary practices of everyday interaction' (Copeland 2002, 187). It is therefore, necessary to interrogate these images for their impact and challenge them when they work against the full flourishing of our bodies, selves and being, as I believe is the case with the image of the Goodas.

THE VIRTUOUS WOMAN IN PROVERBS

In the original Hebrew in which the book of Proverbs was written (circa fourth century BCE), chapter 31, verses 10–31, was actually an acrostic poem of 22 lines; each line begins with a successive letter of the Hebrew alphabet, for example, A-B-C. The opening line is a rhetorical question that emphasises the incomparable value of this extraordinary woman: 'Who can find a virtuous woman?' The rarity of such a find is captured in the explanation of her being more precious than rubies.

This rare woman is described through her activity as a wife (Does this imply that the unmarried woman is not virtuous or as valuable?). Her extraordinary exploits and virtues are extolled. The virtuous wife runs a household distinguished by abundant food and clothing for all within (including her servant girls), by trade (import of raw materials like silk results in the export of finished products), and by the renown of its head, her husband, in the community (US Bishops Conference n.d.). Clearly, her husband's renown is premised on *her* virtue. There is a gender-related division of labour in the Israelite society of which this woman is a part. Without a doubt the husband remains the leader of the household, albeit with special control of the separate external sphere that is men's work – the public sphere. Nonetheless, the division of labour gives the wife an important and perhaps semi-independent role within her own domestic sphere (Lang 2004). She functions in business and at home with the permission of her husband, although he does not interfere in the domestic sphere, which is the woman's domain.

At no point is the woman's sexuality (prowess, behaviour, appeal) mentioned, but her sexual propriety is perhaps implied in her faithfulness to and care of her spouse. Beauty is rejected as vain and the woman is painted as lacking sex appeal and somewhat drab. By implication, sex and sexuality – the erotic – is undervalued or devalued. Indeed, 'the poem celebrates female efficiency, not erotic attraction. Marriage, after all, is for economic purposes and not for satisfying a man's romantic appetite for female beauty' (Lang 2004, 207).

The voice of the poem changes at verse 28. The voice is no longer that of the narrator (or the Queen Mother as Wilson [2011] sees it), but of the woman's children and husband, who, in their turn, heap praises upon her. The poem is often interpreted as an encomium, that is, a formal expression of high praise, to women in order to offset the sometimes negative portrayal of women in the book of Proverbs (US Catholic Bishops Conference). This marvellous woman is an ideal for women to strive to become and a worthy companion to be sought by eligible bachelors (hence its use in weddings; although one colleague of mine used it at her mother's funeral). Her desirable qualities are male-defined and important inasmuch as they benefit the male, providing him with respect, status and wealth within the community. Indeed, 'the good wife is a profitable investment for her husband – and we should keep in mind here that a marriage is not a matter of the "heart", but of the "head" (for in Hebrew parlance, the man's trusting heart is the seat not of his emotions but of his intellect)' (Lange 2004, 198). You can't help but get the impression that most women will fall far short of rare ideal of Proverbs 31. Indeed, Lang (2004) argues that this woman, who is a member of the

Israelite elite, is depicted by the poet in 'perfection what exists only in imperfection' (189).

THE IMMORAL WOMAN IN PROVERBS

Professor of Old Testament Studies, Christopher Lensch (2003) notes that the Book of Proverbs is addressed principally to young men with the intent of preparing them for life and leadership: 'My son, pay attention to my wisdom; listen carefully to my wise counsel.' The Book has a lot to say to the male reader/listener about women, especially immoral seductresses who prey on simpletons and fools (men generally?). The woman glimpsed in chapter 31 differs significantly from women seen in the rest of the book. 'On the whole the women outside of Proverbs 31 are seen as inconsequential, disreputable, untrustworthy and fatal to the well-being of men' (Wilson 2011, 115). More than half of the first nine chapters issue dire warnings against the prostitute and the adulteress/'strange woman', the two types of immoral women denounced in the Book. Such warnings against these evil women are a major theme in chapters 5, 6, 7 and 9. 1). The Prostitute (6:26; 23:27) presents the obvious danger of poverty, as keeping company with harlots leads to wasting of wealth (23:27; 29:3). Although the outward danger of being with a prostitute is not as great as being with a married 'strange woman', a liaison with a prostitute is still dangerous. 2). The 'strange woman' is strange because she belongs to another man and perhaps, worse yet, is a Gentile (she is of what Jennifer Wright Knust [2011] calls 'strange flesh'). Getting involved with a married woman presents the potential danger of poverty and despair (5:1–14) but there is also the danger of death at the hands of the cuckolded husband (2:18; 6:20ff; 7:22–23; 22:143). Interestingly, Proverbs notes that the nature of the temptation presented by such women is not in their beauty or seductive appearance; rather it is in their words. Words are the immoral woman's greatest means of seduction: (2:16 – 'flatters with her words'; 5:3 – lips drip honey, speech is smoother than oil; 6:24 – smooth tongue; 7:5 – flatters with her words; 9:15 – calls to those who pass by; 22:14 – mouth of the adulterous is a deep pit). This is unlike her virtuous rival who speaks wisdom and kind words only and appears to be lacking in sexual desire or sex appeal. The centrality of the power of words cannot therefore be lost upon us. (Dancehall is often chastised for its lyrical content [words], which oftentimes glorifies violence [guns] and male sexual prowess and promiscuity [girls]. The words of the Dancehall express and engender the objectification of women.)

In spite of the lyrical seductiveness of these immoral women, they are also physically attractive and take steps to enhance this artificially (6:25 – Do not desire her beauty 'in your heart'; 7:10 – Dressed as a harlot). The array of tools and techniques used by such women is outlined in 7:1–23: 7:13 – brazenness and boldness; 7:15 – flattery; 7:16 – appeal to the senses like smell; 7:18 – the promise of fulfilment; 7:19 – anonymity, no strings attached; 7:21 – seductive charms; 9:17 – intrigue, pleasure of taking what does not belong to you ('forbidden fruit').

According to Christopher Lensch, 'The warnings [against immoral women in Proverbs] are extensive because of man's vulnerability to sexual temptation. He should never think that he can take fire into his bosom without being burned' (Lensch 2003, 2). Clearly, the Bible has one view of women as the potential downfall of men and biblical stories to support this abound (Adam and Eve; Samson and Delilah; David and Bathsheba, etc.). It will, therefore, take wisdom to avoid the wiles of these women. (Wisdom, of course, is also personified as a woman in Proverbs and has an allure all her own.) This places the burden of maintaining sexual propriety at the feet of women and in a sense robs men of their agency and control in such matters. Of course, ironically, in another sense, men control the process of defining the nature of the women whom they are powerless to resist (the male gaze and the sexual objectification of women are implicated in this patriarchal process). At the same time, this setting of the good woman against the immoral woman is a regular biblical trope, perhaps the best known being the Whore of Babylon versus the Holy Woman Clothed in the Sun in the Book of Revelation. As we will see below, such oppositional categories of women exist also within the Dancehall. Perhaps the biblical perspective on the existence of the two antithetical kinds of women may have been filtered through the cultural lens of folk and Dancehall cultures. It is the recasting of this opposition in the Dancehall context, especially, that is central to this discussion.

CARIBBEAN INTERPRETATIONS OF THE VIRTUOUS WOMAN

As the earlier reference to the yearnings of Jamaican Christian men for the right woman ('Christian Catches') shows, there are allusions to the Virtuous Woman in Proverbs, but with some decided expectations of attractiveness and perhaps passion. The physical attributes of the ideal Christian wife, as detailed above, include: modesty, being dark skinned, slim, physically well proportioned, sharing dreams and [sexual?] passions. However, the importance of such physical characteristics is downplayed by one Jamaican evangelist, Steve Lyston, who admonishes unmarried Christian young men (and the women they are to seek) thus in his explanation of Proverbs 31:10ff:

> Putting 'a ring on it' is not what makes a woman a wife; and it is not about practising regular sexual encounters, or your capacity to 'keep house'! It is her grace under pressure, her capacity to go through hardship and difficult times without jumping ship or 'bailing out'. It is her strength of character, integrity and capacity to keep a unit of differing personalities together under all circumstances; it is the qualities she possesses and her spiritual, mental and emotional maturity that prepare her for that long-term role (Lyston 2013).

In the first sentence, Lyston is probably alluding to Beyonce's very popular song, 'Single Ladies/Put a Ring on It', in which the artiste declares to her former par amour, 'If you liked it then you should have put a ring on it' (of course, the 'it' is left to the imagination but sex and sexiness is somewhere in the mix). Notably, Lyston also downplays or even rejects the sexual dimension of marriage, which he later describes as spiritual; the expected domestic skills of the woman who is the ideal wife of the Christian young man is also dismissed. Lyston is focused on other traits: grace under fire, stick-to-it-tiveness, emotional maturity. Perhaps the necessity of these is implied in the success of the virtuous woman in Proverbs, but I doubt that the writer of the poem in Proverbs would be totally comfortable with the downplaying of the ability to keep house as well as her industriousness, which are desired by the two Christian Catches quoted previously.

A contrary Caribbean female reading of the poem is seen in Guyanese Methodist deacon, Gillian Wilson's Bible Study on the text (2011). Wilson identifies the speaker in vv1 9 as the 'Queen Mother', who is providing advice to her son. According to Wilson, the advice provided 'reflects the dominant values of the patriarchal society in which she lives' (117). The advice provided is therefore critiqued as contributing to and supporting the gender bias of Israelite society. Further, Wilson argues that reading the text from a Caribbean perspective presents both aspects of liberation and oppression. Nonetheless, she argues that the ideal woman described in Proverbs is not to be seen as outside the reach of Caribbean women. She, however, calls for a focus not on the specific attributes or marital status of the woman, but rather on her relationship with God. Wilson, therefore, rejects the focus of the Proverbs text for exalting a woman who brings honour to her husband in public life rather than 'fearing Yahweh'. She, therefore, pulls the focus away from the male, who is defining of the virtue of the woman, and places it on God, who is truly defining of the worth of a person.

GOODAS GIRL IN THE DANCEHALL REPERTOIRE

Turning specifically to the Virtuous Woman in Dancehall, many Dancehall artistes, both male and female, extol the virtues of the Goodas. An instructive but far from exhaustive list includes, Beenie Man, 'Goodas Gal'; General Levy, 'Goodas Gal and Good As Gal'; King Shadrock, 'Goodas Gyal'; Touchless, 'Goodas Gyal'; Vybz Kartel (featuring Marlene), 'Goodas Gal'; Harry Toddler, 'Goodas Gal'; Pamputtae, 'It Goody Good' and 'Good Good'; Liquid, 'Goodas Walk'; TOK, 'Goodas'; Stacious, 'Goodas Clap'; Baby Cham, 'Goodas'. Other tracks which do not mention Goodas in the title but reference the Goodas or the characteristics of the Goodas include, Terror Fabulous, 'Woman Yu Wanted' and Kiprich, 'Ring'. Many of these tracks are of the 'tracing' genre where one party denounces and details the negatives of the rival party. The intent of such songs is to show/establish superiority and gain the goods, which are oftentimes a man and his resources. Many of these Goodas songs involve the male artiste 'tracing' some women on behalf of other women; that is, the NotGoodas/NoGoodas is told off on behalf of the Goodas.

The Goodas is extolled for: being better than the rest (No gal test), knowing what a good man is about, having soft skin (no like leda (leather)/grapefruit) and an 'eva redi body' (always ready body), being independent, not being involved in any legal wrangling, not 'pop down' (being tired looking, unattractive), being good from birth, worthy of being married/taken home for the night. The NotGoodas/NoGoodas is the exact opposite yet often attempts to masquerade as the real deal. Yet, interestingly and ironically, the Goodas has much about her that is similar to the Immoral Woman of Proverbs and perhaps can be seen to possess characteristics of both the Virtuous Woman and her opposite number, the Immoral Woman. Sex appeal, sexual prowess, industriousness, independence of a sort, an attractive body, charming personality, faithfulness to her partner, etc., are all desirable in the Goodas.

At the same time, there is some overlap with the description of the NoGoodas as she is either a poor copy of the Goodas or the exact opposite, depending on who you listen to: 'Pee pee cluck cluck dem a follow yu every trend' (TOK) or, 'You a lead the swagger thing a gal a follow you/A wa do she and her knock off crew' (Liquid). TOK metaphorically recreates the sound of chicks following a hen with onomatopoeic sounds 'pee pee cluck cluck' to give a sense of how closely the NotGoodas both follows in the footsteps of the Goodas and sets out to imitate her. Similarly, Liquid, chastises the NoGoodas for imitating the trend (swagger) set by the Goodas. No wonder the NoGoodas and her friends are described as the 'knock off[s] crew'. Legitimate or illegitimate similarities aside, perhaps what we are looking at is a continuum with the Virtuous Woman being on one end and the Immoral Woman being on the other then the Goodas and NoGoodas are in the middle shading into each other. Nonetheless, there is a sense of unreality about those portraits. One is too perfectly perfect and the other is too perfectly imperfect.

PECULIAR FIXATION

Dancehall is a characteristically male-dominated space in which identity and status are negotiated through dominance of female sexuality, femininity and women (Hope 2006). This is even the case where the virtues of a woman are being extolled, as in the Goodas Gyal. Indeed, the central vision of the Goodas Gyal is tied to her body/shape/figure/profile. The male who defines and describes/bestows the title 'Goodas' is, like many Caribbean men, fixated on the female form with the ultimate goal of sexual congress. The quotidian experience of women in the rural parish of St Lucy, Barbados is telling and representative of the experience of many Caribbean women:

> On the streets casual gender interaction frequently includes sexual banter or taunting (depending on the recipient's point of view). Virtually any woman who is not elderly who walks by a group of men can expect to have her body surveyed, be hissed at, and/or receive sexual offers (Bohn Gmelch and Gmelch 2012, 81).

This casual banter which is public in one form becomes even more potent when it is publicly transformed and delivered on the Dancehall stage. Women patrons of the Dancehall are 'forced' to 'difen' (defend) the state of their body and its desirability in a fashion that no man has to.

This fixation on the female body is described by Donna Hope (2006) as the desire to court and conquer the punaany, that is, the vagina. The male either courts or derogates the woman via her vagina: 'extolling the virtues or negatives of female sexuality' (Hope 2006, 50). As is often the case, the woman is reduced to or identified with one part of her anatomy, usually her genitals, the source of sexual pleasure and progeny for the conquering male. The female body is identified as being for the pleasure of the male courtier, who expresses his desire for the desirable body that is described as 'eva redi' (for sex?). Jamaican masculine identity is tied up with possession of such bodies in numerous quantities.

GOODAS VS NONGOODAS (SKETEL)

The implicit competition/comparison between the Virtuous Woman in Proverbs and the Immoral Woman finds echo in the Dancehall culture/space. The usual Dancehall trope of women in competition with each other for a man's attention and economic resources is also present in the Goodas songs (wifey vs matey, goodas vs pop dung/sketel). Hope (2006) sees a parallel in the wifey vs matey confrontation with the Madonna vs Whore, 'where women are subtly encouraged by traditional, patriarchal mores to identify with the deified and idolized Madonna or wife, seen as the epitome of feminine beauty, attitudes and behaviours by men' (2006, 59). The Virtuous Wife versus the Immoral Woman is of the same biblical order. The labelling of a woman as whore/sketel benefits the man since he is provided with willing bodies and numerous opportunities to play out and reinforce his identity and status.

Hope lists the many characteristics that the wifey persona exhibits, which are in direct contrast to the 'vices' of the matey. The wifey works hard, can read and has education, is independent and can take care of herself and her offspring and the man, keeps only one man, has a well-cared for vagina, does not practise abortion, knows who the father of her child is, has a nice body, smells good, and dresses well. These are the *very* characteristics extolled in the Goodas. Beenie Man, for example, in 'Goodas Gal', addresses the Goodas directly and praises her:

> Gyal yu no kill no baby, and yu no tek abortion/And yu have you owna Jacuzzi, and yuh no bathe inna bath pan/And yu a independent lady, and yu no inna prostitution/Caas yu a goodas gal and no gal cyan flap yuh/Goodas gal so mek dem gwan chat yu/Goodas gal and a gal cyan watch yu.
>
> (Girl, you have not killed any baby and you have not had an abortion*/you have your own Jacuzzi and you don't take a bath in an aluminium basin/You are an independent woman and you are not involved in prostitution/Because you are a Goodas Girl and no other Girl can make you look like a flop/[You are] a Goodas Girl so let them keep on talking about you/[You are a] Goodas Girl and no other girl can waste time looking for bad things to say [*repetition for effect].)

Beenie's ideal woman is independent and high class – having her own Jacuzzi and no abortions. The presence of a Jacuzzi rather than outdoor bathing facilities, epitomized by the poverty of needing to bathe in a 'bath pan', marks the Goodas as being of a certain social class and places many ordinary Jamaican women out of that classification (similar to the elite status of the Virtuous Woman). The need to undertake an abortion is widely condemned in Jamaica, but especially by men for whom fathering children is an important marker of masculinity. Abortions are considered a direct attack on the man. For TOK, that independence is seen in having her 'owna close' (own clothes) and 'owna dough' (own money) and 'not wearing boogas' (cheap crepe sole shoes). In stark contrast, the NonGoodas/Sketel has markers that are the direct opposite of the Goodas. She is said to be lazy and does not want to work, has no education, is dependent on others for financial support and sustenance, has many and multiple sex partners, has a loose vagina, has had more than one abortion, is willing to give her child to the wrong father, is poorly shaped, has offensive bodily and vaginal odours, dresses poorly and lacks style and engages in displays designed to lure weak and unwilling men. She is the very spectre of the Immoral Woman in more graphic Dancehall styling. So, Tony Matterhorn, for example, in 'Goodas Fi Dem' can trumpet:

> Well! Look pon dat one yah chip up like a pisspot (Woooiii!!)/Har face so brown and har whole body black (Woooiii!! Toe pedicure but check out di heel back/How it full up a spot, and now it full up a crap (Woooiii!!)/Fight ova man and now di man no come back (A wah dat).

> (Well! Look at that girl who has scars all over like a dented chamber pot (Woooiii!!)/Her face is so brown and her whole body is black# (Woooiii!!)/Her toes have been pedicured but look at her heel/ It is covered in dark spots, and now it is full of crap (Woooiii!!)/ You are fighting over a man and now the man has left and hasn't returned (What is that about?). [# a sign of the skin bleaching that is increasingly common in Jamaica today].)

Matterhorn, of course, is in defensive mode on behalf of the Goodas. He is actually 'tracing' (cursing out) the rival on her behalf. He is telling the Goodas the reasons she is a better, more desirable object of affection than her rival who has engaged in significant skin bleaching and has rough, dry skin, especially on her feet, which defies the effects of even a good pedicure (the tracing of the other woman about the state of her heel [back] (tough, etc.) is a well-known trope in Jamaican folk culture perhaps coming out of the experience of enslavement, where probably only domestic slaves could have had shoes. There is an implicit field slave versus house slave conflict beneath this as well. TOK also uses a similar reference to the Sketel being like Muta[baruka], a well-known Jamaican Rastafarian poet and cultural critic, who is assumed to have heavily calloused feet from not wearing shoes ('Goodas Gal'). Muta's unshod status is unique, self-chosen and ideological, however. And, ironically, his feet are well-cared for unlike the popular belief. Unlike Matterhorn, Beenie Man appears to support skin bleaching in Goodas as well as wearing 'false' hair: 'Rock to the beat from yu false hair fit yuh den/

Bleach a no nothing from the bleaching fit yu den' (Rock to the beat if your weave looks nice/Skin bleaching is not an issue so long as it makes you look good). The Goodas is clearly designed to fit the taste of the individual male consumer, whose gaze focuses on the external surface and creates the object he desires.

General Levy paints an even more complex and perhaps contradictory picture of his Goodas Girl. He appears to desire a more Afrocentric Goodas (rather like the eligible Christian young man who desires a dark-skinned woman):

> Up inna my chariot a dis a gyal mi haffi carry/Mi African Queen with the cultural body/ shi full a etiquette wid education fi bak i/ Di vital statistics mi know se shi have i/She clear the clouds and mek mi day look sunny/Up inna mi love life dis a gal affi tarry.

> I have to carry this girl in my chariot (car)/She is My African Queen with a culturally-appropriate figure**/ She is well mannered and educated/She has the vital statistics that I think are relevant/She clears up the clouds and brightens up my day/This girls needs to remain in my love life. [**Perhaps a referencing of her African-woman shaped body, which often includes a prominent derriere.])

There appears to be no artifice such as weaves or bleached skin in this Goodas who is an African Queen with a cultural body. The image is of a curvaceous Afrocentric woman with locs, good manners and a university degree. Such an image seems to be out of place in the context of the Dancehall. The General's image is even more jarring as he places his adoration in a religious frame:

> From yu a Goodas gyal mean clean heart yu have/Yu can't stop yu vibes cause yu get it from God/Yu get inspired by the almighty rod/Yu no mix up people yet dem ask fi yu bad/Yu come a dance hall and just rejoice like yu glad/Show dem a righteous path yu a trod/Yu wine up yu front doan mean yu bad/Yu jus a give tanks ca yu proud a wha yu have.

> (Being a Goodas Girl means you have a good heart/You can't prevent the good energy you possess as it was given to you by God/You are inspired by the almighty rod/You don't get into confrontations with people but they keep wishing you ill/You come to dance hall and just rejoice/Show them that you are living in a righteous way/Because you like to wine doesn't mean you are a bad person/You are just giving thanks because you are proud of what you have.)

The reason for the African Queen Goodas' participation in Dancehall is to show off her God-given attributes – her beauty ('pretty like flowers'), her sexy body, her ability to dance (do the Butterfly). Indeed, her public displays are her way of rejoicing and revelling in these attributes. Unlike many Christians, Levy sees no contradiction in being conscious/religious while engaging in such public displays of overtly sexualized behaviour. It is unclear, however, whether and how her righteous path differs significantly from the path of those who do not claim such a path. Perhaps her display and participation may serve to undermine the very path she wants to tred. What is clear, however, is that even among the courtiers of the female body, there are a variety of oftentimes contradictory tastes. Ambiguities abound in the Goodas space.

In his tracing (literally, drawing the outline of the other; describing their shape/body in less than complimentary terms), Matterhorn, and other male DJs, continue to set the meaning of the woman and the value she has by virtue of certain physical attributes that are pleasing to men.

> Gwey!/Fix up yuself mi gal fix up yu place [Woooiii!!]/Yu sexy body and show dem yu cute face [LORD!!!]/All dem a talk yu know a time dem a waste/No bwoy caan point yu out and seh yu point and taste [RAE!!!]/Walk out mi gal and hold up yu head [RAE!!!]/Caw yu a goodas yu no run yu body red (RAE!!!)/Put on yu clothes come out di whole a dem a dead/Nuff a dem a seh dem a hot gyal an no bathe/Talk bout yu kids and how di whole a dem cute [HUH!!!]/Yu baby fadda him no stop send di loot/Look pon dat one deh look like old grapefruit/Dem a big old woman and dem a run di likkle yute [A Wah Dat].

> (Go away!/Fix up yourself, gal. Fix up your home [Woooiii!!]/Your sexy body and show them your cute face [LORD!!!]/Let them keep saying what they want. They are only wasting time/ No man can point you out and say that you have engaged in oral sex with him [RAE!!!]/Walk around with your head held high [RAE!!!]/Because you know that you are not wearing out your body through sexual activities [RAE!!!]/Dress yourself and your enemies will die of envy/Many of them say they are 'hot' girls but they don't even bathe/Talk about your children and how they are all cute [HUH!!!]/Your children's father provides for them financially/Look at your rival, she looks like an old grapefruit/She is an older woman yet she is chasing after a young boy. [What is that about?])

Women adapt/imbibe such characteristics as desirable and several female artistes have taken on board the descriptions of the Goodas. Female DJ, Pamputae, speaks up for herself and others when she declares:

> Hot gyal pat yu pussy and call yu man name/ some gyal cyan do that dem wi shame/ ca' she could call too much man name and every man know shi kitty cyan tame/ Hot gyal wine no play freaky game/ No carry wealth fi no man come strain/ Him tell mi sey him no waan lef mi lane/Afta di bull's eye ah one man a aim.

> (Hot gal pat your pussy and say your man's name/ some gals can't do that as they will feel ashamed [for having more than one man]/ because she would name too many men and every man would know she is sexually insatiable / Hot gal wine don't engage in strange sexual activities/ Don't allow any man to make your beautiful body become worn out/A man is saying he doesn't want to leave the lane where I live/He is very interested in getting my tight vagina.)

She proclaims further:

> (Chorus) It good it good it good it good good good/ So him a sey when mi a step out a di road/It good it good it good it good good good/Ca mi a quint it just like me should.

> ([Chorus] It [my vagina] is good, it is good, it is good, it is very very good/ So the suitor says when I step out/It is good, it is good, it is good, it is very very good/Because I am able to flex my vaginal muscles like I should.)

Women attempt to appropriate the characteristics of the Goodas for themselves as Pamputae does in asserting that she can make her vagina 'quint' (wink) like *she should*. Her use of 'should' emphasizes the obligatory nature of such a performance and the obligation is clearly imposed by the dominant male demands. The imagery behind such an assertion is of the vagina as an eye (also bullseye), which is able to wink (perhaps mischievously). Of course, the direct physical reference is to a well-toned vagina that is able to grip and release to bring added pleasure for the male partner. Such declarations, nonetheless, clearly highlight women taking on meanings given to them by the male rather than making meaning for themselves. The woman does not speak up for herself in her own terms and on her own terms. Indeed, African American theologian, M. Shawn Copeland would accuse such women as being in collusion with their male counterparts in debasing, diluting and defiling the 'real mysterious joy of passion and erotic power' of black women (Copeland 2002, 186).

Of course, there are other readings of the characteristics and actions that are the Goodas. Carolyn Cooper (2004) argues that for the working-class Jamaican women, the exhibitionist performances (for example, of the Goodas) epitomize sexual liberation. Such women, who are extolled as Goodas, are freed from the 'airy-fairy' Judeo-Christian notions of proper female behaviour. Cooper goes so far as to describe the Dancehall as a female fertility rite. As such, the Dancehall is a space in which men are pushed to the margins and serve as mere spectators to women as they parade their bodies. The sexual power of women is affirmed in the Dancehall. Of course, the possibility for the objectification of women by the viewing power of the men who gaze cannot be ignored, especially in a patriarchal space like Jamaica.

HOW IT GO?

In conclusion, it may be too easy to reject the dancehall as a misogynist space 'that reduces women to bare essentials: mindless bodies, (un)dressed and on display exclusively for male sexual pleasure' (Cooper 2004, 262). There may be elements of liberation in the performance of women who are able to present themselves as financially independent, monogamous, sexually attractive, a good mother and wifey. Yet, the lyrical word-images and performance of many male dancehall artistes, who work out their masculinity via an ideology that dominates and oftentimes derogates the feminine other, can be seen to do just that. Indeed, it can be argued that the entreaties of DJs like Toddler, Beenie Man, Matterhorn and Pamputae normalize and legitimize beliefs and practices that value women according to their outward appearance and their sexual and economic value to the dominant, dominating male.

The presence and prevalence of the Goodas in the Dancehall repertoire as well as the Goodas vs NoGoodas rivalry raises several concerns:
 1. Women are constantly presented with an ideal of physical desirability, sexual prowess, virtue, economic success that they have to measure up to. We have to measure ourselves against

these ideals and many women may fall short in one area or the other or for one reason or the other, often beyond the woman's control; this can raise issues of self-worth.

2. Women's bodies are inevitably placed in relation to males' power-over. Importance is placed on how women use their bodies; women are not beautiful for themselves or each other, but are only beautiful to ensure male attention (Charles 2004).

3. Women have been socialized to accept and prepare for their bodies to be on display, especially for men, but certainly for their female rivals. The dominant popular discourse, in Dancehall, accentuates the fact that Jamaican women along with their Caribbean sisters, live lives of spectacle (Carnival, for example). As such, they rarely are the ones to make meaning, but, more often than not, are the bearers of meanings imposed by the male spectator. 'Not only does such a system compromise women's economic power, it compromises their power of self-definition and reduces them from the role of active participant in the creation of themselves to the passive recipient of a construct that often fits them ill, if at all' (Charles 2004, 525). Undue emphasis on the exterior denies women possession of their uniqueness (Charles 2004) and this can only be damaging.

4. Certain women are made into pariahs, as are the NoGoodas, or are given privileges, like the Goodas, for looking a certain way or acquiring certain resources, much of which may be incidental or beyond their control. The possibility, therefore, remains that women continue to remain the objects upon which men place meanings.

5. The independence of the desirable Goodas is belied by how dependent she is on having that vaunted independence recognized by a man, oftentimes, a man who praises that trait in order to avoid his responsibilities. This is often the man who praises her for her faithfulness to one partner while abrogating to himself a right to promiscuous polygamy. The independence may therefore be described as illusory.

6. The setting up of oppositional categories of women fosters invidious competition between women. This may be compounded by the contradictory and varied images and dimensions that go into the Goodas, which seems designed to suit the tastes of the consuming male. This can only serve to break down the bonds of mutuality which have been important in the lives of many inner city men and women, especially in child rearing and economic survival. Clearly, a high psychic price is paid by both women and men in this situation. The challenge is to reclaim personal agency in the creation and understanding of the female body in a fashion that affirms the erotic potential of the body while maintaining bonds of mutuality among women and men. Only then can we speak of a virtuous woman in Dancehall.

References

Bohn Gmelch, Sharon, and George Gmelch. 2012. *The Parrish Behind God's Back: The Changing Culture of Rural Barbados*. 2nd ed. Long Grove, Illinois: Waveland Press, Inc.

Charles, Suzanne Marguerite. 2004. Mirror Mirror: A Feminist Examination of the Construction of Beauty and Body Image.' In *Gender in the 21st Century: Caribbean perspectives, Visions and Possibilities*, ed. Barbara Bailey and Elsa Leo-Rhynie, 509–27. Kingston: Ian Randle Publishers.

Christian Catches. 2008. *Jamaica Gleaner*. Retrieved from http://jamaica-gleaner.com/gleaner/20080825/flair/flair4.html.

Cooper, Carolyn. 2004. *Soundclash: Jamaican Dancehall Culture at Large*. Basingstoke: Palgrave McMillan.

Copeland, M. Shawn. 2002. Body, Representation, and Black Religious Discourse. In *Postcolonialism, Feminism and Religious Discourse*, ed. Laura E. Donaldson and Kwok Pui-lan. Oxford: Routledg.

Hope, Donna. 2006. *Inna Di Dancehall: Popular Culture and the Politics of Identity in Jamaica*. Kingston: University of the West Indies Press.

Knust Wright, Jennifer. 2011. *Unprotected Texts: The Bible's Surprising Contradictions about Sex and Desire*. New York, NY: Harper One.

Lang, Bernhard. 2004. Women's Work, Household and Property in Two Mediterranean Societies: A Comparative Essay on Proverbs XXXI 10-13. *Vestus Testamentum* LIV 2: 188–207.

Lensch, Christopher K. 2003. Two women in the Book of Proverbs. *WRS Journal* 10/1 (February): 9–11.

Lyston, Steve. 2013. Christians Should Not Date. *Daily Gleaner*. Retrieved from http://jamaica-gleaner.com/gleaner/20130211/cleisure/cleisure5.html.

Perkins, Anna Kasafi. 2013. *Moral Dis-ease Making Jamaica Ill?: Re-engaging the Conversation*. Grace Kennedy Foundation Lecture 2013. Kingston: GraceKennedy.

Right Women and Wrong Women/men. Retrieved from http://epreacher.org/sermons/b-provwrongwomen.pdf.

Tafari-Ama, Imani. 2006. *Bloods, Bullets and Bodies: Sexual Politics below Jamaica's Poverty Line*. Kingston: Multimedia Communications.

United States Catholic Bishops. n.d. Proverbs. (New American Bible) Retrieved from http://usccb.org/bible/proverbs/31.

Wilson, Gillian. 2011. Womanhood: A Bible Study on Proverbs 31. In *Righting Her-Story: Caribbean Women Encounter the Bible Story*, ed. Patricia Sheerattan-Bisnauth. Hannover, Germany: World Communion of Reformed Churches.

Discography

Beenie Man. 'Goodas Gal'.
General Levy. 'Goodas Gal'.
———. 'Good As Gal'.
King Shadrock. 'Goodas Gyal'.
Touchless. 'Goodas Gyal'.
Vybz Kartel (featuring Marlene). 'Goodas Gal'.
Harry Toddler. 'Goodas Gal'.
Pamputtae. 'It Goody Good'.
———. 'Good Good'.
Liquid. 'Goodas Walk'.
TOK. 'Goodas'.
Stacious. 'Goodas Clap'.
Baby Cham. 'Goodas'.
Beyonce. 'Single Ladies'.

The Lyrical Opus of Tommy Lee Sparta: Masculinity, Violence, Sexuality and Conflict

Winston C. Campbell

According to Cultural Studies theoretician, Sonjah Stanley Niaah (2004), the Jamaican dancehall can be understood in spatial terms. As a type of space, dancehall can be approached as a physical, conceptual or experiential entity (Roth 2007). The Jamaican dancehall is characterized by numerous political and aesthetic qualities, which are functions of the various ideologies that govern these spaces and the agents that are so positioned to enforce these ideologies (Storey 1998). This chapter advances the idea of dancehall as a *lyrical space* or a *lyricscape*, which may be approached as a variant of the conceptual space described by L.M. Roth (2007).

The concept facilitates dancehall spaces being approached as lyrical domains, which further contributes to an understanding of the various roles played by performers of the music. To this end, the dancehall *lyricscape* is an environment of continuous challenge to and reinforcement of notions dominance, hegemony (of varying types) and ideologies. Dancehall performers/characters, such as Tommy Lee Sparta, are quite aware of these characteristic features and their attendant maxims. As a newer dancehall character, Tommy Lee Sparta also has to assert his place within the *lyricscape*, hence his assertion:

> Mi foot plant like a tree root
> Yet still Addija a mi faada
> Mi come fi rule an mi nuh response
> If yuh neva kno mi nah lef di Gaza

> Tell every media
> Every news carrier
> Tommy Lee nah look no sorry fa
> Suh all who nuh like mi guh suk yuh maada
> All a who agree unnu buss a blank-a
>
> [Buss A Blank 2012]

In the above excerpt, the dancehall artiste, Tommy Lee Sparta, tackles the issue of continuous dominance within the dancehall *lyricscape*. Like all other dancehall artistes in the twenty-first century, Tommy Lee Sparta is engaged in a struggle for relevance within the lyrical domain. In the extract, he asserts legitimacy and inheritance by way of his musical genealogy. Among the evidence is the fact that his [lyrical] father is Addija, or Vybz Kartel. Further, he asserts that the (conceptual) dancehall empire known as *Gaza* is now his and that he has no intention of giving it up; in fact, his feet are 'plant[ed] like a tree root'. Such assertions show the importance of space, place, lineage and hierarchy within the Jamaican cultural – and lyrical – spaces. It is apparent that Tommy Lee Sparta recognizes the importance of these abstractions to his own status within Jamaican popular culture. He needs to be anchored, and being anchored within the *Gaza* means he is heir to, if not the ruler of one of the lyrical empires in contemporary Jamaican dancehall.

However, his stance, which is aggressive in one sense and defensive in another, seems to recall aspects of the Oedipus complex (Blos 1985). He seems to desire to take the place of the self-proclaimed 'Gaza Emperor' (Vybz Kartel) and he is not apologetic about it. Of course, all must be seen within context. Vybz Kartel is currently incarcerated (exiled) and technically cannot rule the rapidly fragmenting empire. The other heirs apparent are at varying stages of their careers and may not be assertive enough to ensure that the *Gaza* brand is as relevant in Kartel's absence as it was in his presence. Maybe, this aggressiveness is coming from an external source that is attempting to cash in on the popularity of the *Gaza* by using it to ensure Tommy Lee's relevance and popularity. Maybe there is a void that is left within the dancehall space by Kartel's physical absence – though Kartel is still musically very present with the sporadic release of previously unreleased songs – and Tommy Lee

Sparta as the aggressive heir apparent is being positioned to fill this void. Whatever the reason, Tommy Lee Sparta asserts that he is only about his subjects; those who agree should buss a blank in classic dancehall '*stylee*'.

It is also clear that Tommy Lee Sparta's increasing visibility within the dancehall *lyricscape* over the past three years has begged the question about the reason(s) for his success. The demand for his music has also challenged the way in which I now engage a phenomenon of twenty-first century dancehall, called *the winning formula*, which I have been attempting to decode for the past few years. Since 2010, I have been interested in identifying the factors that explain why some dancehall characters who were somewhat visible in the *lyricscape* never got established (such as Hollow Point and K-Queens), why some characters (such as Mr Lexx, Hawkeye, Ward 21, Munga Honourable) got established but seem to lose relevance shortly afterwards, and why other characters (such as Assassin, Busy Signal, Elephant Man, Mavado and Vybz Kartel) seem to emerge and maintain relevance within the *lyricscape*.

While it is too early to say that Tommy Lee has the winning formula that could be associated with the latter grouping, it is apparent that, as an act, he manifests some of the critical variables such as a unique way of vocalizing his lyrics, partnerships with critical stakeholders within the space (Vybz Kartel and Kartel's music production associates initially and later, show promoter 'Heavy D' and publicist, Keona Williams), a distinct musical pitch or role within the dancehall space and a recognizable persona that distinguishes him from other acts (Henry 2012). These factors are central to every major dancehall artiste who has maintained any kind of relevance within the *lyricscape* for a period of time.

In this regard, Tommy Lee Sparta has been presented, as is the case with most new pop culture icons, as the face and image of the younger generation (Campbell 2012a). Based on the reactions that I have observed when he performed at Sting 2011, Reggae Sumfest 2012 and Sting 2012, many younger adult males and females are excited about his persona and lyrics. This attraction makes him a significant force in the analysis of youth culture today. This work tackles this significance, and specifically, focuses on identifying the dominant themes in the lyrics of Tommy Lee Sparta and the ways in which these lyrics can be understood within a framework of performance politics, ideology and hegemony. It responds to the question, 'to what extent does the lyrics of Tommy Lee Sparta contribute to the continuing conversations of counter cultural norms in contemporary Jamaican society, with specific emphasis on notions of gender-derived hegemony and ideology?'

THEORETICAL UNDERPINNING

The idea of gender is critical in conversations about aesthetics. As Schneider Adams (2002) notes, gender is a critical aspect of the creation and reception of artworks. In this work, concepts such as hegemonic masculinity and gender role stress are central. Hegemonic masculinity is the view that males are natural leaders and providers for their social groups or families. This view is, however, dependent on a system of control in terms of the roles played by both males and females, whereby females are prohibited or restricted from actively engaging in roles leadership and providing for their families, as being portrayed in any way as persons who play or should play such roles. According to R.W. Connel (2001), the term refers to the process by which patriarchy is legitimized, the dominant position of men is guaranteed and the women are systematically subordinated.

However, P. Jackson (1991) asserts that the system(s) that create, preserve or maintain hegemonic masculinities are harmful in a number of ways. Essentially, the scholar identifies various forms of economic exploitation and social oppression of a systematic nature in such contexts. This occurs on the ideologies that govern the control and actions of the masculine body, social roles and responsibilities, reproductive activities and approaches to productivity or work. The attempts at maintaining and responding to such systems have created what B. Martin and J. Gnoth (2009), R. Horrocks (1994) and J. Beynon (2002) and others regard as a masculine crisis or a masculine gender stress. This crisis or stress is caused from a continuous pressure to perform one's masculinity within a number of sociocultural contexts.

As this work later asserts, the lyrics of Tommy Lee Sparta were created and performed within a particular hegemonic and ideological framework and his lyrics support and challenge aspects of this hegemony in a number of ways. As a newer member of the Jamaican dancehall *lyricscape*, Tommy Lee Sparta is under pressure to both maintain antecedent masculine hegemonies, while at the same time, asserting some difference so that he can maintain relevance within the space. In this regard, the lyrics can be understood as a means of negotiating these various expectations. This negotiation also creates varying degrees of stratification within the society in terms of the cultural value and response to his work (Collins 1994). The gendered ramifications or implications of his lyrics also create tensions between various social classes, as does the output of all creative persons (Dahrendorf 1994).

SIGNIFICANCE AND DISTINCTION

Active in the dancehall *lyricscape* since 2009, Tommy Lee Sparta is significant to contemporary Jamaican youth culture for a number of reasons (Campbell 2011). Among the more critical variables are his nuanced musical output (lyrics and musicology), nuanced dancehall persona/character, musical genealogy and musical partnerships (with critical stakeholders). It is almost a given that Jamaican popular music is often positioned as the music of not only the masses, but also as the music of the younger members of the society. This ambiguous and somewhat duplicitous marriage is often based on subjective experiences and not on scientific methodologies or surveys.

Notwithstanding, it is undeniable that Jamaican popular musicians do have a large following among the younger members of Jamaican society. My own observations support the view those members of the society that respond favourably to his musical output are those below 40 years old. I have observed young boys (and a few girls), aged ten to 13 years old singing his songs (such as 'A Million' 2011), word for word, while he performed at Reggae Sumfest in 2012. Of course, older members of the audience were at the same time blowing 'vuvuzelas' and jumping in apparent enjoyment of the performance of such lyrics. With these observations in mind, and his ubiquitous presence on dancehall shows around the island (major and minor), there has been little doubt that he has been one of the most visible faces of dancehall in the past years.

His musical output, characterization, genealogy, partnerships and visibility have resulted in greater scrutiny of his songs and visualizations. Desired or not, he was seen as a face of contemporary Jamaican popular music and someone with a social responsibility to the youth sub-culture. In this regard, his musical output has attracted some scrutiny within the media and within the dancehall *lyricscape*. Other dancehall artistes, such as Bounty Killer and his ANG (Alliance Next Generation) group have felt a need to overtly attempt to counter his apparent dark or impious influence on the dancehall space and the wider Jamaican society (Campbell 2012). Others, such as Assassin, Kiprich and I-Octane were a bit more clandestine and subliminal with their retorts to his apparently new but undesired musical output and characterization.

It can be argued that while his delivery or sound is distinctive, the lyrical arrangement and concepts manifested in his work do not provide much that is particularly unique; the latter comment can also be extended to the rhyme schemes and extensiveness of the vocabulary employed in the composition of his songs. In fact, like most other artistes, he uses a combination of generally uncomplicated perfect, internal and slant rhymes (Bradley 2009). What seems to be the magnet is the way in which he delivers the lyrics of his songs. The rhythm with which words are delivered in each of the songs reveal a pattern or style that is uniquely his, within the context of contemporary Jamaican popular music. His approach or delivery has also been documented in the media as a type of fusion music that combines dancehall and a 'gothic' aesthetic. To this end, his persona and presentation is seen as counter-cultural, since it presents a range of aesthetic elements and philosophical orientations that are not common within the contemporary cultural space. This claim requires a bit more scrutiny by informed musicologists.

Apart from his unique delivery, he has attempted to create a peculiar masculine character. This is a requirement of the Jamaican dancehall space, which is a carnivalesque environment that is loaded with opportunities for the masquerade of varying characters that are usually flamboyant, distinctive and sometimes seasonal (Stanley Niaah 2004). In other words, characterization is important for contextualizing that which is said by the performer. In the case of Tommy Lee Sparta, his character[ization] appears to have been influenced by Thomas Lee Bass, the American musician and founding member of metal band, Mötley Crüe and founder of rap-metal band, Methods of Mayhem. Bass is known for his tattoos and eccentric dressing, such as the wearing of black leather pants and accessories (Henry 2012). Characterization apart, it is the messages of his music that some have gravitated towards in their praise and admonition of the artiste, though adornment is a critical aspect of his characterization and performance.

CONTRIBUTIONS TO THE LYRICSCAPE

Generally speaking, dancehall music engages a number of core themes, and these have been consistent over the past 30 years. These themes range from bodily adornment and presentation; relationships with members of the family, including parents and spouse; relationships with the immediate, physical and social communities; relationships with colleagues (which can be harmonious or dissonant); description, critique or endorsement of acts of violence as forms of protest, self-defence, or as evidence of one's social status; interaction with/critique of social institutions; hardships faced in life; issues with social, spiritual and moral currency; sexual encounters, prowess and taboos; hustling/entrepreneurship; and personal and communal entertainment options, including dance fads and places of interest. In twenty-first century dancehall, lyrical versatility requires that artistes produce music that tackles a number of these themes in a given period, though very few artistes have tackled all in terms of their opus. These themes can also be discussed within a framework of gender-derived counter-cultural praxis.

In terms of the assessment of the catalogue of Tommy Lee Sparta, up until the end of 2012, the vast majority of his output (approximately 80 per cent of the 49 songs surveyed) are dominated by two broad themes: (i) the description, critique or endorsement of acts of violence as forms of protest, self-defence, or as evidence one's social status and (ii) sexual encounters, prowess and taboos. Other issues that he tackles to a lesser extent in his music are: (i) social and economic hardships faced in daily life; (ii) hustling and entrepreneurship; (iii) personal and communal entertainment options, including dance fads and places of interest; and (iv) relationships with colleagues (which can be harmonious or dissonant). These latter or lesser issues are engaged in only seven songs from his current 50-song catalogue. Emphasis is placed here on the dominant themes of violence and expressions of sexuality. These will be discussed in order to better understand the extent to which the lyrics of Tommy Lee Sparta contribute to the continuing conversations of counter cultural norms, especially with regards to gender-derived hegemony and ideology.

DESCRIPTION, CRITIQUE OR ENDORSEMENT OF ACTS OF VIOLENCE

With regards to the broad theme of violence, there are a number of songs that fit the rubric. Among the more popular examples based on crowd responses at dancehall events are 'Warn Dem' (November 2010), 'Some Bwoy' (October 2011), 'Shelly Christmas' (December 2011), 'Psycho' (June 2012), 'Dem Nuh Bad' (July 2012), 'Uncle Demon/Shook' (September 2012), 'Nuh Fear Dem' (December 2012) and 'Bravery' (December 2012). Interestingly, his engagement of this theme seems to be more limited to the description and endorsement of violence; in other words, there is no real critique on offer. Also, in his lyrics that seem to endorse violence, the pernicious acts were directed in all instances at [other] masculine forces.

The lyrics of his songs suggest that acts of violence are largely masculine undertakings that are directed at other males. In his contribution to the *lyricscape*, women are to be conceptually excluded from those situations that are essentially violent. It is indicative of a sort of feminine marginalization, which could be based on his own experiences of feminine roles, or based on his own projections of what the feminine roles ought to be, or both. However, the non-feminine female does feature in some acts of violence. Some songs have lines that suggest that the feminine may feature as agents of violence, maybe due to their association with masculine agents of violence, though acts of violence should not be directed at the females. For example, in the song, 'Psycho' (2012), he warns 'min' mi sen one a mi demon gal from Sparta com suck off yuh cock an murda yuh.' Further, in another song, 'Maniac' (December, 2012), he asserts:

> Boy affi dead wen mi gun clap
> a bare demon gal watch mi head-back
> sen one a dem inna yuh place
> mek she cum inna mout an shot out yuh suck pussy face

While from the lines above one could surmise that the female is often required to execute certain acts of violence, even after engaging in the perceptually submissive (and still somewhat taboo) activity of oral sex, it is suggested in another song that the act of executing violence is an essentially masculine one. To this end, the lyrical offering of Tommy Lee Sparta suggests a type of masculine gender stress or crisis that may be affecting young males in contemporary Jamaican society. The lyrics articulate a belief in eliminating as many masculine agents as possible as a means of articulating one's own masculinity. In this regard, masculinity is not automatic, but rather a function of situations of conflict.

From the lyrics presented, violence emanates from conflict and requires, in the masculine sense, decisive action and not the extended verbal jabs, quarrelling or 'tracing' that is associated with women. In the chorus of 'Money Make Friend' (April 2011) he emphasized:

> Money make fren it make enemy
> From tings stawt gwaan dem a penny wi
> Dem a hype an a push bare war enuh man
> But wen it come to di tes dem feminine

From the last line above, any kind of hesitation in warfare or in the execution of violence is a feminine act. In this regard, it is also arguable that his fellatio-performing mercenaries are masculine, though female. Essentially, Tommy Lee Sparta's lyrical definition of the female with regards to acts of violence is ambiguous.

While it is tempting to reduce Tommy Lee Sparta to an individual who is surrounded by androgynous or sexually ambiguous demonic creatures, at least in terms of his psychology, his lyrics suggest that the youth members of Jamaican society may be less concerned with the traditional social roles that are often ascribed to the sexes. It also suggests that these roles are being made even more obscure by various fantasy concepts; these fantasy concepts are being introduced to the youth sub-groupings via a range of mostly visual stimuli that are being produced globally and accessed via the television and the Internet in a range of formats.

Ambiguity also abounds with regards to the specific roles that the fantasy concept of the sometimes masculine/sometimes feminine force of the demon, or its variants, play within the socio-lyrical environment. Undoubtedly, the songs cited above show that the demon is a critical variable in lyrics about acts of violence, though he is not particularly consistent as to what he is speaking of whenever he makes references to the otherworldly force (it could be another person or a tool). Also, he has not sufficiently responded to critics regarding his references to demonic forces. The demonic conceptualization gleaned from his lyrical compositions, as a force in urban warfare in Jamaica, or a name of a fearless gangster who had existed within marginalized cultural spaces for some time prior to his emergence and usage. It is a somewhat common concept in the social environment and does appear to a limited extent in contemporary dancehall lyrics performed by some artistes. However, the responses to his music indicates that the *lyricscape* was not particularly accepting of an apparent plethora of demonic references; it was also not ideologically acceptable within music by members of polite society based on their responses in the print and electronic media.

Apart from the references above to demonic ladies (who may be more masculine than feminine) who are available to do his bidding, demonic references appear in a number of other songs – all of which are associated with acts of violence. These songs include (in chronological order) 'Holding Out Di Pressure' (April 2010), 'Shelly Christmas' (December 2011), 'Psycho' (June 2012), 'Dem Nuh Bad' (July 2012), 'Uncle Demon/Shook' (September 2012), 'Mi Nuh Tek Diss' (September 2012), 'Step Middle Day' (November 2012), 'Bloodbath' (featuring Vybz Kartel, December 2012), 'Nuh Fear Dem' (December 2012), 'Maniac' (December 2012) and 'Bravery' (December 2012). Only 'Maniac' has two or more lines with the word demon. Also, the song 'Uncle Demon/Shook' (September 2012) does not have any line or lyric to demon or a variant and is in the listing solely because of its title. All other songs in the listing have only a singular reference to the problematic word or a variant.

Chronologically, most of these songs were all released in 2012, though he has been actively recording music since April 2010. While it is unclear as to what may have provided the impetus in 2012, the lines seem to suggest that it was possibly part of an attempt to re-pitch the character. The lines also suggest a particular sociocultural leaning with regards to perspectives on death. From the songs, it is apparent that demon is already dead and hence cannot be further eliminated during any act of retaliation or conflict. In Tommy Lee Sparta's own words, 'start war wid di dead a weh u gon do...yuh cyah kill a demon even if yuh try to' ('Dem Nuh Bad', July 2012). In other words, it is impossible to destroy or eliminate one who was already from the netherworld.

In this regard, Tommy Lee Sparta's perceived lyrical invincibility is based on positioning himself as someone with otherworldly traits; his superiority is sourced from metaphorical immortality. This is supported by lines where he refers to himself as 'Gaza demon wid di x' ('Bloodbath', December 2012). He adds, 'everybody get scared when mi rise from the dead/...mi evil suh till Satan seh fi bill' ('Maniac', December 2012). In other songs such as 'Nuh Fear Dem' (December 2012) and 'Bravery' (December 2012), he presents himself as the Grim Reaper, another otherworldly character that is depicted in a number of formats in popular imagery. He extends this otherworldly association by positing that even his guns are otherworldly ('Step Middle Day', November 2012). In these songs, he brings netherworld concepts into the current reality to challenge the hegemony of those who may oppose him in the realm of the living. Engagement with the netherworld is considered an abnormal practice within the wider Jamaican sociocultural space and, in this sense, Tommy Lee Sparta brings a peripheral concept into the mainstream in a manner that is more connected and relatable than depictions found in movies and other media sources.

Importantly, there is a tendency to avoid articulating concern or even offer solutions to address the problem of violence in his lyrics, as has been the case repeatedly in the lyrics of the more dominant members of his lyrical/musical genealogy (Bounty Killer and Vybz Kartel). In this regard, his compositions lack the activism – if even contradictory – that is essential to a career that has longevity, if these other characters are to be used as models. Instead, whenever he apparently comes close to articulating this concern, it is usually pitched as an excuse for young males being armed. For example, in the chorus of 'Graveyard' (May 2011) he chimed:

> Gra-a-a-a-ve yard
> Everyweh wi walk
> In this time people scared
> They will lef u in the dark
> So mi pray to mi saviour
> Hey hey ahh
> Youths protect yourself nuh shadow afta dark

Later in the same song, he posited:

> Mi nuh soft like a Caterpillar wid di Mac-10, mmmm
> Rise di melody pon dem
> Pray God yuh no di deh when di telegram send

Similar observations were made in 'Blood Bath' (December 2012) and 'Jah Watch Over Me' (July 2012) as he seemed to demand protection though he was clearly endorsing a socially insidious act:

> Jah watch over me, guide me every step
> let the heathen crumble when they try to eat my flesh (mmmmm)
> my road mucky and dark
> genuine straight like leather pan Clarks
> any time Grim Rim walk
> any eh any time gremlin walk.

However, in 'Journeys' (March 2012), he was a bit less opaque in his rejection of violence:

> Father, save my soul
> Living in a world so cold
> Everyday is the same thing
> I'm depending on my own
> …
> A nuh time fi no war
> Too much conspiracies
> Circulate love and let the system set wi free
> Start a new life
> We want life no dead body
> Di world without love
> Di system set we free

What is this system of which he speaks? This rather esoteric concept has been a part of Jamaican folk culture and popular expressions for several decades and has been used by most, if not all dancehall and reggae artistes who speak to the social, economic or political hardships extant within the society in various moments. Tommy Lee Sparta's usage of the term suggests either exposure to this aesthetic tradition, or an insight into the fact that not much may have been adjusted in the past decades since many in the society are still caught in a rhythm of existence that necessitates acts of violence and that require supernatural intervention for them to escape.

In this regard, Tommy Lee Sparta's endorsement of acts of violence ought to be taken seriously, not only because of his apparent prescriptive tirades, but also because of the fact that his lyrics may be describing a worldview that indicates the need for serious political, social, religious, cultural and economic intercession. Songs such as 'Shelly Christmas' (December 2011) indicates that violence is a form of resistance for certain groups within the society. As he underscores in the recording 'Reality Story' (April 2011) and 'Holding Out Di Pressure' (April 2010), many young men are caught in an architecture of violence. This dilemma sometimes forces some to seek heavenly intervention to avoid executing acts or terror and menace, given that they are bombarded with negative influences.

> Holding out di pressure
> Trying to do di right
> Some fools nah guh wah it happen
> Come a steam up a bag a vibes
> But tell dem fi humble
> An nuh mek nuh demon rise
> Gwaan guh look inna di mirror an waan yuh self
> ['Holding Out Di Pressure', April 2010]

Among the catalysts for seeking an alternate route are often children and mothers, the latter being a most important feminine force within Jamaican social consciousness. Both 'Holding Out Di Pressure' (April 2010) and 'We Want Paper' (March 2012) speak to the importance of the mother as a positive and restraining force among the younger members of Jamaica's society whenever they are faced with such dilemmas. Given the prevalence of single-parent households within the social environment, which are often marshalled by women, many young men place heavy emphasis on their mothers as important agents of influence. The same applies to

Tommy Lee Sparta:

> When mi did poor and nuh have nutten fi nyam
> Mi mother never have it she ah di only one
> So Father protect mi please
> In this time from mankind (Ahhhh)
>
> We want paper
> big up all money paper (Mmmmm)
> I crown all who rise and nuh drop
> Youths dem a di future
> Wi nuh want nuh 14 shoota
> Fi mess up wi dream llike Freddy Kruger (mmmmmmm)
>
> ['We Want Paper', March 2012]

Clearly, the body of work produced by Tommy Lee Sparta to date does provide important and useful descriptions, critiques and endorsements of acts of violence. What is less clear is whether or not these can be reasonably accepted as forms of protest, self-defence, or as evidence of one's social status. While it may be problematic to expect an artiste to tackle all aspects of a theme, it fair to conclude that based on Tommy Lee Sparta's body of work he projects himself in the *lyricscape* as someone who believes that violence is an important element of social status for young masculine agents and is justifiable at least as a form of self-defence. It is, however, not particularly clear that his work reasonably supports the projection of acts of violence as a means of protest against socio-political or other inequities and injustices that exists within the Jamaican space(s), especially by the masculine agents that his lyrics ubiquitously associate with executing and receiving violence. Of course, violence is just one of the broad themes that dominate his body of work.

SEXUAL ENCOUNTERS, PROWESS AND TABOOS

Sexuality is another important recurrent and definitive theme in Tommy Lee Sparta's musical opus. His lyrics endorse a common masculine performance of sexual identity, sexual expectation and sexual performance that is essential heterosexual. For example, Tommy Lee Sparta asserts that sexual encounters require compatible female partners (for him) who are of the highest possible sexual standards (which are defined by a masculine defined system of desired performances or actions). Not surprisingly, self-praise is often the tabled recommendation. This praise takes a number of formats. Maybe the most distinctive is his assertion that he is *the* 'Pussy Mechanic.'

> Pussy Mechanic, Mi a Pussy Mechanic
> When pussy bruk dung a me fix it
> Mi tek out mi cock an inject it
> …
> Me a di pum pum killer
> Beat up yuh pussy mek pum pum swell yah
> Open up yuh foot gal, like umbrella
> KY Jelly den hood unda cellar
> When di cocky reach yuh, yuh run an fella
> Backshot, bruck-dung, pum pum shella
> Fuck inna di room get hot like a hella
> Buss inna yuh mouth like a gun from Dela
> ['Pussy Mechanic', August 2012]

As was pointed out earlier, characterization is an important aspect of the dancehall performer's persona. Many artistes have several personas that are activated within certain contexts. Of note was the earlier indication that during moments of conflict or violence, Tommy Lee Sparta activates the demon or Grim Reaper personas; for sexual encounters, he activates the *mechanic* persona. Whilst the language is metaphoric, it maintains the ideal of masculine-determined heterosexuality. In fact, this masculine-dominance is executed in a cycle of breaking and fixing and may, in this sense, be taken literally, given that many mechanics are known to break things so that they can be called on to fix it later. This breaking and fixing may also attract the criticism as a form of misogyny, given that the lyric suggests that the female's role is to respond submissively to the impulses of a violent, domineering and cock-armed masculine mechanic.

In the lyrics of other songs, Tommy Lee Sparta maintains the roles suggested in 'Pussy Mechanic'. In 'A Million' (August 2011), he again points to the sexual act an encounter between compatible partners and the cycle of breaking and fixing. Armed in this instance with the infamous hammer, the self-professed *mechanic* declares:

> Gal yuh mek mi pressure rise, yuh nuh mek it fall
> Brace up yuh bed pon di wall
> Mek mi knock it wid di hammer, wid di hammer weh tall
> Mek mi knock it wid di hammer, wid di hammer weh tall
> Gal, suh wi fix di edge a di bed
> Jus mek mi rev di hammer red an mek it bun up di edge
> Oh god, mi sorry fi mash up yuh bed
> She seh yuh neva affi run di hammer hammer so wicked
>
> ['A Million', August 2011]

These lyrical contributions to the dancehall *lyricscape* apart, his engagement of sexuality promotes the constantly challenged (dancehall-promoted) stereotypes of heterosexual unions, visiting relationships and an abhorrence of cunnilingus and homosexual exchanges. In this regard, he appears to be the typical dancehall artiste whose masculinity is a function of one's sexual associations with submissive females, avoidance of sexual taboos, and sexual prowess with females. Some sexual taboos can create a masculine crisis, such as performing cunnilingus. Even if done, the act must be vehemently denied if he is to command respect across the masculine defined and dominated dancehall *lyricscape*. This assertion appears in songs such as 'Buss A Blank' (October 2012) where he chimed 'mi neva go low fi nuh polo,' though receiving fellatio is permissible ('Party Non Stop', September 2012). Based on these lyrics, Tommy Lee Sparta does not challenge the inequity in masculine-feminine performance of oral sex activities that exists in the dancehall *lyricscape*. This may be due to the fact that such a challenge will result in a challenge to his gender identity as the masculine agent he purports to be. The challenging or questioning of one's gender is quite common in feuds (lyrical and otherwise) between dancehall and non-dancehall characters and is generally avoided given the importance of the being on the right side of the dominant binary of masculine and feminine, male and female in most contexts.

In Tommy Lee Sparta's lyrical contribution, male and female relationships were defined by a masculine gaze that often prescribed that females present themselves physically in a manner that was sexually attractive to males (in terms of dress and movement). Males often reward this visual pleasure with monetary offerings. The performance of masculinity, therefore, requires that females also subject themselves to a number of performed femininities, for which they are then rewarded. These performances allow the members of either group to maintain the system of masculine hegemony in an economic sense. Such lyrics also echo the findings of the late social anthropologist, Barry Chevannes, who documented the view that boys are taught that being able to give girls money, to be a provider, was part of the definition of manhood/masculinity within the Caribbean space (Chevannes 2001). Another aspect of the definition of Caribbean manhood which is described by Chevannes and endorsed by Tommy Lee Sparta is polygamous relationships.

While his lyrics made it clear that women should not be victims of violence, his role for women seems rather limited. They were to have children – 'hol a one daughta, hol a one son' ('Pussy Mechanic', August 2012), wait on men for money – maybe for use to repair a broken bed, perform lascivious dancing, be accepting of violent sex, and willingly offer fellatio. In this regard, the lyrical limitations and myopia are obvious, especially when compared to the catalogue of longer-established contributors to the dancehall *lyricscape*, such as Vybz Kartel, Bounty Killer, Assassin and Beenie Man. In essence, women are not presented in his lyrics as compatriots, comrades, or partners with an equal economic and political role within the family and society. This is unlike the catalogue of his more celebrated mentor, Vybz Kartel, who has recorded several songs about his mother and the various roles that women play in the political, social and economic arenas.

In this regard, it is apparent that within the dancehall *lyricscape*, Tommy Lee Sparta does not challenge the prevailing hegemonic systems that limit the role of women to that of sexual recipient or domestic furniture. The lyrics also indicate the kind of ideas that are prevalent among certain youth communities within the Jamaican social environment; the statements made are systemic. They are symptomatic of larger sociocultural issues that must be systemically addressed. Unfortunately, it is quite likely the case that Tommy Lee Sparta is but one of several males within the society with these limiting ideas for the (sexual) role of females within Jamaican society. In the conflict for a broadening of those roles to include other social, economic, religious and political roles, he has chosen to be an advocate for the projection and endorsement of a woman who is a child-having and sexually submissive homebody.

SYSTEMS OF CONFLICT AND RESISTANCE

As indicated in the introduction, there are a number of other themes that can be gleaned from the lyrics of Tommy Lee Sparta. For example, social and economic difficulty and conflict is identifiable in a number of songs ('Holding Out', April 2010; 'We Want Paper', March 2012). Such songs highlight inadequate rest, insufficient financial resources, warfare and divine intersession as things necessitated based on these socio-economic pressures. He asserts that access to increased financial resources makes it possible to not only improve the living circumstances of family members or friends, it also increases access to personal and communal entertainment options, such as clubbing ('Inna Di Club', March 2011; 'Live Wi Life', May 2012; 'Live My Life', October 2012; and 'Party Time', November 2012). In works such as these, Tommy Lee Sparta seems to tackle the issue of the meaning of life, and provides the pursuit of pleasure as the answer.

With regards to his relationships with colleagues within the dancehall space, Tommy Lee Sparta appears to be a somewhat marginal artiste, who was sometime engaged in conflict with other members of the dancehall *lyricscape* (Brooks 2012; Campbell 2012a; Campbell 2012f). This is evidenced in the content of songs such as 'Goathead' (September 2012), 'Betray Informer' (May 2012) and 'Di Gaza Boss' (September 2012), 'Hear My Cry' (December 2011), 'Lyrical Bomber' (July 2012) and 'Tom and Jerry' (August 2012), 'Fi Get A Forward' (November 2012). These latter songs speak of no particular member of the dancehall *lyricscape,* but suggest that there is always some challenge to his achievement, as well as suggestions of jealousy over material possessions and female companions. Such expressions may be symptomatic of an increased materialism that Hope (2006) identifies as a feature of the musical consciousness since the late 1980s. As has been articulated by dancehall and hip hop artistes alike, achievement seems to attract unwanted negative attention.

However, the emphasis here was on the lyrics that specifically engaged ideas of violence and sexuality, especially within the ideology of masculine hegemony. In this final section, it is critical then to consider the larger systems of conflict and resistance that Tommy Lee Sparta apparently exists within, based on his lyrics. Like other dancehall artistes, the lyrics performed by Tommy Lee Sparta are often taken as a reflection of his worldview and beliefs, at least in the moments within which such songs are performed. In this regard, it is also imperative to acknowledge the fact that his experiences are not shared with all members of the Jamaican society, and his experiences also help to shape issues that he chose to emphasize. Thus, his lyrics suggest a lifestyle filled with continuous crisis of a masculinity defined by unavoidable enemy creation, enemy avoidance, violence, parties and sexual encounters with various females. That apart, his world consists of music making, marijuana smoking and attempts at avoiding jail (as indicated in the lyrics). It is the case that this is not the lifestyle that most members of the society profess or have even witnessed first-hand.

His lyrics describe a world that runs counter to the script of regular attendance up to secondary school, participation in school sanctioned extra-curricular activities such as sports or service clubs, a possible matriculation to tertiary studies, and eventual employment within the private or public sector business space based on one's formal training. The lyrics instead describe a reality whereby many young males and females have resisted the state-prescribed lifestyle. They resist, in search of an alternative lifestyle, even if it comes with sanctions. Therefore, his perspective on acts of violence, sexuality and sexual expression (as well social and economic hardships, hustling and entrepreneurship and personal and communal entertainment options) can be seen as running counter to that which is endorsed by 'polite society'. It challenges that which is endorsed by the State, as an instrument of the ruling classes of the society (Barnard and Burgess 1996; Macionis 2007).

In the state endorsed lifestyle, violence is to be avoided even in self-defence. To ensure this, the state has the help of legislative and judiciary arms, as well as the police force (Barnard and Burgess 1996; Macionis 2007; Schneider Adams 1996). These state arms predate the artiste for centuries, which makes his endorsement of violence in his songs a flagrant resistance of pre-existing mores of social engagement. Even more so, such alternate lifestyle choices represent not just resistance of the state, but also articulations of masculine and feminine roles within the social environment. If it is the case that he is a reflection of his background, then his works are both descriptive and prescriptive can be used to understand many underlying issues of social identity affecting the society currently. Polite society also polices and regulates sexual expression and norms. His songs endorse a masculinity that is partly defined by multiple sexual (female) partners and challenges the attempts by the Ministry of Health to control the spread of HIV by discouraging such behaviour. The encouragement of lascivious dancing (as a prescribed feminine expression which facilitates a particular type of masculine hegemony) is also in direct opposition to promoted standards of decency by schools, the church and other agents of moral maintenance. A similar position can be held of the aesthetic sensibilities that drive the aesthetic output and lyrical content of dancehall music, which is unlike that which is played at formal events or at the soirées photographically documented in the Sunday newspapers.

Equally problematic for some commentators are his references to 'demon' (and its variants) and a perceived 'darkness' in his work (et cetera), which have been partly inspired by the pursuit of distinctiveness and in articulating a particular type of masculine dancehall character. For some critics (inside and outside of the dancehall space), this distinctiveness is also prescriptive and is capable of leading the youth subgroup within Jamaican society down a path that is apparently new and dangerous (Campbell 2012b; Campbell 2012f). Such masculinities and their associated femininities, whether real or imagined, are understood as types of resistance that must be resisted as well. Such conversations resurrect concerns about the negative impacts of dancehall music on the younger members of Jamaican society. Interestingly, there is an unexplained dearth of commentary on whether or not the music of artistes such as Tarrus Riley, Romaine Virgo, Protégé or Etana is having a positive influence. The response to his songs, therefore, raises the question as to whether or not songs that seem to promote harmonious existence, solidarity, frugal spending, moderate entertainment and modesty are having equal impact on our youth.

It is equally true that Tommy Lee Sparta has not said anything that has not been heard in communities within the past 30 years. In many respects, he is not the architect of these phrases, terminologies or notions of gender. What he has done is to popularize what was parochial, and this is where his lyrics become problematic. Undeniably, his lyrics will be supported by those who already have a predisposition for such ideas and rejected by those who do not have the requisite ideological predisposition. Nonetheless, it also allows us to raise the issue of why some members of our society would be predisposed in the first instance. In other words, there are some systemic issues that must be examined and the demand for content such as that being offered in 80 per cent of Tommy Lee Sparta's recordings is an indictment against our social conscience. Unsurprisingly, his apparent response to critics and adversaries appear to be:

> I wanna live some more
> I wanna be able sleep at night
> Without feeling insecure
> I don't really wanna loose my life
> Really wanna live some more
>
> Mi waan buy my mother two house inna life
> So mi sing till mi throat sore
> I don't wanna go to jail no more
> I just wanna live my life
> I don't wanna be harmed or victimised
> I don't want to take your life
>
> ['Live My Life', October 2012]

Finally, it may be the case that Tommy Lee Sparta really does not care about the remarks made in this chapter in response to his work, or those offered by other critics. Unfortunately for him, attention has been paid to his musical output and he will have to deal with the varying perspectives on the music that he contributes to the *lyricscape*. For him to keep his feet planted like tree root, he will have to respond appropriately to such concerns and to recognize his role as an advocate within the Jamaican cultural space of nuanced ideals.

His output describes, and for some prescribes, the roles of the various genders that make up our society and what he offers in his music cannot be disregarded. Also, he records lyrics that are endorsed by his fans, which makes him their agent and their mouthpiece. He facilitates their resistance of norms and values that are extant within the social environment, and he is at the centre of their conflicts with polite society.

References

Barnard, A., and T. Burgess. 1996. *Sociology Explained*. Cambridge: Cambridge University Press.

Beynon, J. 2002. *Masculinities and Culture*. Philadelphia, PA: Open University Press.

Blos, P. 1985. *Son and father: Before and Beyond the Oedipus Complex*. New York, NY: Free Press.

Brooks, S. 2012. Ryno Attacks Popcaan, Tommy Lee. *Star*, May 12. Retrieved from http://jamaica-star.com/thestar/20120512/ent/ent1.html

Campbell, C. 2011. Tommy Lee Happy with Career. *Star*, November 9. Retrieved from http://jamaica-star.com/thestar/20111109/ent/ent8.html.

———. 2012a. Bounty Lashes out at Tommy Lee - Others also voice concern about demonic songs. *Star*, September 11. Retrieved from http://jamaica-star.com/thestar/20120911/ent/ent1.html.

———. 2012b. Christian man says...Tommy Lee needs prayer. *Star*, August 31. Retrieved from http://jamaica-star.com/thestar/20120831/ent/ent1.html.

———. 2012c. Tommy Lee says he will not clash Bounty...and apologises to Rum Blood. *Star*, October 4. Retrieved from http://jamaica-star.com/thestar/20121004/ent/ent1.html.

———.2012d. Tommy Lee Sparta, Aidonia advocates for peace. *Star*, September 11. Retrieved from http://jamaica-star.com/thestar/20121023/ent/ent1.html.

———. 2012e. Tommy Lee, Bounty, square off in Riverton? *Star*, November 8. Retrieved from http://jamaica-star.com/thestar/20121108/ent/ent1.html.

———. 2012f. War on the horizon? – ANG throws down challenge to Tommy Lee. *Star*, September 24. Retrieved from http://jamaica-star.com/thestar/20120924/ent/ent3.html.

Chevannes, B. 2001. *Learning to be a Man*. Kingston: University of the West Indies Press.

Collins, R. 1994. A Theory of Stratification. In *Four Sociological Traditions: Selected Readings*, ed. R. Collins, 109–32. New York, NY: Oxford University Press

Connell, R.W. 2001. *The Social Organization of Masculinity*. Berkeley and Los Angeles, CA: Polity.

Dahrendorf, R. 1994. Power Divisions as the Basis of Class Conflict.' In *Four Sociological Traditions: Selected Readings*, ed. R. Collins, 58–80. New York, NY: Oxford University Press.

Henry, D. 2012. Tommy Lee trademarks name. *Star*, September 28. Retrieved from http://jamaica-star.com/thestar/20120928/ent/ent1.html.

Hope, D. 2006. *Inna di Dancehall: Popular Culture and the Politics of Identity in Jamaica*. Kingston: University of the West Indies Press.

Horrocks, R. 1994. *Masculinities in Crisis: Myths, Fantasies, and Realities*. New York, NY: St Martin's Press.

Jackson, P. 1991. The Cultural Politics of Masculinity: Towards a Social Geography. *Transactions of the Institute of British Geographers* 16, no. 2:199–213.

Lenski, G. 1994. Theory of Inequality. In *Four Sociological Traditions: Selected Readings*, ed. R. Collins, 81–108. New York, NY: Oxford University Press.

Macionis, J.J. 2007. *Sociology*.12th ed. Upper Saddle River, NJ: Prentice Hall.

Martin, B., and J. Gnoth. 2009. Is the Marlboro man the only alternative? The Role of Gender Identity and Self-Construal Salience in Evaluations of Male Models. *Marketing Letters* no. 20:353–67.

Roth, L.M. 2007. *Understanding Architecture: Its Elements, History, and Meaning*. Boulder, CO: Westview Press.

Schneider Adams. 1996. *The Methodologies of Art*. Boulder, CO: Westview Press.

Stanley-Niaah, S. 2004. *Kingston's Dancehall: A Story of Space and Celebration*. Diss. University of the West Indies.

Storey, J. 1998. *An Introduction to Cultural Theory and Popular Culture*. Athens, GA: University of Georgia Press.

List of Contributors

Heather Augustyn is a newspaper correspondent for the *Times of Northwest Indiana* and an English instructor at Purdue University. She is also author of three books: *Ska: An Oral History* and *Don Drummond: The Genius and Tragedy of the World's Greatest Trombonist* and *Ska: The Rhythm of Liberation.*

Winston C. Campbell holds a PhD in Cultural Studies from the Institute of Caribbean Studies, UWI (Mona). Among his interests are the lyrics of contemporary (or new millennium) dancehall songs, and the ways in which these lyrics contend with peculiar political agencies within the Jamaican society. He is working on a larger manuscript of his findings for publication in the near future.

Alan 'Skill' Cole 'A great, great friend. A confidant.' That is how Bob Marley described Alan 'Skill' Cole. A legendary Jamaican footballer, he was so adept at the game that he gained the moniker 'Skill'. Cole made an indelible mark in Jamaica's history as the youngest senior football player at the international level, donning national colours against a Brazilian team at the mere age of 15. Marley and Cole's friendship began in the late 1960s when they first met at a football match in Trench Town and continued for the rest of Marley's life. Cole was at the peak of his playing career in the mid-1970s when he doubled as Marley's road manager. He is credited as the writer of 'War', from Marley's 1976 *Rastaman Vibration* album. Cole's friendship with Marley will be documented in his forthcoming book, *The Bob Marley That I Know.*

Brent Hagerman teaches in the Music Faculty and the Religion & Culture Department at Wilfrid Laurier University in Waterloo, Ontario. His research interests are interdisciplinary and include religion and gender/sexuality/race, the religion and culture of the Black Atlantic with a specialization on

Rastafari and Jamaican popular music, and the cultural studies of popular music.

Patrick Helber is a research assistant and doctoral candidate in Contemporary History at Heidelberg University. His thesis analyses the controversy on homophobic dancehall music in the Jamaican press. In 2011, he was a visiting researcher at the University of the West Indies, Mona. He is also a radio show host and author of '"Ah My Brownin' Dat."' His publications include 'A Visual Discourse Analysis of the Performance of Vybz Kartel's Masculinity in the Cartoons of the Jamaica Observer,' in *Caribbean Quarterly* (2012).

Donna P. Hope is a Cultural Analyst, and Director and Senior Lecturer, at the Institute of Caribbean Studies & the Reggae Studies Unit, University of the West Indies, Mona. She has presented in multiple fora across the world and published widely on her work on Jamaican popular music and culture. Dr Hope's book publications include *International Reggae: Current and Future Trends in Jamaican Popular Music* (2013), *Man Vibes: Masculinities in the Jamaican Dancehall* (2010) and *Inna di Dancehall: Popular Culture and the Politics of Identity in Jamaica* (2006).

David Katz is author of *People Funny Boy: The Genius of Lee 'Scratch' Perry, Solid Foundation: An Oral History of Reggae*, and Caribbean *Lives: Jimmy Cliff*. In addition, he contributed to *The Rough Guide to Reggae: A Tapestry of Jamaica* and also to *The Story of Island Records*. Katz's work has appeared in many periodicals and books, and he has annotated over one hundred retrospectives of Jamaican music. He has also co-hosted radio programmes, released original records, and contributed to documentaries, and DJs regularly.

Anna Kasafi Perkins is currently Senior Programme Officer, Quality Assurance Unit, University of the West Indies, and Research Fellow UWI Ethics Centre Initiative. A theologian by training, she is a former Dean of Studies of St Michael's Theological College, Jamaica. She has a wide range of research interests, including, sex and sexuality, popular culture (especially dancehall), faith and political life, and ethics in business. She is the author/editor of three books and numerous articles and chapters.

Shara Rambarran is an assistant professor in music and cultural studies at the Bader International Study Centre, UK (Queen's University, Canada). Her main research interests include: popular music analysis, remix, technology, digital cultures, IPR, events management, industry and critical theory. Currently, she is researching on music and virtuality, digital media, electronica and British Caribbean music. She is currently on the editorial board for the academic publication: *The Journal on the Art of Record Production*.

José Luis Fanjul Rivero is a musicologist with training in Hispanic Music from the Universidad de Valladolid, Spain, and the Instituto Superior de Arte, Havana, Cuba. He is a member of the International Musicological Society IMS, a piano professor and musician at Luis Casa Romero Vocational School of Arts, 'José White' Music Conservatoire of Camagüey, pianist of the Danzón Orchestra 'La Bella Época' of Camagüey and Musical Analysis professor at the Havana National School of Arts.

Livingston A. White is a lecturer at the Caribbean Institute of Media and Communication (CARIMAC) at the University of the West Indies, Mona, where he teaches courses at the undergraduate and graduate levels in Social Marketing, Communication Analysis and Planning, and Communication Research Methodology. He has conducted research and training in communication planning for, as well as consulted with, various regional Caribbean-based agencies in areas ranging from knowledge, attitude and practice surveys to media campaign message pretest and recall studies.

Index

Adams, Glen, 31
African Queen, 177–78
Afro-Cuban, xi, 131
American
    Musician, 190
    Popular music, 130
Andy, Bob, 12
Audioweb, 72–80
Auto-Tune, 45

Babylon, 57, 62, 170
Back-A-Wall, 9, 13, 25
Bangarang, 31–32, 47
Beenie Man, 105, 143, 159, 166, 172, 175–76, 180, 183, 200
Belcher, Earl, 19, 27
Bible, 62, 153, 164, 170–71
Blackness, 56–57, 142, 145–46, 149, 156
Black people, 143
    Sexualized, 151
Black urban popular culture, 155–56
Bodies, female, 167, 175, 180–81
Boys Town, 1–2
British
    Britpop, 64, 69–71, 73–79
    Culture, 64–5, 69, 79
    Identity, 70, 77
    Media, xii, 64, 68, 77–79
    Brother Gad, 18, 26
Banton, Buju, 143, 153
Bucknor, Syd, 7, 25

Caribbean
    In Britain, 209
    Music, 65–66, 68, 78–80
    Music, history of, 65
    Women, 172, 174
Centre for Contemporary Cultural Studies, 66
Christian, Catches, 164–65, 171

Clarke, Johnny, 34, 36
Clash – Musical/Dancehall, xii, 100–21
Cliff, Jimmy, 66, 89–90, 93–94, 208
Colonizers, 147, 151, 157,
Cooper, Carolyn, 104, 112, 115, 144, 149, 159, 180
Creativity, xii, 19, 132
Creole, 117, 123, 145–47, 149, 156
Crisis discourse, 152–53, 141, 146
Cuban
    Identity, 55, 61
    Society, 54, 55, 52
Cultural
    Identity, 57, 96, 145–47, 155
    Practices, 155–56

Dance fads, 190
Dancehall, 44, 92, 98, 103–105, 107, 110–11, 113–16, 118–19, 121, 128, 130, 132–33, 136, 144, 149, 152–56, 160, 165–67, 170, 172–74, 176–78, 180–82, 184–86, 189–90, 196, 198–99, 201
    Culture, 100, 102–103, 105, 114, 118, 120, 149, 154, 155, 160, 167, 170, 174
    Lyrics
    Lyrics, Contemporary, 200
    Music, 38, 43–4, 100, 102–3, 106, 109–13, 118–19, 121, 142–43, 146, 155, 190, 203, 208
    Music: Homophobic, 141–43, 145, 208
    Music: Anti-homosexual Dancehall lyrics, 142–45, 16
    Space, 104, 119, 149, 184–87,

189, 201, 203
Dancers, 57, 87, 93–95
Deejays, 41–42, 66–67, 71, 73, 76, 114, 127, 130–33, 135, 137
Deep Roots Music, 38
Diamond, Macka, 149
Digital, Bobby, 28, 30, 32, 36–42, 45–46
Digital
   Reggae, 128, 129, 134, 136, 137
   Revolution, 135
   Technology, 128–29, 133, 136
Dodd, Sir Coxsone, 11, 26, 29, 46, 67, 104
Downtown, 85-6, 92–93, 96–97
   Kingston, 2, 25, 85
   Musicians, 94
Dub plates, 127, 133, 137
Dynamic Sounds, 3, 25–26

Electronica, 71, 73–74, 78, 209
England, 13, 25, 31–32, 35, 47, 66, 70, 73, 85, 89
Environment, social, 193, 196, 200, 203, 205

Family Man, 6–7, 12, 25, 34
Federal Recording Studios, 87
Female sexuality, 173–74
Feminine, 73, 174, 180, 191–93, 196, 199, 203
   Roles: Acts of violence/Social environment, 191, 203
Festival, 87, 91, 96–97
Feuds, *See clash*
Fraser, Eddie, 13–14, 26

Gaza, 100–101, 103, 105, 115–16, 119–21, 184–85, 194, 201
Gaza/Gully, xii, 100–101, 105, 115–16, 119–21
Gender, 71, 105, 122, 145, 147, 149, 154, 159, 160, 168, 172, 174, 187–88, 190–92, 199, 204–205, 207

Genealogy, musical, 132, 135, 185, 188–89, 194
Genres
   Popular music, 73, 75
   Jamaican Music, 51, 53,
Goodas, 164–67, 172–82
   Songs, 172, 174,
Gully, 100, 103, 115

Half-Way-Tree, 19
Hall, Gary, 3–4
Hanna, Lisa, 141–42
Harriott, Derrick, 89
Havana, 52–54, 61,
Hegemony, 145–46, 148–9, 184, 187–88, 191, 194, 200, 202–203
Heterosexuality, 147, 149, 151, 153, 198
Homophobia, 143, 145, 148, 150–51, 154–55, 157–58
Homosexuality, 105, 142, 147–50, 153, 156, 158
Homosexuals, 143–45, 148, 150–51, 153, 155, 157–58, 199

Ifrica, Queen, 141–42
Independent Jamaica, 85, 89, 96
Independence song, 89
Inner city areas, 71

J-FLAG (Jamaican Forum For Lesbians All Sexuals and Gays), 143–44, 158–59
Jamaican
   Music, x, xi, 29, 38, 40, 51, 53–54, 66, 85–86, 92, 101, 102, 106, 111, 120, 128–30, 135, 208
   Folk songs, traditional: Second World War, 78
   Government, xii, 26–27, 45, 86–87, 89, 93, 95–97, 100
Jack, 77–78
Jammy, King, xi, 28, 30, 32, 35, 40–42, 45, 128, 133–35,
Jamaican
   Masculine identity, 174

Media, 100, 107, 111, 120–21, 144
Society, Contemporary, 187, 192
Jamaica's music
  History, 25
  Music producers, 28
Jamaican music
  Industry, xi
  Original: *See Jamaica Ska*
  Press: dancehall music, 142, 208
  Reggae, 127
Jamaican studios, legendary: Channel One, Studio One, Dynamic Sounds, 25
John Crow Skank, 30–31
Junior, David, 5
Jazz, 31, 65–66, 78, 131, 155

Kingston
  Cultural Transformation in the 1970s, 26
  Western, 13, 93
Kartel, Vybz, xii, 100, 102, 105, 115, 116, 143, 172, 185, 186, 193, 194, 200
Katz, David, xi, 28–46

LGBTI-organizations (Lesbian, Gay, Bi-sexual, Transsexual and Intersexual), 143–45, 148, 150, 153, 155
Lee, Byron, 3, 11, 89, 92–97
  Dragonaires, 26 89, 92–93, 95–97
Lee, Striker, xi, 28, 32, 36–38, 43, 46
Lord Creator, 89

Male gaze, 166, 170
Malcolm, Carlos, 87
Marley, Bob, x, 1, 8–9, 12, 17, 20, 24–27, 34, 47, 56, 65, 68–69, 97
  Wailers, 18, 25, 47, 65, 68
Mavado: Artiste, xii, 100–103, 106, 112, 115–16, 119, 186

Media, x, xi, xii, xiii, 54, 64–69, 72–80, 100–103, 106–107, 110–16, 118–22, 128–30, 132, 141–42, 144–45, 156,185, 189, 194
  Agenda Setting, xii, 101, 106, 107, 113, 115, 120–21
  Alternative, 129
  Electronic, 101–102, 105, 107, 111, 119, 193
  Mass, 105, 112, 119–20
  New, 107, 111, 128–29
  Print/Visual, 101, 110, 152, 167
  Social, 105, 121
Merchant, Martin 'Sugar', 64–80
Miss Jamaica: Jimmy Cliff, 90–91
Morgan, Derrick, 29, 89, 90–91, 102–103
Malcolm, Carlos: festival orchestra, 87
Matterhorn, Tony: "Goodas fi dem", 166, 176, 178, 180
Masculine hegemony, 200, 202–203
Murder music, 141, 143–44, 158–60
Music business, 3, 10
Music industry
  Local, 27
  Pre-digital Jamaican, 128
Music, calypso, 33, 65, 66, 89, 131
Music video, 64, 76, 78–79,141
Musical
  Crossovers: in Britain, 68–69
  Performance: Shifting identities and inter-genre, 54–62
Multi-racial groups, 66, 69–70, 78

Natty Dread: album, 18, 25
Natural mystic, 11, 14
Nasralla, Ronnie, 93–95
National anthem: Jamaica Military Band, 87
National identity, xii 70, 75 85, 90, 97,148

Outrage!, 143–44, 148, 150–51, 159

Pamputae: Good, Good Goodas, Gal, 179, 180
Popular music,
  Discourse, 127
  Early British, 69
  Genre-blended, 71
  Music in Jamaica, 85
  Western, 130
Poverty: Jamaica, 25, 90, 169, 175
Proverbs: Book of, xiii, 164–74
Pussy Mechanic: Tommy Lee Sparta, 198, 200

Ranks, Shabba, 41, 43,
Rastafarians, 9, 25, 26, 52–58, 60–61, 94, 176
Rastafarian culture, 52, 55
Reggae
  Music, xi, 28–29, 31, 52, 57, 67, 68, 97, 127, 130, 132, 134
  Songs, 128–30, 132, 134
  Sumfest, 118, 186, 188
  Groups: Madness, UB40, 69
  Industry, 129, 136
  Production, 128, 136
Roots, 35, 39, 68, 75, 137
  Sounds, 131
Reid, Duke, 29, 31, 34, 37–38 102, 104
Remanente, 54, 56–62
Resistance: Systems of Conflict, 201–205,
Reid, Junior, 36, 38–39
Riddims, xii, 127, 130–37
  New, 135–36
  Older, 130, 132
Rocksteady, xi, 26, 29–32, 38, 92, 98, 130

Seaga, Eddie, 26, 92–96
Selectors, 133
Sexual
  Encounters, 190, 197–200
  Taboos, 199
Sexuality, 105, 142, 145, 149, 150–51, 153, 154, 168, 173, 174, 191, 197, 199, 202, 207, 208
Shottas, 142, 155

Silk, Garnett, 42
Ska, xii, 26, 29–32, 34, 38, 65, 69–70, 72, 78, 85–86, 88–89, 91–98, 103, 130
Skatalites: Freedom Sound, 89, 91, 97
Slackness, 114, 141, 142, 154, 156, 159
Sleng Teng: Wayne Smith, 33, 35, 38, 39, 40, 42, 47
Spanish Town, 37, 88
Sparta, Tommy Lee, xii, 184, 205
Sting: Dancehall Festival, 104–105, 110–11, 114–15, 118, 152, 154, 186
Studio One, 25–26, 37–38, 46, 130, 133

Taboos, sexual, 199
Tatchell, Peter: *See Outrage!*
TOK: Goodas, 172, 173, 175, 176
Tourism: Jamaica, 94, 95, 145
Trench Town Rock: Bob Marley, 6
Tubby, King: Studio, 30, 34, 38, 39, 46
Tuff Gong, 5–6, 10
Twelve Tribes, 18, 26–27

Uptown, xii, 85–86, 88–89, 92–93, 96–97
Uptown and Downtown: *See Downtown / Uptown*

Violence, 115, 117, 118 , 142, 143, 144, 145, 152, 157, 170, 184–205
  and Sexuality, xiii, 197–205
Vulgarity: Dancehall, 142, 154

West Indies Recording Limited (WIRL), 26, 97
Woman
  Immoral, 147, 165, 169–70, 173–74, 176
  Virtuous, xiii, 164–67, 171–73, 174–75, 182

Yellowman: From Dub plate to Dancehall, 127, 132, 133, 137

www.ingramcontent.com/pod-product-compliance
Lightning Source LLC
Chambersburg PA
CBHW070611170426
43200CB00012B/2654